ACCA

Paper

F5

Performance
management

Welcome to IFP's study text for Paper F5 *Performance management* which is:

- Written by tutors
- Comprehensive but concise
- In simple English
- Used around the world by Emile Woolf Colleges including China, Russia and the UK

 **International Financial Publishing**

in association with

 **Emile Woolf** International
Training Professionals

First edition published by
International Financial Publishing Limited
Hitherbury House, 97 Portsmouth Road, Guildford, Surrey GU2 5DL
Email: info@ifpbooks.com
www.ifpbooks.com

Notice
International Financial Publishing Limited has made every effort to ensure that at the time of writing the contents of this study text are accurate, but neither International Financial Publishing Limited nor its directors or employees shall be under any liability whatsoever for any inaccurate or misleading information this work could contain.

British Library Cataloguing in Publications Data
A catalogue record for this book is available from the British Library.

ISBN: 978-1-905623-32-7

Printed and bound in Great Britain.

Acknowledgements
The syllabus and study guide are reproduced by kind permission of the Association of Chartered Certified Accountants.

C

Contents

International Financial Publishing Limited

Contents

		Page

International Financial Publishing Limited

S

Syllabus and study guide

Aim

To develop knowledge and skills in the application of management accounting techniques to quantitative and qualitative information, for planning, decision-making, performance evaluation and control.

Main capabilities

After completing this examination paper, students should be able to:

A   Explain, apply and evaluate cost accounting techniques

B   Select and appropriately apply decision-making techniques to evaluate business choices and promote efficient and effective use of scarce business resources, appreciating the risks and uncertainty inherent in business and resolving those risks

C   Apply budgeting techniques and evaluate alternative methods of budgeting, planning and control

D   Use standard costing systems to measure and control business performance and to identify remedial action

E   Assess the performance of a business from both a financial and non-financial viewpoint, appreciating the problems of controlling divisionalised businesses and the importance of allowing for external aspects.

Rationale

This syllabus builds on the knowledge introduced in the Management Accounting syllabus from the Knowledge module. It also prepares candidates for more specialist capabilities which are covered in the Advanced Performance Management paper.

The syllabus begins by introducing more specialised management accounting topics. There is a little knowledge assumed from the Management Accounting paper – primarily overhead treatments. The objective here is to ensure candidates have a broader background in Management Accounting techniques.

The syllabus then considers decision-making. Candidates need to appreciate the problems surrounding scarce resource, pricing and make or buy decisions and how this relates to the assessment of performance. Risk and uncertainty are a factor of real life decisions, candidates need to understand risk and be able to apply some basic methods to help resolve the risks inherent in decision-making.

Budgeting is an important aspect of many accountants' lives. The syllabus explores different budgeting techniques and the problems inherent in them. The behavioural aspects of budgeting are important for accountants to understand and the syllabus includes consideration of the way individuals react to a budget.

Standard costing and variances are then built on. All the variances examined in the Management Accounting paper are examinable here. The new topics are mix and yield variances and planning and operational variances. Again the link is made to performance management. It is important for accountants to be able to interpret the numbers that they calculate and ask what they mean in the context of performance.

The syllabus concludes with performance measurement and control. This is a major area of the syllabus. Accountants need to understand how a business should be managed and controlled. They should appreciate the importance of both financial and non-financial performance measures in management. They should also appreciate the difficulties in assessing performance in divisionalised businesses and the problems caused by failing to consider external influences on performance. This section leads directly to the Advanced Performance Management syllabus at the higher level.

Syllabus

A   Specialist cost and management accounting techniques
1   Activity based costing

2   Target costing

3   Life cycle costing

4   Backflush accounting

5   Throughput accounting

B   Decision-making techniques

1   Multi-limiting factors and the use of linear programming and shadow pricing

2   Pricing decisions

3   Make-or-buy and outsourcing decisions

4   Dealing with risk and uncertainty in decision-making

C   Budgeting

1   Objectives

2   Budgetary systems

3   Types of budgets

4   Quantitative analysis in budgeting

5   Behavioural aspects of budgeting

D   Standard costing and variances analysis

1   Budgeting and standard costing

2   Basic variances and operating statements

3   Material mix and yield variances

4   Planning and operational variances

5   Behavioural aspects of standard costing

E   Performance measurement and control

1   The scope of performance measurement

2   Divisional performance and transfer pricing

3   Performance analysis in not-for-profit organisations and the public sector

4   External considerations and behavioural aspects

Approach to examining the syllabus

Paper F5, Performance Management, seeks to examine candidates' understanding of how to manage the performance of a business.

The paper builds on the knowledge acquired in Paper F2, Management Accounting and prepares those candidates who will decide to go on to study Paper P5, Advanced Performance Management at the Professional level

Examination structure

The examination will contain four compulsory, 25 marks questions. There will be calculation and discursive elements to the paper with the balance being broadly in line with the pilot paper. The pilot paper contains questions from four of the five syllabus sections. Generally the paper will seek to draw questions from as many of the syllabus sections as possible.

Study guide

This study guide provides more detailed guidance on the syllabus. You should use this as the basis of your studies.

A   Specialist cost and management accounting techniques

1   Activity based costing

    (a)   Identify appropriate cost drivers under ABC.

    (b)   Calculate costs per driver and per unit using ABC.

    (c)   Compare ABC and traditional methods of overhead absorption based on production units, labour hours or machine hours.

    (d)   Explain the implications of switching to ABC for pricing, sales strategy, performance management and decision-making.

2   Target costing

    (a)   Derive a target cost in manufacturing and service industries.

    (b)   Explain the difficulties of using target costing in service industries.

    (c)   Explain the implications of using target costing on pricing, cost control and performance management.

    (d)   Suggest how a target cost gap might be closed.

3   Life cycle costing

    (a)   Identify the costs involved at different stages of the life cycle.

    (b)   Explain the implications of life cycle costing on pricing, performance management and decision-making.

4   Backflush accounting

    (a)   Describe the process of backflush accounting and contrast with traditional process accounting.

    (b)   Explain the implications of backflush accounting on performance management and the control of a manufacturing process.

    (c)   Identify the benefits of the introduction of backflush accounting.

    (d)   Evaluate the decision to switch to backflush accounting from traditional process control.

5   Throughput accounting

    (a)   Calculate and interpret a throughput accounting ratio (TPAR).

    (b)   Suggest how a TPAR could be improved.

    (c)   Apply throughput accounting to a multi-product decision-making problem.

B   Decision-making techniques

1   Multi-limiting factors and the use of linear programming and shadow pricing

(a)   Select an appropriate technique in a scarce resource situation.

(b)   Formulate and solve a multiple scarce resource problem both graphically and using simultaneous equations as appropriate.

(c)   Explain and calculate shadow prices (dual prices) and discuss their implications on decision-making and performance management.

(d)   Calculate slack and explain the implications of the existence of slack for decision-making and performance management.

(Excluding simplex and sensitivity to changes in objective functions)

2   Pricing decisions

(a)   Explain the factors that influence the pricing of a product or service.

(b)   Explain the price elasticity of demand.

(c)   Derive and manipulate a straight line demand equation. Derive an equation for the total cost function (including volume-based discounts).

(d)   Evaluate a decision to increase production and sales levels considering incremental costs, incremental revenues and other factors.

(e)   Explain different price strategies, including:

(i)   all forms of cost plus

(ii)   skimming

(iii)   penetration

(iv)   complementary product

(v)   product-line

(vi)   volume discounting

(vii)   discrimination

(viii) relevant cost

(f)   Calculate a price from a given strategy using cost plus and relevant cost.

3   Make-or-buy and other short-term decisions

(a)   Explain the issues surrounding make vs. buy and outsourcing decisions.

(b)   Calculate and compare "make" costs with "buy-in" costs.

(c)   Compare in-house costs and outsource costs of completing tasks and consider other issues surrounding this decision.

(d) Apply relevant costing principles in situations involving make or buy in, shut down, one-off contracts and the further processing of joint products.

4   Dealing with risk and uncertainty in decision-making

(a) Suggest research techniques to reduce uncertainty e.g. Focus groups, market research.

(b) Explain the use of simulation, expected values and sensitivity.

(c) Apply expected values and sensitivity to decision-making problems.

(d) Apply the techniques of maximax, maximin, and minimax regret to decision-making problems including the production of profit tables.

(Excluding decision trees and the value of perfect information)

C   Budgeting

1   Objectives

(a) Outline the objectives of a budgetary control system.

(b) Explain how corporate and divisional objectives may differ and can be reconciled.

(c) Identify and resolve conflicting objectives and explain implications.

2   Budgetary systems

(a) Explain how budgetary systems fit within the performance hierarchy.

(b) Select and explain appropriate budgetary systems for an organisation (Systems to include: Top down, bottom up, rolling, zero based, activity based, incremental and feed-forward control).

(c) Describe the information used in budget systems and the sources of the information needed.

(d) Explain the difficulties of changing a budgetary system.

(e) Explain how budget systems can deal with uncertainty in the environment.

3   Types of budgets

(a) Indicate the usefulness and problems with different budget types (Zero based, activity based, incremental, master, functional, flexible).

(b) Explain the difficulties of changing the type of budget used.

4 Quantitative analysis in budgeting

(a) Analyse fixed and variable cost elements from total cost data (High Low and regression). Evaluate these methods.

(b) Explain the use of forecasting techniques. (Techniques: Time series, simple average growth models and estimates based on judgement and experience). Predict a future value from provided time series analysis data using both additive and proportional data.

(c) Estimate the learning effect and apply the learning curve to a budgetary problem. This includes calculations on steady states.

(d) Discuss the reservations with the learning curve.

(e) Apply expected values and explain the problems and benefits.

(f) Explain the benefits and dangers inherent in using spreadsheets in budgeting.

5 Behavioural aspects of budgeting

(a) Identify the factors which influence behaviour.

(b) Discuss the issues surrounding setting the difficulty level for a budget.

(c) Explain the benefits and difficulties of the participation of employees in the negotiation of targets.

D Standard costing and variances analysis

1 Budgeting and standard costing

(a) Explain the use of standard costs.

(b) Outline the methods used to derive standard costs and discuss the different types of costs possible.

(c) Explain the importance of flexing budgets in performance management.

(d) Prepare budgets and standards that allow for waste and idle time.

(e) Explain and apply the principle of controllability in the performance management system.

(f) Prepare a flexed budget and comment on its usefulness.

2 Basic variances and operating statements

(a) Calculate, identify the cause of and interpret all basic variances:

(i) Sales price and volume

(ii) Materials total, price and usage

(iii) Labour total, rate and efficiency

(iv) Variable overhead total, expenditure and efficiency

(v) Fixed overhead total, expenditure and, where appropriate, volume, capacity and efficiency.

(b)   Explain the effect on labour variances where the learning curve has been used in the budget process.

(c)   Produce full operating statements in both a marginal cost and full absorption costing environment, reconciling actual profit to budgeted profit.

(d)   Calculate the effect of idle time and waste on variances including where idle time has been budgeted for.

(e)   Explain the possible causes of idle time and waste and suggest methods of control.

(f)   Calculate using a simple situation ABC based variances.

(g)   Explain the different methods available for deciding whether or not too investigate a variance cause.

3   Material mix and yield variances

(a)   Calculate, identify the cause of and explain mix and yield variances.

(b)   Explain the wider issues involved in changing mix e.g. cost, quality and performance measurement issues.

(c)   Identify and explain the interrelationship between price, mix and yield.

(d)   Suggest and justify alternative methods of controlling production processes.

4   Planning and operational variances

(a)   Calculate a revised budget.

(b)   Identify and explain those factors that could and could not be allowed to revise an original budget.

(c)   Calculate planning and operational variances for sales, (including market size and market share) materials and labour.

(d)   Explain and resolve the manipulation issues in revising budgets.

5   Behavioural aspects of standard costing

(a)   Describe the dysfunctional nature of some variances in the modern environment of JIT and TQM.

(b)   Discuss the behavioural problems resulting from using standard costs in rapidly changing environments.

(c)   Discuss the effect that variances have on staff motivation and action.

E   Performance measurement and control
1   The scope of performance measurement

(a)   Describe and calculate and interpret financial performance indicators (FPIs) for profitability, liquidity and risk in both manufacturing and service businesses. Suggest methods to improve these measures.

(b) Describe, calculate and interpret non-financial performance indicators (NFPIs) and suggest method to improve the performance indicated.

(c) Explain the causes and problems created by short-termism and financial manipulation of results and suggest methods encourage a long term view.

(d) Explain and interpret the Balanced Scorecard, and the Building Block model proposed by Fitzgerald and Moon.

(e) Discuss the difficulties of target setting in qualitative areas.

2   Divisional performance and transfer pricing

(a) Explain the basis for setting a transfer price using variable cost, full cost and the principles behind allowing for intermediate markets.

(b) Explain how transfer prices can distort the performance assessment of divisions and decisions made.

(c) Explain the meaning of, and calculate, Return on Investment (ROI) and Residual Income (RI), and discuss their shortcomings.

(d) Compare divisional performance and recognise the problems of doing so.

3   Performance analysis in not for profit organisations and the public sector

(a) Comment on the problems of having non-quantifiable objectives in performance management.

(b) Explain how performance could be measured in these sectors.

(c) Comment on the problems of having multiple objectives in these sectors.

(d) Outline Value for Money (VFM) as a public sector objective.

4   External considerations and behavioural aspects

(a) Explain the need to allow for external considerations in performance management. (External considerations to include stakeholders, market conditions and allowance for competitors).

(b) Suggest ways in which external considerations could be allowed for in performance management.

(c) Interpret performance in the light of external considerations.

(d) Identify and explain the behaviour aspects of performance management

Formulae

Learning curve

$Y = ax^b$

Where y = average cost per batch

a = cost of first batch

x = total number of batches produced

b = learning factor (log LR/log 2)

LR = the learning rate as a decimal

Regression analysis

$y = a + bx$

$$b = \frac{n \sum xy - \sum x \sum y}{n \sum x^2 - (\sum x)^2}$$

$$a = \frac{\sum y}{n} - \frac{b \sum x}{n}$$

$$r = \frac{n \sum xy - \sum x \sum y}{\sqrt{\left(n \sum x^2 - (\sum x)^2\right)\left(n \sum y^2 - (\sum y)^2\right)}}$$

Demand curve

$P = a - bQ$

$$b = \frac{\text{change in price}}{\text{change in quantity}}$$

a = price when Q = 0

CHAPTER

1

Costing systems

Contents
1   Activity based costing
2   Target Costing
3   Product life cycle costing
4   Backflush accounting
5   Throughput accounting
6   Throughput accounting and the Theory of Constraints

Activity based costing (ABC)

- Activity based costing, overhead costs and cost drivers
- When using ABC might be appropriate
- The measurement of costs with ABC
- ABC and traditional absorption costing
- Advantages and disadvantages of ABC
- Implications of switching to ABC

---

1 Activity based costing (ABC)

1.1 Activity based costing, overhead costs and cost drivers

Activity based costing (ABC) is a form of absorption costing. However, it differs from traditional absorption costing, in which production overhead costs are traced to production departments and production activities, and absorbed at a direct labour hour rate.

Activity-based costing is based on the following assumptions:

- In a modern manufacturing environment, a large proportion of total costs are overhead costs, and direct labour costs are relatively small.
- Because overhead costs are large, it is appropriate to trace these costs as accurately as possible to the products that create the cost.
- Since direct labour is a fairly small element of cost, it is inappropriate to trace production overhead costs to products by absorbing overheads at a rate per direct labour hour.

Further assumptions are that:

- Many overhead costs are attributable to activities, such as customer order handling or product warehousing and despatch. These activities are not necessarily confined to single functional departments within the organisation.
- The costs of each of these activities are driven by one or more factors, called cost drivers. The cost driver for an activity is not necessarily production volume. For example, the cost driver for order handling costs might be the number of orders, not the quantity of items in each order.

Overhead costs are therefore caused by activities, and the costs of activities are driven by factors other than production volume.

ABC is a system of costing that attempts to:

- Identify the activities that create overhead costs
- Identify the cost driver or cost drivers for each of these activities

---

- Charge overheads to products on the basis of the activities that are required to provide the product: each product should be charged with a fair share of overhead cost that represents the activities that go into making and selling it.

- There is also an argument that in the long run, all overhead costs are variable (even though they are fixed in the short-term). Measuring costs with ABC might therefore provide management with useful information for controlling activities and long-term costs.

1.2   When using ABC might be appropriate

Activity based costing is a form of absorption costing, in which overheads are absorbed at a rate for each activity, rather than a rate per direct labour hour. It is likely to be suitable as a method of costing in the following circumstances:

- In a manufacturing environment, where absorption costing is required for inventory valuations.

- Where a large proportion of production costs are overhead costs, and direct labour costs are relatively small.

- Where products are complex.

- Where products are provided to customer specifications.

- Where order sizes differ substantially, and order handling and despatch activity costs are significant.

1.3   The measurement of costs with ABC

To measure the cost of products or jobs with ABC, the basic approach is to:

- Identify the activities that create overhead costs.

- Allocate actual overhead expenditure to each of these activities. The costs allocated to each activity are known as a cost pool.

- Identify the factor that drives the cost for each activity (the cost driver). There should be a cost driver for each activity and each cost pool.

- Calculate an absorption rate for each cost pool/activity.

- Absorb overhead costs into the costs of production by absorbing an overhead cost for each activity.

- The total production cost is therefore direct production costs plus absorbed overheads for each activity. (There might also be an absorbed amount for general overheads, which cannot be attributed to any specific activity and cost pool).

 Example

A manufacturing company has identified that a large part of its overhead costs are incurred in handling customer orders, and that the same effort goes into handling a small order as the effort required to deal with a large order. Order sizes differ substantially. The company makes four products, and the estimated costs of order handling are $250,000 per year.

The company uses ABC, and wants to establish an order-handling overhead cost for each product, based on the following budget:

Product	Number of orders	Total number of units ordered
W	15	60,000
X	22	33,000
Y	4	40,000
Z	9	27,000
	50	160,000

If the cost driver for order handling is the number of orders handled, the budgeted order handling cost will be $250,000/50 = $5,000 per order. Overhead costs will be charged to products as follows:

Product	Number of orders	Cost
		$
W	15	75,000
X	22	110,000
Y	4	20,000
Z	9	45,000
	40	250,000

1.4 ABC and traditional absorption costing

Although ABC is a form of absorption costing, the effect of ABC could be to allocate overheads in a completely different way between products. Product costs and product profitability will therefore be very different with ABC compared with traditional absorption costing.

Example

Entity Blue makes and sells two products, X and Y. Data for production and sales each month are as follows:

	Product X	Product Y
Sales demand	4,000 units	8,000 units
Direct material cost/unit	$20	$10
Direct labour hours/unit	0.1 hour	0.2 hours
Direct labour cost/unit	$2	$4

Production overheads are $500,000 each month. These are absorbed on a direct labour hour basis.

An analysis of overhead costs suggests that there are four main activities that cause overhead expenditure.

Activity	Total cost	Cost driver	Total number	Product X	Product Y
	$				
Batch setup	100,000	Number of set-ups	20	10	10
Order handling	200,000	Number of orders	40	24	16
Machining	120,000	Machine hours	15,000	6,000	9,000
Quality control	80,000	Number of checks	32	18	14
	500,000				

Required

Calculate the full production costs for Product X and Product Y, using:

(a)   traditional absorption costing

(b)   activity based costing.

 Answer

Traditional absorption costing
The overhead absorption rate = $500,000/ (4,000 × 0.1 + 8,000 × 0.2) = $250

	Product X	Product Y	Total
	$	$	
Direct materials	20	10	
Direct labour	2	4	
Overhead (at $250 per hour)	25	50	
Cost per unit	47	64	
Number of units	4,000	8,000	
Total cost	$188,000	$512,000	$700,000

Activity based costing

Activity	Total cost	Cost driver		Product X	Product Y
	$		$	$	$
Batch setup	100,000	Cost/setup	5,000	50,000	50,000
Order handling	200,000	Cost/order	5,000	120,000	80,000
Machining	120,000	Cost/machine hour	8	48,000	72,000
Quality control	80,000	Cost/check	2,500	45,000	35,000
	500,000			263,000	237,000

	Product X	Product Y	Total
	$	$	$
Direct materials	80,000	80,000	
Direct labour	8,000	32,000	
Overheads	263,000	237,000	
Total cost	351,000	349,000	$700,000
Number of units	4,000	8,000	
Cost per unit	$87.75	$43.625	

In this example, the unit cost with a traditional absorption costing approach differs substantially from the unit costs with activity based costing.

1.5   Advantages and disadvantages of ABC

Advantages

- ABC provides useful information about the activities that drive overhead costs. Traditional absorption costing and marginal costing do not do this.

- ABC therefore provides information that could be relevant to long-term cost control and long-term product selection or product pricing.

- ABC can provide the basis for a management information system to manage and control overhead costs.

- It might be argued that full product costs obtained with ABC are more 'realistic', although it can also be argued that full product cost information is actually of little practical use or meaning for management.

Disadvantages

- The analysis of costs in an ABC system may be based on unreliable data and weak assumptions. In particular, ABC systems may be based on inappropriate activities and cost pools, and incorrect assumptions about cost drivers.

- ABC provides an analysis of historical costs. Decision-making by management should be based on expectations of future cash flows. It is incorrect to assume that there is a causal relationship between a cost diver and an activity cost, so that increasing or reducing the activity will result in higher or lower activity costs.

- In some cases, ABC may be little more than a sophisticated absorption costing system.

- Within ABC systems, there is still a large amount of overhead cost apportionment. General overhead costs such as rental costs, insurance costs and heating and lighting costs may be apportioned between cost pools. This reduces the causal link between the cost driver and the activity cost.

- Many ABC systems are based on just a small number of cost pools and cost drivers. More complex systems are difficult to justify, on grounds of cost.

- Many activities and cost pools have more than one cost driver. Identifying the most suitable cost driver for a cost pool/activity is often difficult.

- Traditional cost accounting systems may be more appropriate for the purpose of inventory valuation and financial reporting.

- It might be a costly system to design and use. The costs might not justify the benefits. It must be remembered that full product costing is of little relevance for management decision-making.

1.6   Implications of switching to ABC

The information produced using ABC can be used to improve
- Pricing decisions
- Sales strategy
- Performance measurement
- Decision-making

Organisations may adopt various pricing strategies but in the long run price must exceed average total cost to result in a profit. Absorption costing often leads to too much overhead allocated to high volume standardised products and too little overhead being allocated to low volume, complex products. ABC costs may more accurately reflect the costs incurred to produce a product and therefore provide better information for managers when deciding on price and product mix.

Activity based costing may be used to analyse costs of product lines, customer groups and distribution outlets to more accurately assess profitability and determine where management attention should be focused. Sales strategy may be to improve the profitability of low margin products and customers, increase marketing to high margin products and customers with the intention of increasing market share or even to change the mix of products or distribution outlets.

ABC information may improve understanding of how costs are incurred in overhead departments. It is difficult to control overhead costs in an absorption costing system as often responsibility is not assigned to specific managers. By understanding the activities which drive costs, responsibility for monitoring key performance indicators can be assigned to specific managers and action can be taken if performance is not as expected.

The benefits of using ABC information for decision-making are mainly due to the improved accuracy of cost information and better understanding of the activities which drive costs. However, short-run decision-making is based on relevant costs, that is, future cash flows which change as a result of the decision, and many commentators argue that marginal costing is more suitable for this purpose.

A five level hierarchy has been developed to help identify costs which vary with different types of cost driver.

Level	Cost driver	Example
1. Unit	Production volume	Machine maintenance
2. Batch	Number of batches	Setup costs
3. Process	Number of processes	Quality control
4. Product	Number of product lines	Product management
5. Facility	Number of production facilities	Rent

The variable product cost can be accumulated by considering each successively higher level of cost and whether it applies to the product. Decisions relating to the product can then be made using the relevant avoidable cost. So, for example, a decision to withdraw a product may result in cost savings at the unit, batch, process and product level but the facility level costs are genuinely fixed costs which are unavoidable and are therefore not relevant.

Target costing
■ The purpose of target costing
■ The target costing method
■ Closing the target cost gap
■ The implications of using target costing

2 Target costing

2.1 The purpose of target costing

Target costing is a method of strategic profit management. It is used mainly for new product development. A company decides the price that it would like to charge for a new product under development, in order to win a target share of the market. The company then decides on the level of profitability that it wants to achieve for the product, in order to make the required return on investment. Having identified a target price and a target profit, the company then establishes a target cost for the product. This is the cost at which the product must be manufactured and sold in order to achieve the target profits and return at the strategic market price.

Keeping the costs of the product within the target level is then a major factor in controlling its design and development. If there is 'gap' between the target cost and the expected cost, the gap must be closed by finding ways of making the product more cheaply – for example, by simplifying the design or using a different material.

2.2 The target costing method

Target costing is based on the idea that when a new product is developed, a company will have a reasonable idea about:

■ the price at which it will be able to sell the product, and

■ the sales volumes that it will be able to achieve for the product over its expected life.

There may also be estimates of the capital investment required, and any incremental fixed costs (such as marketing costs or costs of additional salaried staff).

Taking estimates of sales volumes, capital investment requirements and incremental fixed costs over the life cycle of the product, it should be possible to calculate a target cost. The target cost for the product is the maximum variable cost for the product that will provide at least the minimum required return on investment.

There will be a gap between the cost at which the product can be made now and the target cost. The aim should be to close the gap, and reduce the cost of making the product to the target cost level. The most effective way of closing the gap is to re-design the product, so that it can be produced at less cost.

The elements in the target costing process are shown in the diagram below.

Target costing

```
                                              ┌──────────────┐
                                              │  Define the  │
                                              │   current    │
                                              │ achievable   │
                                              │    cost      │
                                              └──────────────┘

        ┌──────────────┐   ┌──────────────┐              ┌──────────────┐
        │  Define the  │   │  Define the  │              │ Try to close │
        │   required   │──▶│required profit│             │ the cost gap │
        │  invesment   │   │  or return   │              └──────────────┘
        └──────────────┘   └──────────────┘
┌──────────────┐   ┌──────────────┐       ┌──────────────┐   ┌──────────────┐
│ Design/define│   │  Set target  │       │  Define the  │   │ Try to close │
│   product    │──▶│    price     │──────▶│ target cost  │- -│ the cost gap │
│specification │   └──────────────┘       └──────────────┘   └──────────────┘
└──────────────┘
        ┌──────────────┐
        │Define required│
        │ sales volume │
        └──────────────┘
```

Example

A company has designed a new product. It currently estimates that to make the product, an investment of $1,000,000 in machinery would be required. The residual value of this investment would be $300,000 at the end of year 4, when the product is expected to reach the end of its marketable life.

After studying potential demand in the market, the company has set a target selling price of $20. It has been estimated that at this price, the annual sales volume in units would be:

Year	Sales volume
	units
1	20,000
2	30,000
3	40,000
4	10,000

The current estimate of costs is that it would cost $14 to make each unit of the product, but that there would be no incremental fixed costs. The company has a cost of capital of 10% for this type of project.

This data can be used to calculate a target cost for the new product, and to identify the current size of the cost gap.

In the table below, the variable cost per unit of product is shown as V.

Year	Capital cost/ residual value	Revenue	Variable costs	Discount factor at 10%	PV of variable costs	PV of other cash flows
	$	$	$		$	$
0	(1,000,000)			1.000		(1,000,000)
1		400,000	20,000V	0.909	18,180V	363,600
2		600,000	30,000V	0.826	24,780V	495,600
3		800,000	40,000V	0.751	30,040V	600,800
4	300,000	200,000	10,000V	0.683	6,810V	340,500
					79,810V	800,500

In order to make a return of at least 10% on the investment in the project, the maximum variable cost per unit that can be permitted is $800,500/79,810 = $10.03.

The target cost for the product should therefore be $10.03, say $10 per unit. The current estimated cost is $14 per unit; therefore the cost gap is $4.

The company needs to identify ways of closing this cost gap.

2.3 Closing the target cost gap

Target costs are rarely achievable immediately and plans must be put in place to reduce costs. These planned cost reductions are measured against benchmarks or targets and any deviation from the plans is closely controlled by the whole organisation.

Common methods of closing the target cost gap are:

■ To redesign products to incorporate common processes and components

■ To eliminate non value-added activities. Value analysis may be used to systematically examine all aspects of a product cost to provide the product at the required quality at the lowest possible cost.

■ To train staff in more efficient techniques

■ To achieve economies of scale.

■ To achieve cost reductions as a result of the learning curve or, more likely, the experience curve effect. The learning curve is considered in a later chapter and is most likely to exist in a labour intensive environment. It relate to cost savings that are made as labour becomes more familiar with a complex task. The experience curve effect relates to cost savings made in other than labour costs as the organisation becomes more familiar with production of a new product. For example, management of the process and marketing may become more efficient.

2.4 The implications of using target costing

The use of a target costing system has implications for pricing, cost control and performance measurement.

Target costing is used to set a price which the market will bear for the desired market share. The price is derived by deducting the company's target profit from the appropriate market price. It may be used to enable lower prices to be set. This may result in a higher market share as competitors are deterred from entering the market by the lower profits available. Higher volumes can lead to lower average costs through economies of scale and learning/experience curve savings.

Cost control and performance measurement has a different emphasis when target costing is used.

- Cost savings are actively sought and made continuously over the life of the product

- There is joint responsibility for achieving benchmark savings. If one department fails to deliver, other departments find ways to achieve the savings

- Staff are trained and empowered to find new ways to reduce costs while maintaining the required quality

Product life cycle costing

- The product life cycle
- Research and development phase
- Introduction phase
- Growth phase
- Maturity phase
- Decline phase
- The implications of using life cycle costing

3 Product life cycle costing

3.1 The product life cycle

Most products go through a life cycle. A life cycle consists of several stages: **research and development** of the product, **introduction** to the market, a period of **growth** in sales and market size, a period of **maturity** and finally a period of **decline**. Eventually, a product is withdrawn from the market.

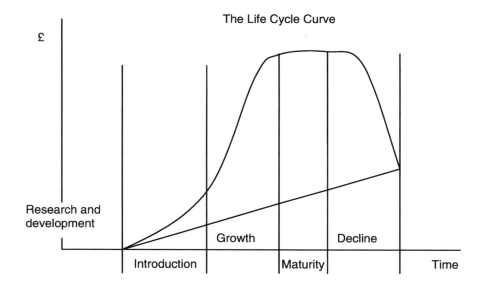

The length of a product life cycle varies. As a general rule:

- a broad type of product may have a long life of several decades
- the product may be produced in several different forms, and the life cycle of each form of the product may be shorter than the total life of the broad product
- companies may produce a form of the product, and the life cycle of a company's product may be shorter than the total life of broad product form.

For example, the life of the television has already been many decades long, and shows no obvious sign of coming to an end. However, the life cycle of the black-and-white picture television set has been shorter, and the end of the life of the analogue television can now be foreseen. Many companies have produced black and white picture televisions in the past, but the life cycle of their particular product will often have been quite short. For example, some companies may have stopped producing black and white televisions and switched entirely to colour televisions, long before other manufacturers stopped making black and white televisions.

As some products of a company reach the end of their life cycle, they need to be replaced with new products. Product innovation is essential to survival. Companies need to have a portfolio of products that:

- provides a profit, and also
- ensures the survival of the company's business in the longer term.

At each phase in its life cycle:

- selling prices will be altered
- costs may differ
- the amount invested (capital investment) may vary
- spending on advertising and other marketing activities may change.

Sales volume, sales revenue, profitability, investment and cash flow will all vary as the product goes through the different stages of its life.

3.2 Research and development phase

During this phase it has been estimated that 70-90% of a product's costs are incurred or committed. The design of the product and the processes that will be used to produce the product will be key in ensuring that the product is cost effective. Target costing may be used to plan the price, cost and target market share of the product over its life.

3.3 Introduction phase

When a product is new to the market, and a competitor has not already established a rival product in the market, a company may be able to choose its pricing strategy for the new product.

- If a 'market penetration' strategy is chosen, the aim should be to sell the product at a low price in order to obtain a large share of the market as quickly as possible. This pricing strategy is therefore based on low prices and high volumes.
- If a 'market skimming' strategy is chosen, the aim is to sell the product at a high price in order to maximise the gross profit per unit sold. Sales volumes will be low, and the product will be purchased only by customers who are willing to pay a high price to obtain a 'unique' item. Gradually, the selling price will be reduced, although it will be kept as high as possible for as long as possible. This approach is often used with high technology products.

During the introduction phase the average cost per unit of production may be high if products are produced in small batches. Marketing costs may be high to establish the product in the market. Profit per unit will be low.

3.4 Growth phase

In the growth phase of a product's life, sales demand grows rapidly, but more competitors enter the market. Companies need to focus on cost control, mainly by achieving economies of scale by producing in larger quantities. However, it is also important to ensure that customers believe that they are receiving good value and quality for the price.

3.5 Maturity phase

In the maturity phase of a life cycle, the objective should be to maintain market share. It may be necessary to use changes in price to sustain market share. Alternatively, a company may look for new distribution channels that offer an opportunity to sell at higher prices or at lower costs.

During this phase the product should break even and generate profit. The longer the maturity phase can be extended, the more profitable the product is likely to be.

3.6 Decline phase

In the decline phase, the market is saturated and demand falls. The product can continue to be sold while price exceeds variable cost. The aim should be to sell any existing inventory and keep production to a minimum. When price falls below variable cost the product should be withdrawn from the market.

3.7 The implications of using life cycle costing

Traditional costing systems do not attempt to measure the profitability of a product over its life.

■ Research and development costs are written off as they are incurred

■ Profits are measured on a time basis rather than on a product basis

■ Non production costs are not linked to products but are written off as expenses.

Life cycle costing compares the revenues and costs of the product over its entire life. This has many benefits.

■ The potential profitability of products can be assessed before major development of the product is carried out and costs incurred. Non profit-making products can be abandoned at an early stage before costs are committed.

■ Techniques can be used to reduce costs over the life of the product.

■ Pricing strategy can be determined before the product enters production. This may lead to better control of marketing and distribution costs.

■ Attention can be focused on reducing the research and development phase to get the product to market as quickly as possible. The longer the company can operate without competitors entering the market the more revenue can be earned and the sooner the product will reach the breakeven point.

- By monitoring the actual performance of products against plans, lessons can be learnt to improve the performance of future products. It may also be possible to improve the estimating techniques used.

> ## Backflush accounting
>
> - The basic concept of backflush accounting
> - The difference between traditional costing and costing with backflush accounting
> - Backflush accounting with two 'trigger points'
> - Backflush accounting with one 'trigger point'
> - Backflush accounting: conclusion

4 Backflush accounting

4.1 The basic concept of backflush accounting

Backflush accounting is a method of accounting that begins by focusing on output and then works backwards, allocating costs between cost of goods sold and inventories. This is the complete opposite to traditional cost accounting, which begins by calculating the cost of production and inventories and works forwards to establish a cost of sales and value for closing inventory.

It simplifies costing accounting, because it ignores labour variances and work-in-progress value.

Backflush accounting is ideally suited to a **JIT philosophy** and is suitable where inventory levels are low and so inventory values are immaterial. Transfers between processes are often made at standard cost, and any variances are taken directly as a total variance to the income statement as a gain or a loss.

4.2 The difference between traditional costing and costing with backflush accounting

Backflush accounting is a method of cost accounting that is consistent with JIT systems.

- Traditional cost accounting systems for manufacturing costs are 'sequential tracking' systems. They track the costs of items as they progress through the manufacturing process, from raw materials, through work in progress to finished goods. At each stage of the manufacturing process, more costs are added and recorded within the cost accounting system.

- The main benefit of sequential tracking costing systems is that they can be used to put a cost to items of inventory. When inventory is large, there is a need to measure inventory costs with reasonable 'accuracy'.

- With a JIT philosophy, this benefit does not exist. Inventory should be small, or even non-existent. The cost of inventory is therefore fairly insignificant. A costing system that measures the cost of inventory is therefore of little or no value, and is certainly not worth the time, effort and expenditure involved.

- Backflush accounting is an alternative costing system that can be applied in a JIT environment. It is ideally suited to a manufacturing environment where production cycle times are fairly short and inventory levels are low.

As the term 'backflush' might suggest, costs are calculated after production has been completed. They are allocated between the cost of goods sold and inventories in retrospect. They are not built up as work progresses through the production process.

4.3 Backflush accounting with two 'trigger points'

A backflush accounting system has one or two trigger points, when costs are recorded. When there are two trigger points, these are usually:

- the purchase of raw materials and
- the manufacture of completed products.

A numerical example will be used to illustrate the costing method.

 Example

Suppose that a manufacturing company operates a JIT system. At the beginning of a period, it has no inventory of raw materials or finished goods. It manufactures a single product, Product P, which has the following standard cost:

	$
Raw materials	20
Direct labour	8
Overheads	22
	50

During the period, it incurred the following costs:

Raw materials purchased	$2,030,000
Direct labour costs incurred	$775,000
Overhead costs incurred	$2,260,000

The company made 100,000 units of Product P and sold 98,000 units.

The company uses a backflush costing system, with trigger points at raw materials purchase and at completion of production.

Trigger point 1

Record the purchase of raw materials:

Raw materials inventory account

	$		$
Creditors	2,030,000		

Trigger point 2

Record the manufacture of the 100,000 units:

Finished goods inventory account

		$		$
Raw materials	(100,000 × 20)	2,000,000		
Conversion costs	(100,000 × 30)	3,000,000		

Raw materials inventory account

	$		$
Creditors	2,030,000	Finished goods inventory	2,000,000
		Closing balance c/f	30,000
	2,030,000		2,030,000

Conversion costs account

	$		$
Bank (labour cost)	775,000	Finished goods inventory	3,000,000
Creditors (overheads)	2,260,000	Balance	35,000
	3,035,000		3,035,000

The closing balance on the raw materials account may represent the cost of closing inventory. If so, it is carried forward as an opening balance to the start of the next period. However, any cost variance (difference between standard and actual material cost) should be taken to the income statement for the period.

Similarly, the balance on the conversion costs account probably represents cost variances for labour and overhead, and this should be written off to the income statement for the period.

Management should identify the cause of any variances, and take control measures where appropriate. However, variances will probably be analysed using non-financial methods of investigation, and it is unlikely that detailed cost variances will be calculated in the backflush costing system.

The cost of sales and closing inventory of finished goods are simply recorded as follows:

Finished goods inventory account

		$			$
Raw materials	(100,000 × 20)	2,000,000	Cost of goods sold	(98,000 × 50)	4,900,000
Conversion costs	(100,000 × 30)	3,000,000	Closing inventory	(2,000 × 50)	100,000
		5,000,000			5,000,000

4.4 Backflush accounting with one 'trigger point'

An even simpler backflush accounting system has just one trigger point, the manufacture of finished units. Using the same example, the cost accounting entries would be as follows:

Finished goods inventory account

		$			$
Creditors	(100,000 × 20)	2,000,000	Cost of goods sold	(98,000 × 50)	4,900,000
Conversion costs	(100,000 × 30)	3,000,000	Closing inventory	(2,000 × 50)	100,000
		5,000,000			5,000,000

Conversion costs account

	$		$
Bank (labour cost)	775,000	Finished goods inventory	3,000,000
Creditors (overheads)	2,260,000	Balance	35,000
	3,035,000		3,035,000

The only difference is that there is no raw materials inventory account. The $30,000 of materials that has been purchased but not used is simply not recorded in the costing system, and is therefore not included in closing inventory at the end of the period.

4.5 Backflush accounting: conclusion

The examples above should illustrate that with backflush accounting, costs are not 'tracked' sequentially from raw materials through work in progress to finished goods and cost of sales. They are applied in retrospect, from finished goods and back to raw materials and conversion costs.

Backflush accounting therefore avoids the need to maintain a detailed cost accounting system, which can be regarded as a non-value added activity.

Management must monitor performance, but performance measurement is more likely to consist of non-financial performance indicators, rather than detailed cost variances.

Throughput accounting

- Assumptions in throughput accounting
- Throughput, inventory and operating expenses
- Profit and throughput accounting
- The value of inventory in throughput accounting
- Comparing throughput accounting with absorption costing and marginal costing

5 Throughput accounting

5.1 Assumptions in throughput accounting

Throughput accounting is associated with the Theory of Constraints (TOC) and is also based on the view that the only variable cost in operations is the cost of materials bought from external suppliers.

- In traditional marginal costing, it is assumed that direct labour costs are a variable cost, but in practice this is not usually correct. Employees are paid a fixed weekly or monthly wage or salary, and labour costs are a fixed cost.
- The only variable cost is the purchase cost of materials and components purchased from external suppliers.
- A business makes real profit by adding value. Value is added by selling goods or services to customers whose market value is more than the cost of the materials that go into making them. However, value is not added until the sale is actually made.
- Value added should be measured as the value of the sale minus variable cost, which is the cost of the materials.

5.2 Throughput, inventory and operating expenses

Throughput accounting is therefore based on three concepts:

- throughput
- inventory (investment) and
- operating expenses.

Throughput

Throughput is defined as 'the rate of production of a defined process over a stated period of time. Rates may be expressed in terms of unit of products, batches produced, turnover or other meaningful measurements' (CIMA **Official Terminology**).

Value is added by creating throughput. The value of throughput can be measured as follows:

Throughput = Sales minus Variable costs

Throughput differs from contribution in traditional marginal costing because variable costs consist only of real variable costs, which are (mainly) materials costs.

It is therefore appropriate to define throughput as:

Throughput = Sales minus Cost of raw materials and components

Inventory (or investment)

Inventory or investment is all the money that is tied up in a business, in inventories of raw materials, WIP and finished goods. Inventory is eventually converted into throughput.

Operating expenses

Operating expenses are all the expenditures incurred to produce the throughput. They consist of all costs that are not variable costs, and so include labour costs.

5.3   Profit and throughput accounting

Profit in throughput accounting is measured as throughput minus operating expenses.

Example

	$
Sales	800,000
Raw materials and components costs	350,000
Throughput	450,000
Operating expenses	340,000
Net profit	110,000

A feature of throughput accounting that makes it different from other methods of costing, such as absorption costing and marginal costing, is that operating expenses are not charged to products, The throughput from individual products is measured, but nothing else except net profit.

5.4   The value of inventory in throughput accounting

Inventories do not have value, except the variable cost of the materials and components. Even for work-in-progress and inventories of finished goods, the only money invested is the purchase cost of the raw materials. No value is added until the inventory is sold.

- In throughput accounting, all inventory is therefore valued at the cost of its raw materials and components, and nothing more.

- It should not include any other costs, not even labour costs. No value is added by the production process, not even by labour, until the item is sold.

■ It is **impossible** to make extra profit simply by producing more output, unless the extra output is sold.

5.5 Comparing throughput accounting with absorption costing and marginal costing

The difference between throughput accounting and the traditional methods of accounting can be illustrated with an example.

Example

A company makes 1,000 units of a product during May and sells 800 units for $32,000. There was no inventory at the beginning of the month. Costs of production were:

	$
Raw materials	6,000
Direct labour	8,000
Fixed production overheads	10,000
Other non-production overheads	5,000

Required

Calculate the profit for the period using:

(a)   absorption costing

(b)   marginal costing

(c)   throughput accounting.

Assume for the purpose of absorption costing that budgeted and actual production overheads were the same, and there are no under- or over-absorbed overheads.

Answer

The value of closing inventory:

Absorption costing: $4,800 ($24,000 × 200/1,000)
Marginal costing: $2,800 ($14,000 × 200/1,000)
Throughput accounting: $1,200 ($6,000 × 200/1,000) in throughput accounting.

Profit for the month using each costing method is therefore as follows:

Absorption costing			Marginal costing			Throughput accounting	
	$			$			$
Sales	32,000		Sales	32,000		Sales	32,000
Production costs	24,000		Variable production costs	14,000		Materials bought	6,000
Closing inventory	4,800		Closing inventory	2,800		Inventory	1,200
Cost of sales	19,200		Variable costs of sale	11,200			4,800
Gross profit	12,800		Contribution	20,800		Throughput	27,200
Other overheads	5,000		Fixed overheads	15,000		Operating expenses	23,000
Profit	7,800		Profit	5,800		Net profit	4,200

The differences in profit are entirely due to the differences in inventory valuations.

> ## Throughput accounting and the Theory of Constraints
>
> - The Theory of Constraints
> - Constraints and bottlenecks in the system
> - Dealing with constraints
> - The relevance of the Theory of Constraints to throughput accounting
> - Throughput accounting ratio
> - Throughput accounting and decision-making

6 Throughput accounting and the Theory of Constraints

6.1 The Theory of Constraints

The theory of constraints is derived from system theory.

- Every system, including a business organisation, has inputs. Inputs are processed into outputs from the system. Inputs of a business include resources of materials, labour and capital. Outputs include finished products and services.

- A system consists of many different parts or sub-systems that inter-react with each other. The performance of each sub-system depends on the performance of other sub-systems. The output of one sub-system becomes the input to other sub-systems.

- A system can be affected by conditions or events in its external environment.

- Every system has a goal. A business system, for example, might have the goal of making profits.

6.2 Constraints and bottlenecks in the system

Every system has a constraint. A constraint is anything that limits the output from the system. If a system had no constraint, its output would be either zero or the system would continue to produce more and more output without limit. Therefore for any system whose output is not zero, there must be a constraint that stops it from producing more output than it does.

Constraints in a business system might be caused by any of the following:

- external factors, such as a limit to customer demand for the products made by the business

- weaknesses in the system itself, and the way that its sub-systems operate and interact

- weaknesses in the system's controls.

In a manufacturing system, constraints can be described as **bottlenecks** in the system. A bottleneck is simply a constraint that limits throughput. For example, a bottleneck might be a shortage of materials, or a shortage of machine time.

6.3   Dealing with constraints

The management of business operations should focus on dealing with the key constraints.

The output of a system is restricted by its key constraint. Management must identify what this is.

Action by management to improve operational efficiency is a waste of time and effort if it is applied to any area of operations that is not a constraint. For example, measures to improve labour efficiency are a waste of time if the key constraint is a shortage of machine capacity.

The key constraint limits throughput. The nature of the key constraint might be:

- limitations on sales demand
- inefficiency in production, with stoppages and hold-ups caused by wastage, scrapped items and machine downtime
- unreliability in the supplies of key raw materials, and a shortage of key materials
- a shortage of a key production resource, such as skilled labour.

Goldratt, who developed the Theory of Constraints, argued that:

- Management should identify the key constraint and consider ways of removing or easing the constraint, so that the system is able to produce more output.
- However, when one constraint is removed, another key constraint will take its place.
- The new key constraint must be identified, and management should now turn its attention to ways of removing or easing the new key constraint.
- By removing constraints one after another, the output capacity of the system will increase.

However, there will always be a key constraint.

6.4   The relevance of the Theory of Constraints to throughput accounting

Goldratt argued that if the aim of a business is to make money and profit, the most appropriate methods of doing this are to:

- increase throughput
- reduce operating expenses, or
- reduce inventory (since there is a cost in holding inventory).

He therefore championed throughput accounting. He also argued that the most effective of these three ways of increasing profit is to increase throughput.

Throughput can be increased by identifying the bottlenecks in the system, and taking action to remove them or ease them.

6.5 Throughput accounting ratio

Performance can be measured using three ratios:

- Throughput per unit of the bottleneck resource
- Operating expenses per unit of the bottleneck resource
- Throughput accounting ratio.

The throughput accounting ratio is the ratio of [throughput in a period per unit of bottleneck resource] to [operating expenses per unit of bottleneck resource].

Units of a bottleneck resource are measured in hours (labour hours or machine hours). This means that the throughput accounting ratio can be stated as:

$$\text{Throughput accounting ratio} = \frac{\text{Throughput per hour of bottleneck resource}}{\text{Operating expenses per hour of bottleneck resource}}$$

Example

A business manufactures product Z, which has a selling price of $20. The materials costs are $8 per unit of Product Z. Total operating expenses each month are $120,000.

Machine capacity is the key constraint on production. There are only 600 machine hours available each month, and it takes three minutes of machine time to manufacture each unit of Product Z.

Required

(a) Calculate the throughput accounting ratio.

(b) How might this ratio be increased?

Answer

(a) Through put per machine hour $= \dfrac{\$(20-8)}{\dfrac{3}{60}\text{hours}} = \$240$

Operating expenses per machine hour $= \dfrac{\$120,000}{600 \text{ hours}} = \$200$

Throughput accounting ratio $= \dfrac{\$240}{\$200} = 1.20$

(b) To increase the throughput accounting ratio, it might be possible to:

- Raise the selling price for Product Z for each unit sold, to increase the throughput per unit.

- Improve the efficiency of machine time used, and so manufacture Product Z in less than three minutes.

- Find ways of reducing total operating expenses, in order to reduce the operating expenses per machine hour.

6.6   Throughput accounting and decision-making

In a multi-product situation, throughput per unit of limiting factor can be used to rank products in order of priority of production. The approach is the same as limiting factor analysis with the exception that only materials are treated as a variable cost.

Paper F5
Performance management

CHAPTER

2

Limiting factors and linear programming

Contents	
1	Costs for decision-making
2	Limiting factor decisions: single limiting factor
3	Limiting factor decisions: linear programming
4	Linear programming: graphical solution
5	Linear programming: shadow prices and slack

Costs for decision-making

- Management information for making decisions
- Using marginal costing for decision-making

---

1 Costs for decision-making

1.1 Management information for making decisions

Decisions involve a choice about what should be done. Management might need information about costs and revenues in order to make decisions. By estimating the costs and revenues from each possible course of action, management can identify the choice that will maximise profits.

Information for decision-making is different from information about historical costs.

Decisions are concerned with the future:

- Information about costs and revenues should be about **future costs and future revenues.**
- Decisions should be concerned with **cash and cash flow.** Only those costs and revenues that represent cash flow are relevant to decision-making.
- It is assumed for the purpose of providing cost information for decision-making that the aim or **objective is to maximise profit.**
- **Historical costs are irrelevant** for decision-making, because they are not future costs.
- However, historical costs can provide a guide to what future costs will be.

1.2 Using marginal costing for decision-making

Marginal costs are normally relevant costs for decision-making.

- The marginal cost of a product is the extra cost that would be incurred by making and selling one extra unit of the product.
- Similarly, the marginal cost of an extra hour of direct labour work is the additional cost that would be incurred if a direct labour employee worked one extra hour. When direct labour is a variable cost, paid by the hour, the marginal cost is the variable cost of the direct labour wages plus any variable overhead cost related to direct labour hours.

Examples of the use of marginal costing for decision-making are:

- **Planning decisions:** marginal costing can be used to estimate future profits. This can be very useful when a company prepares its annual budget.
- **Limiting factor decisions.** Marginal costing is also used when there is a shortage of a key resource, such as materials or skilled labour, to identify the output plan that will maximise profits.

- **Make or buy decisions.** When there is a choice between making an item in-house or buying it externally from a sub-contractor, marginal costing can be used to decide on the profit-maximising programme for buying externally.

This chapter focuses on decision-making when there are limiting factors that restrict operational capabilities.

| Limiting factor decisions: single limiting factor |

- Definition of a limiting factor
- Maximising profit when there is a single limiting factor
- Identifying limiting factors

2 Limiting factor decisions: single limiting factor

2.1 Definition of a limiting factor

It is normally assumed in budgeting that a company can produce as many units of its products (or services) as is necessary to meet the available sales demand. Sales demand is therefore normally the factor that sets a limit on the volume of sales in each period.

Sometimes, however, there could be a shortage of a key production resource, such as an item of direct materials, or skilled labour, or machine capacity. In these circumstances, the factor setting a limit to the volume of sales and profit in a particular period is the availability of the scarce resource.

It is assumed in this chapter that a company makes and sells more than one different product. When there is a limiting factor, the problem is therefore to decide how many of each different product to make and sell in order to maximise profits.

2.2 Maximising profit when there is a single limiting factor

When there is just one limiting factor (other than sales demand), total profit will be maximised in a period by maximising the total contribution earned with the available scarce resources.

- The objective should be to maximise total contribution.
- This will be achieved by maximising the contribution in total from the scarce resources.
- Products should therefore be ranked in order or priority for manufacture and sale.
- The priority ranking should be according to the **contribution earned by each product (or service) for each unit of the scarce** resource that the product uses.
- The products or services should be produced and sold in this order of priority, up to the expected sales demand for each product.
- The planned output and sales should be decided by working down through the priority list until all the units of the limiting factor have been used.

In other words, in order to maximise profit, the aim should be to maximise the contribution for each unit of limiting factor used.

Example

A company makes four products, A, B, C and D, using the same direct labour work force on all the products. Budgeted data for the company is as follows:

Product	A	B	C	D
Annual sales demand (units)	4,000	5,000	8,000	4,000
	£	£	£	£
Direct materials cost	3.0	6.0	5.0	6.0
Direct labour cost	6.0	12.0	3.0	9.0
Variable overhead	2.0	4.0	1.0	3.0
Fixed overhead	3.0	6.0	2.0	4.0
Full cost	14.0	28.0	11.0	22.0
Sales price	15.5	29.0	11.5	27.0
Profit per unit	1.5	1.0	0.5	5.0

Direct labour is paid £12 per hour. However, only 6,000 direct labour hours are available during the year.

Required

Identify the quantities of production and sales of each product that would maximise annual profit.

Answer

The products should be ranked in order of priority according to the contribution that they make per direct labour hour.

	A	B	C	D
	£	£	£	£
Sales price/unit	15.5	29.0	11.5	27.0
Variable cost/unit	11.0	22.0	9.0	18.0
Contribution per unit	4.5	7.0	2.5	9.0
Direct labour hours/unit	0.5	1.0	0.25	0.75
Contribution/direct labour hour	9.0	7.0	10.0	12.0
Priority for making and selling	3·	4·	2·	1·

The products should be made and sold in the order D, C, A and then B, up to the volume of sales demand for each product and until all the available direct labour hours (limiting factor resources) are used up.

Profit-maximising budget

Product	Sales units	Direct labour hours	Contribution per unit	Total contribution
			£	£
D (1st)	4,000	3,000	9.0	36,000
C (2nd)	8,000	2,000	2.5	20,000
A (3rd)	2,000 (balance)	1,000	4.5	9,000
		6,000		65,000

2.3 Identifying limiting factors

You might not be told by an examination question that a limiting factor exists, although you might be told that there is a restricted supply of certain resources. You might be expected to identify the limiting factor by calculating the budgeted availability of each resource and the amount of the resource that is needed to meet the available sales demand.

Example

A company manufactures and sells two products, Product X and Product Y. The two products are manufactured on the same machines. There are two types of machine, and the time required to make each unit of product is as follows:

	Product X	Product Y
Machine type 1	10 minutes per unit	6 minutes per unit
Machine type 2	5 minutes per unit	12 minutes per unit

Sales demand each year is for 12,000 units of Product X and 15,000 units of Product Y.

The contribution per unit is £7 for Product X and £5 for Product Y.

There is a limit to machine capacity, however, and in each year there are only 3,000 hours of Machine 1 time available and 4,200 hours of Machine 2 time available.

Required

Recommend what the company should make and sell in order to maximise its annual profit.

Answer

The first step is to identify whether or not there is any limiting factor other than sales demand. To do this we calculate the required machine time to manufacture units of Product X and Y to meet the sales demand in full. We then compare this requirement for machine time with the actual time available.

	Machine type 1	Machine type 2
	hours	hours
Time required		
To make 12,000 units of Product X	2,000	1,000
To make 15,000 units of Product Y	1,500	3,000
Hours needed to meet sales demand	3,500	4,000
Hours available	3,000	4,200
Shortfall	(500)	-

Machine type 1 is a limiting factor, but Machine type 2 is not. To maximise contribution and profit, we should therefore give priority to the product that gives the higher contribution per hour of machine type 1.

	Product X	Product Y
Contribution per unit	£7	£5
Machine type 1 time per unit	10 minutes	6 minutes
Contribution per hour (Machine type 1)	£42	£50
Priority for making and selling	2-	1·

Profit-maximising budget

Product	Sales units	Machine type 1 hours	Contribution per unit	Total contribution
			£	£
Y (1st)	15,000	1,500	5.0	75,000
X (2nd) - balance	9,000	1,500	7.0	63,000
		3,000		138,000

> **Limiting factor decisions: linear programming**
>
> - Two or more limiting factors
> - Formulating a linear programming problem
> - The objective function
> - Formulating the constraints

3 Limiting factor decisions: linear programming

3.1 Two or more limiting factors

When there is more than one limiting factor (other than sales demand for the products), the contribution-maximising plan cannot be identified simply by ranking products in order of contribution per unit of limiting factor.

The problem can be formulated as a linear programming problem.

3.2 Formulating a linear programming problem

A linear programming problem is formulated by:

- identifying an objective function, and
- formulating two or more constraints, one for each limiting factor or other restriction (such as maximum sales demand).

3.3 The objective function

The objective of a linear programming problem is to maximise or minimise the value of something. For the purpose of your examination, it is likely to be the objective of maximising total contribution. (The objective might possibly be something else, such as the objective of minimising costs.)

An objective function expresses the objective, such as total contribution, as a formula.

 Example

A company makes and sells two products, Product X and Product Y. The contribution per unit is £8 for Product X and £12 for Product Y. The company wishes to maximise profit.

If it is assumed that total fixed costs are the same at all levels of output and sales, the objective of the company is to maximise total contribution.

Total contribution can be expressed as a formula, as follows:

Let the number of units (made and sold) of Product X be x

Let the number of units (made and sold) of Product Y be y

The objective function is therefore to maximise:

(Total contribution): $8x + 12y$.

3.4   Formulating the constraints

In a linear programming problem, there is a separate constraint for each item that might put a limitation on the objective function.

Each constraint, like the objective function, is expressed as a formula. Each constraint must also specify the amount of the limit or constraint.

If there is a **maximum limit**, the constraint must be expressed as 'must be equal to or less than'.

For example, if there is a maximum sales demand for Product X of 5,000 units, the constraint for sales demand for X would be expressed as:

$x \le 5{,}000$

Similarly, if there is a **minimum limit**, the constraint must be expressed as 'must be equal to or more than'. For example, if there is a requirement to supply a customer with at least 2,000 units of Product X, this constraint would be expressed as:

$x \ge 2{,}000$

Non-negativity constraints

A requirement of linear programming problems is that there should be no negative values in the final solution. For example, it is not possible to make and sell *minus 4,000* units of Product Y.

Constraints in the linear programming problem should therefore be that each 'variable' must be equal to or greater than 0.

For example:

(Non-negativity constraint): $x, y \ge 0$.

Example

A company makes and sells two products, Product X and Product Y. The contribution per unit is £8 for Product X and £12 for Product Y. The company wishes to maximise profit.

The expected sales demand is for 6,000 units of Product X and 4,000 units of Product Y. However, there are limitations to the amount of labour time and machine time that is available in the period:

	Product X	Product Y
Direct labour hours per unit	3 hours	2 hours
Machine hours per unit	1 hour	2.5 hours

	Total hours
Direct labour hours available, in total	20,000
Machine hours available, in total	12,000

A linear programming problem can be formulated as follows:

Let the number of units (made and sold) of Product X be x
Let the number of units (made and sold) of Product Y be y

The objective function is to maximise total contribution: $8x + 12y$.

Subject to the following constraints:

Direct labour	$3x + 2y$	$\leq$	20,000
Machine time	$x + 2.5y$	$\leq$	12,000
Sales demand, X	x	$\leq$	6,000
Sales demand, Y	y	$\leq$	4,000
Non-negativity	x, y	$\geq$	0

If you do not like figures with fractions in a constraint, the constraint for machine time could be expressed (by doubling it) as:

Machine time	$2x + 5y$	$\leq$	24,000

> **Linear programming: graphical solution**
>
> - Drawing the constraints on a graph
> - Maximising (or minimising) the objective function
> - Calculating the value for the objective function
> - An alternative approach to a solution

4 Linear programming: graphical solution

When there are just two variables in a linear programming problem (x and y), the problem can be solved by a graphical method. The solution identifies the values of x and y that maximise (or minimise) the value of the objective function.

There are three stages in solving a problem by the graphical method:

- **Step 1**: Draw the constraints on a graph, to establish the feasible combinations of values for the two variables x and y that are within all the constraints in the problem.

- **Step 2**: Identify the combination of values for x and y, within this feasible area, that maximises (or minimises) the objective function. This is the solution to the problem.

- **Step 3**: Calculate the value for the objective function that this solution provides.

4.1 Drawing the constraints on a graph

The constraints in a linear programming problem can be drawn as straight lines on a graph, provided that there are just two variables in the problem (x and y). One axis of the graph represents values for one of the variables, and the other axis represents values for the second variable.

The straight line for each constraint is the boundary edge of the constraint – its outer limit (or inner limit, in the case of minimum values).

For example, suppose we have a constraint:
$2x + 3y \leq 600$

The outer limit of this constraint is represented by a line:
$2x + 3y = 600$.

Combinations of values of x and y beyond this line on the graph (with higher values for x and y) will have a value in excess of 600. These exceed the limit of the constraint, and so cannot be feasible for a solution to the problem.

The constraint is drawn as a straight line. To draw a straight line on a graph, you need to plot just two points and join them up. The easiest points to plot are the combinations of x and y:

- where x = 0, and
- where y = 0.

For the equation 2x + 3y = 600:

- when x = 0, y = 200 (600/3). So plot the point x = 0, y = 200 on the graph
- when y = 0, x = 300 (600/2). So plot the point y = 0, x = 300 on the graph

Join these two points, and you have a line showing the values of x and y that are the maximum possible combined values that meet the requirements of the constraint.

 Example

Suppose that we have the following linear programming problem:

The objective function is to maximise total contribution: 5x + 5y

Subject to the following constraints:

Direct labour	2x + 3y	≤	6,000
Machine time	4x + y	≤	4,000
Sales demand, Y	y	≤	1,800
Non-negativity	x, y	≥	0

The non-negativity constraints are represented by the lines of the x axis and y axis. The other three constraints are drawn as follows, to produce a combination of values for x and y that meet all three constraints. These combinations of values for x and y represent the 'feasible region' on the graph for a solution to the problem.

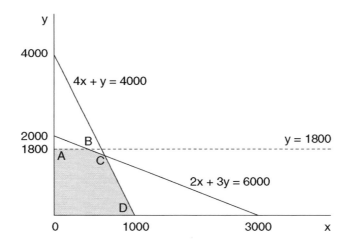

The feasible area for a solution to the problem is shown as the shaded area OABCD. To solve the linear programming problem, we now need to identify the feasible combination of values for x and y that maximises the objective function.

4.2 Maximising (or minimising) the objective function

As a starting point, you might recognise that the combination of values for x and y that maximises the objective function will be a pair of values that lies somewhere along the outer edge of the feasible area.

In the graph above, the solution to the problem will normally be the values of x and y at one of the following points on the graph:

■ A

■ B

■ C, or

■ D

In other words, we will normally expect the solution to be the combination of values for x and y that lies at one of the 'corners' of the outer edge of the feasible area.

(In some cases, the solution might be:

■ any combination of values of x and y along the line AB, or

■ any combination of values of x and y along the line BC, or

■ any combination of values of x and y along the line CD.

However, this would be unusual.)

To identify the combination of values for x and y that are feasible (within all the constraints) and that also maximises the objective function, we need to look at the objective function itself.

We do not know the maximum value (or minimum value) of the objective function. However, we can draw a line that shows all the combinations of x and y that provide the same total value for the objective function.

For example, suppose that the objective function is to maximise contribution $4x + 3y$. We can draw a line on a graph that shows combinations of values for x and y that give the same total contribution, when x has a contribution of 4 and y has a contribution of 3. Any total contribution figure can be chosen, but a convenient multiple of 4 and 3 is simplest and easiest.

■ For example, we could select a total contribution value of $4x + 3y = 12,000$. This contribution line could be found by joining the points on the graph x = 0, y = 4,000 and y = 0, x = 3,000.

■ Instead, we might select a total contribution value of $4x + 3y = 24,000$. This contribution line could be found by joining the points on the graph x = 0, y = 8,000 and y = 0, x = 6,000.

If you draw both of these contribution lines on a graph, you will find that:

■ the two lines are parallel to each other on the graph, and

■ the line with the higher total contribution value for values of x and y (24,000) is further away from the origin of the graph (point 0).

This can be used to identify the solution to a linear programming problem.

■ Draw a line showing combinations of values for x and y that give the same total value for the objective function. (This might be called an 'iso-contribution' line – meaning 'the same' contribution).

■ Look at the slope of the contribution line, and (using a ruler if necessary) identify which combination of values of x and y within the feasible area for the constraints is furthest away from the origin of the graph. This is the combination of values for x and y where an iso-contribution line can be drawn as far to the right as possible that just touches one corner of the feasible area.

This is the combination of values of x and y that provides the solution to the linear programming problem.

Example

Returning to the previous example, we can draw an iso-contribution line for, say, 5x + 5y = 10,000, by joining the points x = 0, y = 2,000 and y = 0, x = 2,000. (The value 10,000 is chosen here as a convenient multiple of the values 5 and 5.)

This should show that the combination of values of x and y that will maximise total contribution lies at point C on the graph.

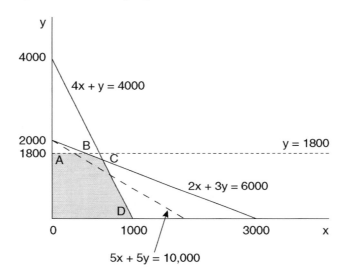

4.3 Calculating the value for the objective function

Having identified which combination of values for x and y provides the solution to the linear programming problem, the final step is to:

■ establish the exact values for x and y at this point, and

■ use these values to calculate the value of the objective function at this point.

You can do this by solving two simultaneous equations for the values of x and y. The simultaneous equations are the equations for the two constraint lines at the point on the graph that provides the solution to the linear programming problem.

Example

In the previous example, the solution is the combination of values of x and y at point C on the graph. At point C, we have the simultaneous equations:

$2x + 3y = 6,000$
$4x + y = 4,000$

We can solve these equations:

(1)	$2x + 3y$	=	6,000
(2)	$4x + y$	=	4,000
Multiply (1) by 2:			
(3)	$4x + 6y$	=	12,000
Subtract (2) from (3):			
	$5y$	=	8,000
Therefore	y	=	1,600
Substitute in equation (2)			
	$4x + 1,600$	=	4,000
	$4x$	=	2,400
	x	=	600

So total contribution is maximised by producing 600 units of X and 1,600 units of Y.

The objective in this problem is to maximise $5x + 5y$.

The total contribution where x = 600 and y = 1,600 is:

$5 (600) + 5 (1,600) = £11,000$.

This is the amount of the maximum achievable contribution.

4.4   An alternative approach to a solution

If you find the iso-contribution line method confusing, there is an alternative method of identifying the solution to a linear programming problem.

When you have drawn the feasible area on a graph, and you have identified the feasible combinations of values for x and y, you will know that the solution lies at one of the corners of the feasible area.

In the previous example, the solution has to be at points A, B, C or D.

You can calculate the values of x and y at each of these points, using simultaneous equations if necessary to calculate the x and y values. Having established the values of x and y at each of the points, calculate the value of the objective function (total contribution) for each.

The solution is the combination of values for x and y at the point where the total contribution is highest.

> ## Linear programming: shadow prices and slack
>
> - Shadow prices and slack
> - The implications for decision-making and performance measurement

5 Linear programming: shadow prices and slack

5.1 Shadow prices and slack

Linear programming is used to find the product mix which maximises contribution given two or more limiting factors and two products. A similar approach can be used when there are more than two products but this can only be solved using simplex which is outside of the scope of your syllabus.

At an optimal product mix there will be some resources which are limiting factors and others which are not binding constraints. A resource which is a limiting factor will have a shadow price.

- The shadow price of a scarce resource is the amount by which the objective function (total contribution) will be increased if one extra unit of the scarce resource could be made available. If direct labour hours are a scarce resource, its shadow price would be the extra total contribution that could be earned if one extra direct labour hour could be made available.

- When sales demand is a constraint in the linear programming problem, it can have a shadow price. For example, if there is a maximum sales demand for Product A of 6,000 units, and in the optimal solution the quantity of Product A to be made and sold is 6,000 units, there would be a shadow price for sales demand for Product A. This is the increase in total contribution that could be achieved if sales demand for Product A could be increased by one unit (to 6,001).

Example
A baker makes two products bread and cakes. A batch of bread earns contribution of £10 and a batch of cakes earns contribution of £18.

The following resources are used:

	Bread per batch	Cakes per batch	Available
Mixing machines	30 minutes	10 minutes	18 hours per day
Ovens	20 minutes	30 minutes	18 hours per day
Skilled labour	20 minutes	20 minutes	10 hours per day

The baker must produce a minimum of 10 batches of bread and 5 batches of cakes to satisfy contracts with local businesses. The maximum demand for bread is 30 batches per day and for cakes 15 batches per day.

Calculate the optimum production plan for the baker and the shadow prices of resources.

Let x = the number of batches of bread baked per day

Let y = the number of batches of cakes baked per day

The objective function is to maximise:

(Total contribution): $10x + 18y$.

Subject to the constraints

Mixing machines	$30x + 10y \leq 1,080 \ (18 \times 60)$
Ovens	$20x + 30y \leq 1,080 \ (18 \times 60)$
Skilled labour	$20x + 20y \leq 600 \ (10 \times 60)$
Demand for bread	$x \leq 30$
Demand for cakes	$y \leq 15$
Minimum production	$x \geq 10, \ y \geq 5$
Non-negativity	$x, y \geq 0$

To graph the constraints calculate two points on each line.

Mixing machines $30x + 10y = 1,080$

If $x = 0, y = 108$

If $y = 0, x = 36$

Ovens $20x + 30y = 1,080$

If $x = 0, y = 36$

If $y = 0, x = 54$

Skilled labour $20x + 20y = 600$

If $x = 0, y = 30$

If $y = 0, x = 30$

The lines $x = 30$, $y = 15$, $x = 10$, $y = 5$ can also be graphed.

Minimum production $x \geq 10, \ y \geq 5$

Batches of cake

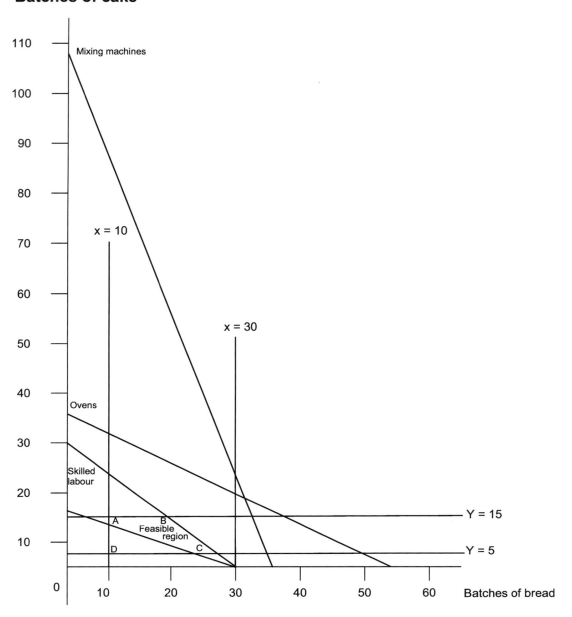

The feasible region is ABCD. The optimum combination can be found by plotting the objective function 10x + 18 y.

Try 10x + 18y = 300

If x = 0, y = 16.7

If y = 0, x = 30

It can be seen from the gradient of the objective function that the optimum solution is point B. At this point the constraints y = 15 and 20x +20y = 600 intersect.

Solving we have y = 15 and x = 15 and the optimum production plan is to make 15 batches of bread and cakes. Contribution earned will be 15 × £10 + 15 × £18 = £420

Shadow prices can be found for the scarce resources, which in this example are skilled labour and demand for cakes.

To find the shadow price for skilled labour assume that one more hour of labour becomes available. The constraint is now
20x + 20y = 660.

The new optimum solution is y = 15 and 20x + 20 × 15 = 660 or x = 18
Contribution earned is now 18 × £10 + 15 × £18 = £450.

Contribution has increased by £30. This is the shadow price of skilled labour.

To find the shadow price for demand for cakes assume that one more batch of cakes could be sold. The new constraints would be:
Y = 16 and
20x + 20 y = 600

Solving these, the optimum solution is y = 16 and x = 14
Contribution earned would be 14 × £10 + 16 × £18 = £428 an increase of £8 compared to the original solution. This is the shadow price for the demand for cakes.

All of the other resources are under-utilised and represent slack at the optimum solution.

For example, at the optimum solution of 15 batches of bread and cakes the mixing machines are used for

30 × 15 + 30 × 10 = 750 minutes or 12.5 hours. They are available for 18 hours so there is slack of 5.5 hours.

Now attempt question 'Proglin' from the questions at the back of the study text.

5.2   The implications for decision-making and performance measurement

The calculation of shadow prices and slack has important implications for decision-making and performance management.

A shadow price represents the highest premium that should be paid for additional units of the scarce resource. In the previous example the shadow price for skilled labour was £30. The baker could afford to pay an overtime premium of up to £30 per hour to obtain more labour. The shadow price for cakes was £8. The baker could afford to increase advertising or delivery costs of the cakes by up to £8 per batch to increase demand.

Shadow prices will not be valid for infinite increases of the scarce resource as at some point another resource will become the binding constraint. In the previous example the shadow price for labour of £30 will be valid until production is increased to such an extent that mixing machine time, oven time or demand becomes in short supply. This point can be calculated using the linear programming diagram by moving the skilled labour line out until it reaches another constraint line.

The existence of slack has important implications for performance measurement as it measures the extent of underutilised resources. It may be possible to find other uses of these resources or reallocate them to areas of scarcity. For example, machines could be utilised in different ways and staff could be retrained.

CHAPTER

3

Pricing

Contents

1	Factors that influence price
2	Cost-based pricing methods
3	Sales demand and price elasticity of demand
4	Market-based approaches to pricing

■ Type of market

■ Cost

■ Product life cycle

■ Other issues

1 Factors that influence price

1.1 Type of market

Perfect competition

When there is perfect competition in the market, there are many different suppliers competing to sell identical products. In the real world, perfect competition is rare, but markets with features similar to those of perfect competition include foreign exchange markets and some commodities markets.

In perfect competition:

■ an individual firm is unable to influence the price for its own goods, because identical products are obtainable from competitors

■ the selling price in the market is determined by the forces of demand and supply

■ the selling price in the market is the price that all suppliers in the market must accept to remain competitive: every supplier can produce and sell as much output as they want to and sell it at this price.

■ Suppliers in a perfectly competitive market are 'price takers' and they must accept the market price.

Imperfect competition

When there is imperfect competition in the market, a supplier has more influence over the selling price that it charges for its products. Imperfect competition exists when there are relatively few suppliers in the market, and suppliers seek to differentiate their products from those of their competitors.

The effect of imperfect competition is that firms are able to decide their selling prices (they are 'price takers'). However, the higher the sales price, the lower the sales demand for their product. In microeconomics terms, firms in imperfectly-competitive markets face a 'downward-sloping demand curve'.

Oligopoly

An oligopolistic market is where there are a few large suppliers, all of which have market power. Examples include the supermarket sector and oil companies. This type of market is characterised by stable prices and intense non-price competition.

Any attempt to lower prices to increase market share is met with fierce competition which results in a lowering of profits for all companies in the market.

Monopoly

A monopoly is where there is only one supplier in the market. Monopolies often exist due to barriers to entry in the market. For example, pharmaceutical companies may patent new drugs to prevent their production by other companies and governments may control key industries such as electricity and water to protect the economy. A monopoly supplier can choose the price set in the market and the customer will have to pay this price to obtain goods or service. Governments often regulate monopoly markets to protect the consumer from unfair exploitation.

It can be seen that one of the key differences between the types of market is the degree of competition. This will have a great impact on the price that a company will be able to charge.

1.2   Cost

In the long run, price must exceed average cost in order to make a profit. Cost is therefore a major determinant of price. Cost will be influenced by:

■ Suppliers' prices.

■ Price inflation

■ Exchange rate movements

■ Quality

Organisations may have to decide where they wish to position their product in the market in terms of quality. Premium pricing can be used for high quality products but consumers may prefer lower quality, lower priced products. A clear understanding of the link between quality and cost will be needed to help management determine the optimum price/quality mix.

1.3   Product life cycle

As a product goes through the different stages of its life cycle, the pricing policy might be changed.

■ **Introduction stage**. During the introduction stage, the product is introduced to the market. If the product is new, and there are no rival products on the market, there is a choice between a market skimming policy for pricing or a market penetration policy. These are explained below.

■ **Growth stage**. During the growth stage of the life cycle, demand for the product increases rapidly, but more competitors enter the market. If the market is competitive, each firm might have to lower its prices to win a share of the growing market. However, because sales demand is strong, prices and profit margins are likely to be fairly high (although falling). Some companies might try to identify a specialist 'niche' in the market, where they have more control over pricing of their products. Similarly, companies might try to keep prices higher by differentiating their product from those of competitors on the basis of quality or other distinguishing features (such as design differences).

- **Maturity stage**. When a product reaches the maturity stage of its life cycle, total sales demand in the market becomes stable, but the product may become a 'commodity'. Firms must then compete for market share, often by cutting prices. Companies might use product differentiation strategies to keep the price of their product higher than it might otherwise be, but prices generally will be lower than during the growth stage of the life cycle.

- **Decline**. Eventually, the market demand for a product declines. When sales demand falls, companies leave the market. Those that remain keep on selling the product as long as they can make a profit. Prices might remain very low. In some cases, however, a product might acquire 'rarity value', allowing companies to raise prices. However, since unit costs will also be higher, it is still difficult to make a profit.

When a business entity is trying to decide whether or not to develop and launch a new product, the **expected sales demand over its life cycle** should be taken into consideration in the DCF analysis.

1.4 Other issues

Other issues which may influence the price chosen are:

- Product range

  Products may be complements, for example computer game consoles and computer games, or substitutes, for example different brands of washing powder. A business often offers a range of products and the pricing decision may be influenced by this. So, for example, a decision may be made to charge a low price for games consoles to increase demand and then to charge a high price for computer games to earn a profit. The low priced product may even be sold at a loss, a loss leader, to gain customers if it is likely that a profit can be made from other purchases in the product range.

- Price perception

  Customers may perceive that price reflects quality and may be prepared to increase demand when price increases.

- Growth in income

  During periods of economic growth, income will be increasing and consumers may be less concerned about price increases and more concerned about the quality of the product and the ease of purchase. In periods of recession, price may become a more important factor.

Cost-based pricing methods

- Pricing decisions
- Full cost plus pricing
- Marginal cost plus pricing (mark-up pricing)
- Return on investment (ROI) pricing
- Opportunity cost pricing (minimum pricing)

---

2 Cost-based pricing methods

2.1 Pricing decisions

Entities have to make decisions about pricing the goods they sell and the services they provide. There are various methods of pricing, and the most suitable method of pricing depends on the circumstances.

There are two broad categories to making pricing decisions:

- calculating a price on the basis of **cost**
- deciding a price on the basis of **market factors**, such as prices charged by competitors for similar items, and the prices that customers are willing to pay

2.2 Full cost plus pricing

With full cost plus pricing, a mark-up or profit margin is added to the fully absorbed cost of the item to obtain a selling price.

Profit is expressed as either:

- a percentage of the full cost (a profit 'mark-up') or
- a percentage of the sales price (a 'profit margin').

	$
Variable production costs	600
Other variable costs	200
Absorbed overheads:	
Production overheads absorbed	800
Non-production overheads absorbed	300
Full cost	1,900
Profit (added to full cost)	380
Selling price	2,280

In this example the profit mark-up is 380/1,900 = 20% and the profit margin is 380/2,280 = 16.7%.

When full cost plus pricing is used to calculate a selling price for standard units of a product, the selling price per unit may be calculated as:

$$\frac{[\text{Total budgeted production costs} \quad + \text{Total budgeted non} \quad - \text{production costs}] + \text{Profit}}{\text{Budgeted sales units}}$$

Notes on calculating the profit:

■ If the mark-up is x% of full cost, the selling price is Full cost + x%.

■ If the profit margin is y% of the sales price, the profit is [y/(100 – y)] × Full cost

Advantages of full cost plus pricing

A business entity might have an idea of the percentage profit margin it would like to earn. It might therefore decide the average profit mark-up on cost that it would like to earn from sales, as a general guideline for its pricing decisions. This can be useful for businesses that carry out a large amount of **contract work** or **jobbing work**, for which individual job or contract prices must be quoted regularly to prospective customers and there is no obvious 'fair market' price.

The percentage mark-up or profit margin does not have to be a fixed percentage figure. It can be varied to suit the circumstances, such as demand conditions in the market and what the customer is prepared to pay.

There are also other possible advantages in using full cost plus pricing:

■ If the budgeted sales volume is achieved, sales revenue will cover all costs and there will be a profit.

■ It is useful for justifying price rises to customers, when an increase in price occurs as a consequence of an increase in costs.

Disadvantages of full cost plus pricing

The main disadvantage of cost plus pricing is that it is calculated on the basis of cost, without any consideration of market conditions, such as competitors' prices.

■ Cost plus pricing fails to allow for the fact that when the sales demand for a product is affected by its selling price, there is a profit-maximising combination of price and demand. A cost plus based approach to pricing is unlikely to arrive at the profit-maximising price for the product.

■ In most markets, prices must be adjusted to market and demand conditions. The pricing decision cannot be made on a cost basis only.

There are also other disadvantages:

■ The choice of profit margin or mark-up is arbitrary. How is it decided?

■ When the entity makes and sells different types of products, the calculation of a full cost becomes a problem due to the weaknesses of absorption costing. The method of apportioning costs between the different products in absorption costing is largely subjective. This affects the calculation of full cost and the selling price.

 Example

Entity Q makes two products, product X and product Y. These products are both made by the same work force and in the same department. The budgeted fixed costs are $900,000. Variable costs per unit are as follows:

		Product X		Product Y
Direct costs		$		$
Materials		6		6
Labour	(2 hours)	12	(3 hours)	18
Expenses	(1 machine hour)	6	(1 machine hour)	6
		24		30

Budgeted production and sales are 15,000 units of product X and 10,000 units of product Y.

Required

Calculate the sale prices for each unit of product X and product Y which give a profit margin of 20% on the full cost, if overheads are absorbed on the following bases:

(a)   on a direct labour hour basis

(b)   on a machine hour basis.

 Answer

(a)   **Direct labour hour basis**

Budgeted direct labour hours = (15,000 × 2) + (10,000 × 3) = 60,000 hours.

Overhead absorption rate = $900,000/60,000 = $15 per direct labour hour.

	Product X	Product Y
Direct costs	$	$
Materials	6.00	6
Labour	12.00	18
Expenses	6.00	6
	24.00	30
Absorbed overhead	30.00	45
Full cost	54.00	75
Mark-up (20%)	10.80	15
Selling price/unit	64.80	90

The budgeted profit would be (15,000 × $10.80) + (10,000 × $15) = $312,000.

(b)   **Machine hour basis**

Budgeted machine hours = (15,000 × 1) + (10,000 × 1) = 25,000 hours.

Overhead absorption rate = $900,000/25,000 = $36 per machine hour.

	Product X	Product Y
Direct costs	$	$
Materials	6.00	6.00
Labour	12.00	18.00
Expenses	6.00	6.00
	24.00	30.00
Absorbed overhead	36.00	36.00
Full cost	60.00	66.00
Mark-up (20%)	12.00	13.20
Selling price/unit	72.00	79.20

The budgeted profit would be (15,000 × $12) + (10,000 × $13.20) = $312,000.

However, the different bases of absorbing overheads would give a significantly different full cost for each product, and a different selling price. It must be doubtful whether the entity can sell 15,000 units of product X and 10,000 units of product Y, no matter which prices are chosen.

2.3   Marginal cost plus pricing (mark-up pricing)

With marginal cost plus pricing, also called mark-up pricing, a mark-up or profit margin is added to the marginal cost in order to obtain a selling price.

	$
Variable production costs	600
Other variable costs	200
Marginal cost	800
Mark-up (added to marginal cost)	400
Selling price	1,200

The mark-up represents contribution.

When marginal cost plus pricing is used to calculate a selling price for standard units of a product, the selling price per unit may be calculated as:

$$\frac{\left[\text{Budgeted variable production costs} + \text{Total budgeted variable non - production costs}\right] + \text{Mark} - \text{up}}{\text{Budgeted sales units}}$$

The total mark-up is the required percentage mark-up on total budgeted variable costs.

Advantages of marginal cost plus pricing

The advantages of a marginal cost plus approach are as follows:

■   It is useful in some industries such as retailing, where prices might be set by adding a mark-up to the purchase cost of items bought for resale. The size of the mark-up can be varied to reflect demand conditions. For example, in a competitive market, a lower mark-up might be added to high-volume items.

■ It draws management attention to contribution and the effects of higher or lower sales volumes on profit. This can be particularly useful for short-term pricing decisions, such as pricing decisions for a market penetration policy (described later).

■ When an organisation has spare capacity, marginal cost plus pricing can be used in the short-term to set a price which covers variable cost. This approach is used by hotels, airlines, railway companies and telephone companies to price off-peak usage. As long as fixed costs are covered by peak users and the lower price set does not affect the main market, a marginal cost price can be set off-peak to increase demand and therefore contribution.

■ It is more appropriate where fixed costs are low and variable costs are high.

Disadvantages of marginal cost plus pricing

A marginal cost plus approach to pricing also has disadvantages.

■ Although the size of the mark-up can be varied according to demand conditions, marginal cost plus pricing is a cost-based pricing method, and does not properly take market conditions into consideration.

■ It ignores fixed overheads in the pricing decision. Prices must be high enough to make a profit after covering all fixed costs. Cost-based pricing decisions therefore cannot ignore fixed costs altogether.

2.4 Return on investment (ROI) pricing

This method of pricing might be used in a decentralised environment where the investment centre is required to meet a target return on capital employed. Prices might be set to achieve a target percentage return on the capital invested.

With return on investment pricing, the selling price per unit may be calculated as:

$$\frac{\text{Budgeted total costs of the division} + \left[\text{Target ROI\%} \times \text{Capital employed}\right]}{\text{Budgeted volume}}$$

■ When the investment centre makes and sells a single product, the budgeted volume is sales volume.

■ When the investment centre makes and sells several different products, budgeted volume might be production volume in hours, and the mark-up added to cost is then a mark-up for the number of hours worked on the product item.

■ Alternatively, the budgeted volume might be sales revenue, and the mark-up is then calculated as a percentage of the selling price (a form of full cost plus pricing).

Advantages of ROI pricing

The advantages of an ROI approach to pricing are as follows:

- ROI pricing is a method of deciding an appropriate profit margin for cost plus pricing.
- The target ROI can be varied to allow for differing levels of business risk.

Disadvantages of ROI pricing

An ROI approach to pricing also has disadvantages.

- Like all cost-based pricing methods, it does not take market conditions into sufficient consideration, and the prices that customers will be willing to pay.
- Since it is a form of full cost plus pricing, it shares most of the other disadvantages as full cost plus pricing.

Example

A manufacturer is about to launch a new product.

The non-current assets needed for production will cost $4,000,000 and working capital requirements are estimated at $800,000.

The expected annual sales volume is 40,000 units.

Variable production costs are $60 per unit.

Fixed production costs will be $600,000 each year and annual fixed non-production costs will be $200,000.

Required

(a) Calculate selling price using:

  (i) full cost plus 20%

  (ii) marginal cost plus 40 %

  (iii) pricing based on a target return on investment of 10% per year.

(b) If actual sales are only 20,000 units and the selling price is set at full cost plus 20%, what will the profit be for the year?

Answer

(a)

(i) Full cost plus 20%	$ per unit
Variable cost	60
Fixed costs ($600,000 + $200,000)/40,000 units	20
Full cost	80
Mark-up: 20% on cost	16
Selling price	96

(ii) Marginal cost plus 40%	$ per unit
Variable cost	60
Mark-up: 40% on variable cost	24
Selling price	84

(iii) Target ROI pricing	$
Non-current assets	4,000,000
Working capital	800,000
Capital employed	4,800,000
Profit required ($4,800,000 × 10%)	480,000
Profit required per unit (40,000 units)	$12

	$
Variable cost	60
Fixed costs (see above)	20
Full cost	80
Profit	12
Selling price	92

(b)

Profit for the year	$
Sales (20,000 units × $96)	1,920,000
Variable costs (20,000 units × $60)	(1,200,000)
Fixed costs	(800,000)
Net loss	(80,000)

2.5 Opportunity cost pricing (minimum pricing)

Opportunity cost pricing might be used for pricing a product or a service in special circumstances. In some circumstances, an entity might be prepared to charge a price for an item that leaves it no worse off than if it were to choose the next most profitable course of action. This is the marginal price or **minimum price** of an item.

A minimum price of an item is the total of the **relevant costs** of making and selling it.

A profit margin can be added to the minimum price, to obtain an opportunity cost price. The profit margin added to the relevant costs is the additional profit the entity will earn from selling the item, instead of choosing the next most profitable course of action.

■ Minimum price = Relevant costs of making and selling the item

■ If a margin is added for incremental profit:

Price = Relevant costs + Profit margin.

If resources are in scarce supply (limiting factors), minimum prices must include an allowance for the opportunity cost of using the resources for making and selling the item.

Example

Southampton is a shipbuilding company. It uses two materials, steel and fibreglass.

It needs to complete a shipping order using 500 tonnes of steel and 1,000 tonnes of fibreglass.

The work force will have to work 2,000 hours on making the boat: 1,200 hours will be in the assembly process and the remainder will be in the finishing (painting the boat and other finishing tasks).

Southampton will quote a price of relevant cost plus 50%.

Southampton has 200 tonnes of steel held in inventory. This originally cost $10 per tonne. It now has a current price of $12 and could be sold for $8 per tonne. Southampton no longer produces steel boats and has no other use for steel. It only produces fibreglass boats on a regular basis.

There are 400 tonnes of fibreglass held in inventory. This originally cost $20 per tonne. It currently has a purchase price of $23 per tonne and a selling price of $15 per tonne. (Selling price and net realisable value can be assumed to be the same figure).

All labour is paid $4 per hour. To complete the contract on time, labour for the finishing process will have to be transferred from other work which produces contribution at a rate of $3 per hour (after labour costs). There is currently surplus capacity for assembly labour amounting to 1,000 hours for the duration of the contract. Owing to other work requirements, however, any further assembly labour hours in excess of these 1,000 hours will have to be hired on a temporary basis at a rate of $5 per hour.

Required
Calculate the price Southampton will quote on the contract.

Answer

		$
Steel	– lost net realisable value (200 × $8)	1,600
	– purchases (300 × $12)	3,600
Fibreglass	(1,000 × $23)	23,000
Finishing labour	– cost (800 × $4)	3,200
	– lost contribution (800 × $3)	2,400
Assembly labour	(200 × $5)	1,000
Relevant cost		34,800
Mark-up (50%)		17,400
Quoted price		52,200

2.6 Limitations of cost-based pricing

Cost-based approaches to pricing all ignore external market factors such as the prices that customers are prepared to pay and what competitors are charging for rival products or services.

Cost based pricing does not ensure a profit, because sales volume must be sufficient to cover all fixed costs, and not even full cost plus pricing can ensure that sufficient sales volumes will be achieved to cover all fixed costs.

Sales demand and price elasticity of demand

- Level of sales demand
- Price elasticity of sales demand
- Elastic and inelastic demand
- Elasticity and setting prices

3 Sales demand and price elasticity of demand

Pricing decisions should take into consideration market factors. Two aspects of the market for a product or service are:

- The level of sales demand at a given price
- The sales elasticity of demand: this is a measurement of how sales demand varies with a change in the sales price.

3.1 Level of sales demand

Sales demand is the quantity of a product or service that customers want to buy, and are willing and able to pay for. This is known as **effective demand**.

The influences on sales demand are:

- The selling price of the item: demand is normally higher at lower selling prices and lower at higher selling prices.
- For consumer goods, household income also affects total sales demand. When consumers are earning more income (or have access to more cheap credit) sales demand will rise.
- The price of 'substitute goods': substitute goods are goods that customers could buy as an alternative.
- The price of 'complementary goods': complementary goods are items that customers will have to buy in addition to complement the product. For example, the demand for mobile telephone handsets will be affected by the price of mobile telephone services and calls.
- Consumer tastes and fashion. High prices might be obtained for 'fashion goods'.
- Advertising and marketing. Sales demand can be affected by sales and marketing activities.

3.2 Price elasticity of sales demand

The price elasticity of sales demand (PED) is a measurement of the change in sales demand that would occur for a given change in the selling price.

It is measured as;

$$\frac{\text{The change in quantity demanded as a percentage of original demand}}{\text{The change in price as a percentage of the original price}}$$

Example

The following estimates have been made for demand for a product X:

■ An increase in the price from $9 to $10 will result in a fall in daily demand from 2 to 1 batches

■ An increase in the price from $4 to $5 will result in a fall in daily demand from 6 to 5 batches

■ An increase in the price from $1 to $2 will result in a fall in daily demand from 10 to 9 batches.

Required

Calculate the price elasticity of demand for product X at a price of:

(a)　$9

(b)　$4

(c)　$1.

 Answer

(a)　If price is increased from $9 to $10

The change in quantity demanded as a percentage of original demand
= -1/2 = -0.5 or 50%

The change in price as a percentage of the original price = 1/9 = 0.111 or 11.1%

PED = -0.5/0.111 = - 4.5

(b)　If price is increased from $4 to $5

The change in quantity demanded as a percentage of original demand
= -1/6 = -0.16667 or 16.7%

The change in price as a percentage of the original price = 1/4 = 0.25 or 25%

PED = -0.16667/0.25 = - 0.67

(c)　If price is increased from $1 to $2

The change in quantity demanded as a percentage of original demand
= -1/10 = -0.1 or 10%

The change in price as a percentage of the original price = 1/1 = 1 or 100%

PED = -0.1/1 = - 0.1

3.3 Elastic and inelastic demand

Demand is elastic if PED > 1 and inelastic if PED < 1.

If demand is highly elastic, increasing the sales price will lead to a fall in total sales revenue, due to a large fall in sales demand. Similarly, a reduction in the sales price will result in an increase in total sales revenue, due to the large rise in sales demand. Profit might increase or decrease when the sales price is changed, depending on changes in total costs as well as the change in total revenue.

If demand is inelastic, increasing the sales price will result in an increase in total sales revenue, because the fall in sales volume is fairly small. Similarly, reducing the sales price will result in lower total sales revenue, because the increase in sales demand will not be enough to offset the fall in price.

The same product might have a high price elasticity of demand at some sales prices and a low price elasticity at other selling prices.

3.4 Elasticity and setting prices

A knowledge of PED will assist managers in making pricing decisions:

- If demand is inelastic, prices can be increased as this will lead to increased revenue from the sale of fewer units which should result in lower costs. It may be necessary to consider the cost function however because lower output may result in few cost savings and may lead to excess capacity.

- If demand is inelastic, reducing price will lead to lower overall revenues. Increasing sales volume will be better achieved through changing customers perception of the product through marketing, service and distribution.

- If demand is elastic, increases in price will lead to a fall in overall revenues. Managers will have to determine whether the fall in market share can lead to cost savings which can offset the fall in revenue.

- If demand is elastic, reducing price can lead to a price war at the end of which all sellers are worse off. Suppliers must try to reduce elasticity by non price methods, such as quality, service and promotions.

> **Market-based approaches to pricing**
>
> - The economist's demand curve and profit-maximising model
> - Using mathematical models to decide the profit-maximising price
> - Market skimming prices
> - Market penetration prices
> - Price discrimination (differential pricing)
> - Loss leaders
> - Going rate pricing
> - Target pricing

4 Market-based approaches to pricing

There are various methods of pricing based on market conditions and marketing strategies.

4.1 The economist's demand curve and profit-maximising model

In the economist's model, a firm maximises its profits by setting the sales price at a level where:

[The marginal revenue from selling an extra unit] = [The marginal cost of making and selling the unit].

In other words, **profit is maximised where MR = MC**.

You might be expected to calculate the formula for MR, given a demand curve.

Calculating a demand curve

A demand curve is a graph showing the quantity demanded at different sales prices. A straight-line demand curve has the basic formula.

$P = a - bQ$

Where

P = the sales price
Q = the quantity demanded
a = the sales price when the quantity demanded is 0
b = a constant value.

Example

The sales demand curve for a product is straight-line. When the sales price is $0, the sales demand is 80,000 units. When the sales price is $40, sales demand is 0 units. For every $0.50 increase in price, the sales demand falls by 1,000 units.

The demand curve is therefore:

$P = 40 - (0.50/1,000)Q$

$P = 40 - 0.0005Q$

Note

For every $0.50 increase in price, sales demand changes by 1,000 units; therefore b in the formula is $0.50/1,000 = 0.0005$.

Calculating MR

The value of marginal revenue is found from the formula for total revenue.

- Total revenue = Price × Quantity
- The price is represented by the demand curve, $P = a - bQ$
- Total revenue = $(a - bQ) Q, = aQ - bQ^2$
- Marginal revenue MR is found using differential calculus.

However, if you are not familiar with differential calculus, whenever there is a total revenue formula:

- Total revenue (TR) = $aQ - bQ^2$
- Marginal revenue = $a - (2b)Q$

Example

Returning to the previous example:

- the demand curve is $P = 40 - 0.0005Q$
- $TR = (40 - 0.0005Q)Q = 40Q - 0.0005Q^2$
- $MR = 40 - (2 \times 0.0005)Q = 40 - 0.001Q$.

Profit-maximisation, MR = MC

It is normally assumed that total costs consist of fixed and variable costs; therefore the formula for total costs =

$TC = FC + vQ$

Where
FC = fixed costs
V = the variable cost per unit sold
Q = the number of units sold

Whenever the total cost line consists of fixed and variable costs, the marginal cost MC is the variable cost, so MC = V.

Example

Suppose that the monthly demand curve for a product is P = 40 – 0.0005Q. Fixed costs per month are $500,000 and the variable cost per unit is $2.

Required

Calculate the sales price and output quantity that maximise the profit each month, and calculate the amount of that profit.

Answer

MR = 40 – 0.001Q
MC = 2
Profit is maximised when MR = MC
40 – 0.001Q = 2
0.001Q = 38
Q = 38,000 units.
The sales price when Q = 38,000 is:
P = 40 – 0.0005(38,000) = $21.

	$
Sales (38,000 × $21)	798,000
Variable costs (38,000 × $2)	76,000
Contribution	722,000
Fixed costs	500,000
Profit	222,000

4.2 Using mathematical models to decide the profit-maximising price

In order to use a mathematical model to decide the profit-maximising selling price, at the price where MC = MR, the following conditions must be met:

■ There must be a reliable estimate of both the cost function and the sales revenue function. It is often possible to prepare an estimate of total cost as fixed costs plus variable costs (TC = F + Vx, where x is the number of units sold). However, it is much more difficult to obtain a reliable estimate of the demand function, and express the relationship between price and quantity demanded as a mathematical formula.

■ The purpose of using a mathematical model would be to decide the selling price for a product. This is only possible if the selling price is an 'endogenous' variable in the model.

- An **endogenous variable** is a variable in the model that is under the control of management. It would normally be assumed, for example, that the variable costs are an endogenous variable, and that management can make sure that actual variable costs can be controlled at the level stated in the model.

- An **exogenous variable**, in contrast, is a variable in a model that is outside the control of management. Exogenous variables might include variables such as long-term market trends or sales tax (value added tax) on the product. Changes in an exogenous variable can sometimes affect the value of an endogenous variable.

When using a mathematical model, management make decisions about the value of an endogenous variable, to maximise or optimise the value of the results from the model. For example, a mathematical model to determine the price where MC = MR would be used to decide the selling price. This assumes that the selling price is an endogenous variable in the model.

In reality, the selling price may be partly an endogenous variable and partly an exogenous variable. Management may be able to decide the selling price for its product (therefore selling price = endogenous variable), but the price they can charge may be restricted by considerations of the prices that competitors are charging for rival products (therefore selling price = exogenous variable). Since selling price may not be an entirely endogenous variable in the model, it is questionable whether using a mathematical model to decide the selling price for a product would be a useful exercise.

4.3 Market skimming prices

When a company introduces a product to the market for the first time, it might choose a pricing policy based on 'skimming the market'.

When a new product is introduced to the market, a few customers might be prepared to pay a high price to obtain the product, in order to be one of the first people to have it. Buying the new product gives the buyer prestige, so the buyer will pay a high price to get it.

In order to increase sales demand, the price must be gradually reduced, but with a skimming policy, the price is reduced slowly and by small amounts each time. The contribution per unit with a skimming policy is very high.

To charge high prices, the firm might have to spend heavily on advertising and other marketing expenditure.

Market skimming will probably be more effective for new 'high technology' products, such as digital televisions and plasma screen televisions. Other examples in the past have been personal computers and laptop computers.

Firms using market skimming for a new product will have to reduce prices later as new competitors enter market with rival products.

Skimming prices and a product differentiation strategy

It is much more difficult to apply a market skimming pricing policy when competitors have already introduced a rival product to the market. Customers in the market will already have a view of the prices to expect, and might not be persuaded to buy a new version of a product in the market unless its price is lower than prices of existing versions.

However, it may be possible to have a policy of market skimming if it is possible to differentiate a product from its rivals, usually on the basis of quality. This is commonly found in the market for cars, for example, where some manufacturers succeed in keeping prices very high by producing and selling a high-quality product. High-quality cars cost more to produce, and sales demand may be fairly low: however, profits are obtained by charging high prices and earning a high contribution for each unit sold.

4.4 Market penetration prices

Market penetration pricing is an alternative pricing policy to market skimming, when a new product is launched on to the market for the first time.

With market penetration pricing, the aim is to set a low selling price for the new product, in order to create a high sales demand as quickly as possible. With a successful penetration pricing strategy, a company might 'capture the market'.

A firm might also use market penetration prices to launch their own version of a product into an established market, with the intention that offering low prices will attract customers and win a substantial share of the market.

Penetration pricing and a cost leadership strategy

A cost leadership market strategy is a strategy of trying to become the lowest-cost producer of a product in the market. Low-cost production is usually achieved through economies of scale and large-scale production and sales volumes.

Penetration pricing is consistent with a cost leadership strategy, because low prices help a company to obtain a large market share, and a large market share means high volumes, economies of scale and lower costs.

4.5 Price discrimination (differential pricing)

With price discrimination (or differential pricing), a firm sells a single identical product in different segments of the market at different prices.

For price discrimination to work successfully, the different market segments must be kept separate. It might be possible to charge different prices for the same product:

■ in different geographical areas – for example, in the US and in China

■ at different times of the day – for example, travel tickets might be priced differently at different times of the day or the week

■ to customers in different age groups – for example, offering special prices to individuals over a certain age, or to students or to children.

4.6 Loss leaders

Some products might be sold for a short time as 'loss leaders'. This type of pricing is used in retailing, where some products are offered at very low prices (below cost, or possibly below marginal cost) in order to attract customers into the store, where they will also buy other items as well as the low-priced items.

4.7 Going-rate pricing

Many firms charge a price that is the 'going rate' in the market. This is a pricing policy for 'price followers'. Companies must often accept the going market price when they produce a fairly standard product (or service) and they are not in a particularly strong competitive position.

4.8 Target pricing

Target pricing has been described in an earlier chapter, in relation to target costing. When a company develops a new product, it might decide during the design stage of development what the price needs to be.

The decision about price may be based on a study of the existing market and prices for similar products. A target price is the price that a company thinks it will have to charge for a new product in order to be competitive in the market.

Having established a target price, the company can then establish a target cost. This is the maximum amount that the new product must cost to make and sell, so that the return on investment from the new product will be sufficient to justify its development.

The designers of the product are then required to design the product so that it costs no more than the target cost, and it can be sold for an appropriate return at the target price.

CHAPTER

4

Relevant costs

Contents

The concept of relevant costing

- Information for decision-making
- Marginal costing and decision-making
- Relevant costs and decision-making
- Terms used in relevant costing
- Opportunity costs

1 The concept of relevant costing

1.1 Information for decision-making

Management make decisions about the future. When they make decisions for economic or financial reasons, the objective is usually to increase profitability or the value of the business, or to reduce costs and improve productivity.

Costing information should help managers to make well-informed decisions about the best course of action to take.

- Decisions affect the future, but cannot change what has already happened. Decision-making should therefore look at the future consequences of a decision, and should not be influenced by historical events and historical costs.
- Decisions should consider what can be changed in the future. They should not be influenced by what will happen in the future that is unavoidable, possibly due to commitments that have been made in the past.
- Economic or financial decisions should be based on future cash flows, not future accounting measurements of costs or profits. Accounting conventions, such as the accruals concept of accounting and the depreciation of fixed assets, do not reflect economic reality. Cash flows, on the other hand, do reflect the economic reality of decisions. Managers should therefore consider the effect that their decisions will have on future cash flows, not reported accounting profits.

1.2 Marginal costing and decision-making

Marginal costing might be used for decision-making. As explained in previous chapters, marginal costing is used for limiting factor analysis and linear programming.

It is appropriate to use marginal costing for decision-making when it can be assumed that future fixed costs will be the same, no matter what decision is taken, and that all variable costs represent future cash flows that will be incurred as a consequence of any decision that is taken.

These assumptions about fixed and variable costs are not always valid. When they are not valid, relevant costs should be used to evaluate the economic/financial consequences of a decision.

1.3   Relevant costs and decision-making

Relevant costs should be used for assessing the economic or financial consequences of any decision by management. Only relevant costs and benefits should be taken into consideration when evaluating a decision.

A relevant cost is a future cash flow that will occur as a direct consequence of making a particular decision.

The key concepts in this definition of relevant costs are as follows:

- Relevant costs are **costs that will occur in the future**. They cannot include any costs that have already occurred in the past.

- Relevant costs of a decision are **costs that will occur as a direct consequence of making the decision**. Costs that will occur anyway, no matter what decision is taken, cannot be relevant to the decision.

- Relevant costs are **cash flows**. Notional costs, such as depreciation charges, notional interest costs and absorbed fixed costs, cannot be relevant to a decision.

1.4   Terms used in relevant costing

Several terms are used in relevant costing, to indicate how certain costs might be relevant or not relevant to a decision.

Incremental cost

An incremental cost is an additional cost that will occur if a particular decision is taken. Provided that this additional cost is a cash flow, an incremental cost is a relevant cost.

Differential cost

A differential cost is the amount by which future costs will be different, depending on which course of action is taken. A differential cost is therefore an amount by which future costs will be higher or lower, if a particular course of action is chosen. Provided that this additional cost is a cash flow, a differential cost is a relevant cost.

 Example

A company needs to hire a photocopier for the next six months. It has to decide whether to continue using a particular type of photocopier, which it currently rents for £1,000 each month, or whether to switch to using a larger photocopier that will cost £1,800 each month. If it hires the larger photocopier, it will be able to terminate the rental agreement for the current copier immediately.

The decision is whether to continue with using the current photocopier, or to switch to the larger copier. One way of analysing the comparative costs is to say that the larger copier will be more expensive to rent, by £800 each month for six months. The differential cost of hiring the larger copier for six months would therefore be £4,800.

Avoidable and unavoidable costs

An avoidable cost is a cost that could be saved (avoided), depending whether or not a particular decision is taken. An unavoidable cost is a cost that will be incurred anyway.

Avoidable costs are relevant costs. Unavoidable costs are not relevant to a decision.

 Example

A company has one year remaining on a short-term lease agreement on a warehouse. The rental cost is £50,000 per year. The warehouse facilities are no longer required, because operations have been moved to another warehouse that has spare capacity.

If a decision is taken to close down the warehouse, the company would be committed to paying the rental cost up to the end of the term of the lease. However, it would save local taxes of £8,000 for the year, and it would no longer need to hire the services of a security company to look after the empty building, which currently costs £20,000 each year.

The decision about whether to close down the unwanted warehouse should be based on relevant costs only. Local taxes and the costs of the security services (£28,000 in total for the next year) could be avoided and so these are relevant costs. The rental cost of the warehouse cannot be avoided, and so should be ignored in the economic assessment of the decision whether to close the warehouse or keep it open for another year.

Sunk costs

Sunk costs are costs that have already been incurred (historical costs) or costs that have already been committed by an earlier decision. Sunk costs must be ignored for the purpose of evaluating a decision, and cannot be relevant costs.

For example, suppose that a company must decide whether to launch a new product on to the market. It has spent £500,000 on developing the new product, and a further £40,000 on market research.

A financial evaluation for a decision whether or not to launch the new product should ignore the development costs and the market research costs, because the £540,000 has already been spent. The costs are sunk costs.

1.5 Opportunity costs

Relevant costs can also be measured as an opportunity cost. An opportunity cost is a benefit that will be lost by taking one course of action instead of the next-most profitable course of action.

Example

A company has been asked by a customer to carry out a special job. The work would require 20 hours of skilled labour time. There is a limited availability of skilled labour, and if the special job is carried out for the customer, skilled employees would have to be moved from doing other work that earns a contribution of £30 per labour hour.

A relevant cost of doing the job for the customer is the contribution that would be lost by switching employees from other work. This contribution forgone (20 hours × £30 = £600) would be an opportunity cost. This cost should be taken into consideration as a cost that would be incurred as a direct consequence of a decision to do the special job for the customer. In other words, the opportunity cost is a relevant cost in deciding how to respond to the customer's request.

> # Identifying relevant costs
>
> - Relevant costs of materials
> - Relevant costs of labour
> - Relevant costs and overheads

2 Identifying relevant costs

There are certain rules or guidelines that might help you to identify the relevant costs for evaluating a management decision.

2.1 Relevant costs of materials

The relevant costs of a decision to do some work or make a product will usually include costs of materials. Relevant costs of materials are the additional cash flows that will be incurred (or benefits that will be lost) by using the materials for the purpose that is under consideration.

If **none of the required materials are currently held as stock**, the relevant cost of the materials is simply their purchase cost. In other words, the relevant cost is the cash that will have to be paid to acquire and use the materials.

If **the required materials are currently held as stock**, the relevant costs are identified by applying the following rules:

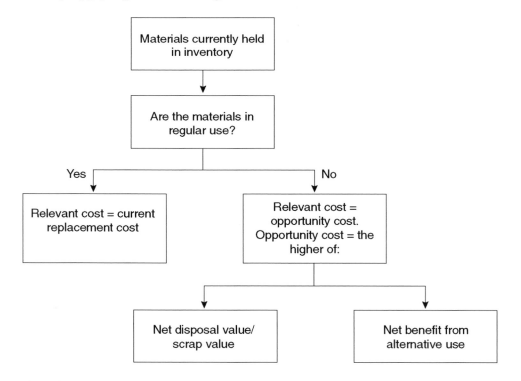

Note that the historical cost of materials held in stock cannot be the relevant cost of the materials, because their historical cost is a sunk cost.

The relevant costs of materials can be described as their 'deprival value'. The deprival value of materials is the benefit or value that would be lost if the company were deprived of the materials currently held in stock.

■ If the materials are regularly used, their deprival value is the cost of having to buy more units of the materials to replace them (their replacement cost).

■ If the materials are not in regular use, their deprival value is either the net benefit that would be lost because they cannot be disposed of (their net disposal or scrap value) or the benefits obtainable from any alternative use. In an examination question, materials in stock might not be in regular use, but could be used as a substitute material in some other work. Their deprival value might therefore be the purchase cost of another material that could be avoided by using the materials in stock as a substitute.

 Example

A company has been asked to quote a price for a one-off contract.

The contract would require 5,000 kilograms of material X. Material X is used regularly by the company. The company has 4,000 kilograms of material X currently in stock, which cost £2 per kilogram. The price for material X has since risen to £2.10 per kilogram.

The contract would also require 2,000 kilograms of material Y. There are 1,500 kilograms of material Y in stock, but because of a decision taken several weeks ago, material Y is no longer in regular use by the company. The 1,500 kilograms originally cost £7,200, and have a scrap value of £1,800. New purchases of material Y would cost £5 per kilogram.

What are the relevant costs of the materials, to assist management in identifying the minimum price to charge for the contract?

 Answer

Material X

This is in regular use. Any units of the material that are held in stock will have to be replaced for other work if they are used for the contract. The relevant cost is their replacement cost.

Relevant cost = replacement cost = 5,000 kilograms × £2.10 = £10,500.

Material Y

This is not in regular use. There are 1,500 kilograms in stock, and an additional 500 kilograms would have to be purchased. The relevant cost of material Y for the contract would be:

	£
Material held in stock (scrap value)	1,800
New purchases (500 × £5)	2,500
Total relevant cost of Material Y	4,300

2.2 Relevant costs of labour

The relevant costs of a decision to do some work or make a product will usually include costs of labour.

The relevant cost of labour for any decision is the additional cash expenditure (or saving) that will arise as a direct consequence of the decision.

■ **If the cost of labour is a variable cost**, and labour is not in restricted supply, the relevant cost of the labour is its variable cost. For example, suppose that part-time employees are paid £10 per hour, they are paid only for the hours that they work and part-time labour is not in short supply. If management is considering a decision that would require an additional 100 hours of part-time labour, the relevant cost of the labour would be £10 per hour or £1,000 in total.

■ **If labour is a fixed cost and there is spare labour time available**, the relevant cost of using labour is 0. The spare time would otherwise be paid for idle time, and there is no additional cash cost of using the labour to do extra work. For example, suppose that a new contract would require 30 direct labour hours, direct labour is paid £15 per hour, and the direct workforce is paid a fixed weekly wage for a 40-hour week. If there is currently spare capacity, so that the labour cost would be idle time if it is not used for the new contract, the relevant cost of using 30 hours on the new contract would be £0. The 30 labour hours must be paid for whether or not the contract work is undertaken.

■ **If labour is in limited supply**, the relevant cost of labour should include the opportunity cost of using the labour time for the purpose under consideration instead of using it in its next-most profitable way.

 Example

A company is considering the price to charge for a contract that will require labour time in three departments.

Department 1. The contract would require 200 hours of work in department 1, where the workforce is paid £10 per hour. There is currently spare labour capacity in department 1 and there are no plans to reduce the size of the workforce in this department.

Department 2. The contract would require 100 hours of work in department 2 where the workforce is paid £12 per hour. This department is currently working at full capacity. The company could ask the workforce to do overtime work, paid for at the normal rate per hour plus 50% overtime premium. Alternatively, the workforce could be diverted from other work that earns a contribution of £4 per hour.

Department 3. The contract would require 300 hours of work in department 3 where the workforce is paid £20 per hour. Labour in this department is in short supply and all the available time is currently spent making product Z, which earns the following contribution:

	£	£
Sales price		90
Labour (2 hours per unit)	40	
Other variable costs	30	
		70
Contribution per unit of product Z		20

Required

What is the relevant cost for the contract of labour in the three departments?

 Answer

Department 1. There is spare capacity in department 1 and no additional cash expenditure would be incurred on labour if the contract is undertaken.

Relevant cost = £0.

Department 2. There is restricted labour capacity. If the contract is undertaken, there would be a choice between:

- overtime work at a cost of £18 per hour (£12 plus overtime premium of 50%) – this would be an additional cash expense, or

- diverting the labour from other work, and losing contribution of £4 per hour – cost per hour = £12 basic pay + contribution forgone £4 = £16 per hour.

It would be better to divert the workforce from other work, and the relevant cost of labour is therefore 100 hours × £16 per hour = £1,600.

Department 3. There is restricted labour capacity. If the contract is undertaken, labour would have to be diverted from making product Z which earns a contribution of £20 per unit or £10 per labour hour (£20/2 hours). The relevant cost of the labour in department 3 is:

	£
Labour cost per hour	20
Contribution forgone	10
Relevant cost per hour	30

Relevant cost of 300 hours = 300 × £30 = £9,000.

Summary of relevant costs of labour:

	£
Department 1	0
Department 2	1,600
Department 3	9,000
	10,600

2.3 Relevant costs and overheads

Relevant costs of expenditures that might be classed as overhead costs should be identified by applying the normal rules of relevant costing. Relevant costs are future cash flows that will arise as a direct consequence of making a particular decision.

Fixed overhead absorption rates are therefore irrelevant, because fixed overhead absorption is not overhead expenditure and does not represent cash spending

However, it might be assumed that the overhead absorption rate for **variable** overheads is a measure of actual cash spending on variable overheads. It is therefore often appropriate to treat a variable overhead hourly rate as a relevant cost, because it is an estimate of cash spending per hour for each additional hour worked.

The only overhead fixed costs that are relevant costs for a decision are extra cash spending that will be incurred, or cash spending that will be saved, as a direct consequence of making the decision.

> **Applications of relevant costing**
>
> - Make-or-buy decisions
> - Make-or-buy decisions with scarce resources
> - Other issues surrounding the make-or-buy decision
> - Shutdown decisions
> - Joint product further processing decisions

3 Applications of relevant costing

The principles of relevant costing can be applied to any type of management decision. Examples of management decisions where relevant costing is used are:

- One-off contract decisions: management might want to decide whether or not to undertake a contract for a specified fixed price. If it is a one-off contract, rather than regular production work, it would be worthwhile undertaking the contract if the extra revenue from the contract is higher than the relevant costs of doing the work (including any opportunity costs).
- Make-or-buy decisions
- Shutdown decisions
- Joint product further processing decisions.

3.1 Make-or-buy decisions

A make-or-buy decision is a decision about:

- whether to make an item internally or to buy it from an external supplier, or
- whether to do some work with internal resources, or to contract it out to another organisation such as a sub-contractor or an outsourcing organisation.

The economic basis for the decision whether to make internally or buy externally should be based on relevant costs, and the selected option (from a financial viewpoint) should be the one that has the lower relevant costs.

 Example

A company manufactures a component that is included in a final product that it also manufactures. Management have identified an external supplier who would be willing to supply the component.

The variable cost of manufacturing the component internally is £5 and the external supplier would be prepared to supply the components for £6.50 each. It has been estimated that cash savings on general overhead expenditure will be £24,000 each year if internal production is ended. The company needs 10,000 units of the component each year.

Required

Should the company make or buy the component?

Answer

The annual relevant costs and benefits of a decision to buy the components externally can be presented as follows:

	£
Extra costs of purchasing externally (10,000 units × (£6.50 - £5))	(15,000)
Cash savings in overhead expenditures	24,000
Net benefit from external purchasing per year	9,000

Conclusion: The company would increase its profit by purchasing externally instead of making the items in-house. The recommendation is therefore to buy, not make.

3.2   Make-or-buy decisions with scarce resources

If a company has scarce resources total costs will be minimised if the units are bought out from a sub contractor in order of the lowest extra variable cost of buying out per unit of scarce resource.

Example

Superclean Ltd is a contract cleaning company. It provides three services; daily office cleaning, intensive cleaning of office space and minor repairs.

Information relating to the different type of work is as follows:

	Average labour Hours per job	Variable cost per job(£)	Budgeted jobs	Sub-contractor Quote per job (£)
Daily office cleaning	4	30	1,500	40
Intensive cleaning	6	54	400	100
Minor repairs	3	28	650	50

There are 8,000 labour hours available. Which services should be sub-contracted?

Answer

Using variable cost per labour hour

A knowledge of limiting factor analysis may suggest that the approach should be to calculate the variable cost per labour hour and make the cheapest product first, sub-contracting the remainder.

The ranking would be as follows:

	Average labour Hours per job	Variable cost per job(£)	Variable cost per Labour hour	Ranking
Daily office cleaning	4	30	7.5	1
Intensive cleaning	6	54	9	2
Minor repairs	3	28	9.33	3

The plan would be to carry out the following work:

	Budgeted jobs	Total labour hours	Total variable cost (£)
Daily office cleaning	1,500	6,000	45,000
Intensive cleaning	333	<u>1,998</u>	17,892
		7,998	
Sub-contract			
Intensive cleaning	67		6,700
Minor repairs	650		<u>32,500</u>
			102,092

This is not the cheapest way to carry out the work.

Using the extra variable cost of buying out per labour hour.

	Daily office cleaning	Intensive cleaning	Minor repairs
In-house variable cost (£)	30	54	28
Sub-contractor variable cost (£)	<u>40</u>	<u>100</u>	<u>50</u>
Extra variable cost	10	46	22
Labour hours saved	4	6	3
Extra variable cost per labour hour	2.50	7.67	7.11

It is cheaper to sub-contract office cleaning then minor repairs. It is most expensive to sub-contract intensive cleaning and this is the first choice to be carried out in-house.

The plan would be to carry out the following work:

	Budgeted jobs	Total labour hours	Total variable cost (£)
Intensive cleaning	400	2,400	21,600
Minor repairs	650	1,950	18,200
Office cleaning	912	<u>3,648</u>	27,360
		7,998	
Sub-contract			
Office cleaning	588		<u>23,520</u>
			90,680

There is a cost saving of £11,412.

3.3 Other issues surrounding the make-or-buy decision

Outsourcing or sub-contracting is the use of external suppliers for finished products, services or components. There has been a significant trend in the 1990s for private and public sector organisations to outsource non-core functions. The advantages of this are:

■ companies can concentrate on their core competencies – activities which are fundamental to their business.

■ Specialist contractors can be used which may result in higher quality and efficiency

■ Capital can be freed up to invest in core activities

■ It may offer greater flexibility in response to fluctuations in demand

There may be significant disadvantages

■ Loss of direct control over the work. Quality and reliability may suffer and this may impact on the reputation of the business.

- Loss of expertise within the business
- Vulnerability to price increases
- Redundancies may lower staff morale throughout the organisation

3.4 Shutdown decisions

A shutdown decision is a decision about whether or not to shut down a part of the operations of a company. From a financial viewpoint, an operation should be shut down if the benefits of shutdown exceed the relevant costs.

Example

Company V makes four products, P, Q, R and S. The budget for next year is as follows:

	P	Q	R	S	Total
	£000	£000	£000	£000	£000
Direct materials	300	500	400	700	1,900
Direct labour	400	800	600	400	2,200
Variable overheads	100	200	100	100	500
	800	1,500	1,100	1,200	4,600
Sales	1,800	1,650	2,200	1,550	7,200
Contribution	1,000	150	1,100	350	2,600
Directly attributable fixed costs	(400)	(250)	(300)	(300)	(1,250)
Share of general fixed costs	(200)	(200)	(300)	(400)	(1,100)
Profit/(loss)	400	(300)	500	(350)	250

Directly attributable fixed costs are cash expenditures directly attributable to each individual product. These would be saved if operations to make and sell the product were shut down.

Required

State with reasons whether any of the products should be withdrawn from the market.

Answer

From a financial viewpoint, a product should be withdrawn from the market if the savings from closure exceed the benefits of continuing to make and sell the product. If a product is withdrawn from the market, the company will lose the contribution, but will save the directly attributable fixed costs.

Product P and product R both make a profit even after charging a share of general fixed costs. On the other hand, product Q and product S both show a loss after charging general fixed costs, and we should therefore consider whether it might be appropriate to stop making and selling either or both of these products, in order to eliminate the losses.

Effect of shutdown	P	Q	R	S
	£000	£000	£000	£000
Contribution forgone	(1,000)	(150)	(1,100)	(350)
Directly attributable fixed costs saved	400	250	300	300
Increase/(reduction) in annual cash flows	(600)	100	(800)	(50)

Although product S makes a loss, shutdown would reduce annual cash flows because the contribution lost would be greater than the savings in directly attributable fixed costs.

However, withdrawal of product Q from the market would improve annual cash flows by £100,000, and withdrawal is therefore recommended on the basis of this financial analysis.

Decision recommended: Stop making and selling product Q but carry on making and selling product S.

3.5 Joint product further processing decisions

Joint products produced from a common process might be sold when they emerge from the process. Alternatively, a joint product might be processed further, and sold after further processing.

A joint product further processing decision is a decision whether to sell a joint product at the end of the common process, or whether to process it further before sale.

Applying relevant costing, the costs of the common process are irrelevant to the decision, because these costs will be incurred anyway, whatever the decision. A joint product should undergo further processing if the extra revenue from further processing exceeds the extra (relevant) costs of the further processing.

Example

A company produces two joint products from a common process. For every 100 kilograms of input to the common process, output consists of 40 kilograms of joint product 1 (JP1) and 60 kilograms of joint product 2 (JP2). The costs of the common process are £200 per 100 kilograms of input.

JP1 can be sold for £5 per kilogram and JP2 can be sold for £8 per kilogram. Alternatively, JP1 can be processed to make a finished product, FP1. Costs of further processing consist of variable costs of £3 per kilogram and fixed costs of £40,000 per year. Of these fixed costs, £32,000 would be directly attributable to the further processing operations, and the remaining £8,000 would be an apportionment of general fixed overhead costs. The further processed product (FP1) would have a selling price of £14 per kilogram.

It is estimated that 15,000 kilograms of JP1 will be produced each year. There are no losses in any process.

Required

Should JP1 be sold as soon as it is produced from the common process, or should it be further processed into Product FP1?

Answer

The common processing costs are irrelevant to the further processing decision. The annual relevant costs and benefits of further processing JP1 are as follows:

	£
Revenue from selling FP1 (per kilogram)	14
Variable further processing cost	(3)
Additional variable revenue from further processing	11
Opportunity cost: sales of JP1 forgone	(5)
Benefit per kilogram from further processing	6
Number of kilograms produced each year	15,000
	£
Total annual benefits before directly attributable fixed costs	90,000
Directly attributable fixed costs of further processing	(32,000)
Net annual benefits of further processing	58,000

Recommendation: The joint product should be processed to make FP1, because this will increase annual profit by £58,000.

CHAPTER

5

Decision-making with risk and uncertainty

Contents	
1	Risk and uncertainty
2	Decision-making with uncertainty
3	Using probabilities
4	Sensitivity analysis

> ## Risk and uncertainty
>
> ■ Decision-making and risk and uncertainty
> ■ Risk preference

1 Risk and uncertainty

1.1 Decision-making and risk and uncertainty

Decision-making, particularly long-term decision-making, has to be taken under conditions of risk and uncertainty.

■ **Uncertainty** occurs when there is insufficient information about what will happen, or what will probably happen, in the future. It is therefore likely that estimates of future values (future sales, future costs, and so on) will be inaccurate.

■ **Risk** occurs when future events of the future outcome could be any of several different possibilities. However, the probabilities of each possible outcome can be assessed with reasonable accuracy.

Uncertainty in decision-making can be reduced by obtaining more reliable information. This may be achieved through market research or by analysing costs and processes in focus groups. Risk cannot be removed from a decision, because risk exists in the situation itself. A decision-maker can try to analyse the risk, and must make a decision on the basis of whether the risk is justified or acceptable.

1.2 Risk preference

Risk preference describes the attitude of a decision-maker towards risk. Decision-makers might be described as risk averse, risk-seeking or possibly risk neutral.

■ A **risk averse decision maker** considers risk in making a decision, and will not select a course of action that is more risky unless the expected return is higher and so justifies the extra risk. It is not correct to state that a risk-averse decision maker seeks to avoid risk as much as possible. However, a risk-averse decision maker might expect a substantially higher return to make the extra risk worth taking.

■ A **risk neutral decision maker** ignores risk in making a decision. The decision of a risk neutral decision maker is to select the course of action with the highest expected return, regardless of risk. The highest expected return could mean the highest EV of contribution, profit or NPV.

■ A **risk-seeking decision maker** also considers risk in making a decision. A risk seeker, unlike a risk-averse decision-maker, will take extra risks in the hope of earning a higher return. Given two options with the same EV of profit, a risk seeker will prefer the option with the higher return even if this has a higher risk.

> ## Decision-making with uncertainty
>
> - Worst, most likely and best possible outcomes
> - Constructing a pay-off table
> - Maximax, maximin and minimax regret decision rules

2 Decision-making with uncertainty

2.1 Worst, most likely and best possible outcomes

The choice between two or more alternative courses of action might be based on the worst, most likely or best expected outcomes from each course of action. A pay-off table can be produced which records all possible profit values from the different courses of action.

Example

A company must make a decision between three possible courses of action, 1, 2 and 3. A pay-off table has been produced which shows the expected profit or loss from each course of action.

Course of action	Worst possible outcome	Most likely outcome	Best possible outcome
Course 1	- 1,000	+ 4,000	+ 5,000
Course 2	- 500	+ 2,500	+ 7,000
Course 3	- 3,000	+ 1,000	+ 9,000

The course of action chosen by the company will depend on the attitude to risk of its decision-maker.

- A decision might be taken to select the project where the possible loss is the lowest. This would be course of action 2, where the worst outcome is – 500. This is not as bad as the worst outcome for courses of action 1 and 3. A risk-averse decision-maker might choose this course of action.

- A decision might be taken on the basis of the most likely outcome. The preferred course of action would then be the one where the expected return is highest. In this example, the preferred course of action would be course 1, where the most likely return is + 4,000. This is better than course 2 (+ 2,500) or course 3 (+ 1,000).

- A decision might be taken on the basis of the best possible return. The preferred course of action would then be the one that offers the highest return. Here, the preferred course of action would be course 3 (+ 9,000). This course of action would be the choice of a risk-seeking decision-maker.

The main disadvantage of choosing between mutually-exclusive courses of action on the basis of the worst, most likely or best possible outcome is that the choice **ignores the likelihood or probability** of the worst, most likely or best outcomes actually happening.

2.2   Constructing a pay-off table

Pay-off tables can be constructed from information given.

Example

A greengrocer must decide how many boxes of apples to buy each day. A box of apples earns contribution of £30 and costs £15. Demand is uncertain and could vary from 30 boxes to 10 boxes. The most likely demand is considered to be 20 boxes.
Required; produce a pay-off table and suggest how many boxes of apples the greengrocer should buy each day.

Course of action	Demand 10 boxes	Demand 20 boxes	Demand 30 boxes
Buy 10 boxes	300	300	300
Buy 20 boxes	150	600	600
Buy 30 boxes	0	450	900

Entries in the pay-off table are calculated as follows:

Buy 10 boxes - sell 10 boxes   Contribution = $10 \times £30 = £300$
             - The greengrocer cannot meet the demand of 20 or 30 boxes. The maximum contribution is £300

Buy 20 boxes - sell 10 boxes   Contribution = $10 \times £30 - 10 \times £15 = £150$
             - sell 20 boxes   Contribution = $20 \times £30 = £600$
             - demand is unmet.

Buy 30 boxes - sell 10 boxes   Contribution = $10 \times £30 - 20 \times £15 = 0$
             - sell 20 boxes   Contribution = $20 \times £30 - 10 \times £15 = £450$
             - sell 30 boxes   Contribution = $30 \times £30 = £900$

A risk averse green grocer may choose to buy 10 boxes as this gives the best result if the lowest level of demand occurs. A risk neutral greengrocer may choose to buy 20 boxes as this gives the best outcome at the most likely level of demand. A risk seeking green grocer may choose to buy 30 boxes as this gives the opportunity of making the highest contribution.

Note that the greengrocer cannot choose the level of demand as this is determined by factors outside of his control. He may be able to predict the likelihood of each level of demand which may help the decision by reducing the uncertainty.

2.3   Maximax, maximin and minimax regret decision rules

Choosing between mutually-exclusive courses of action can be stated as 'decision rules'. The choice may be based on a maximax, maximin or a minimax regret decision rule.

- **Maximax decision rule**. The decision-maker will select the course of action with the highest possible pay-off. The decision-maker seeks the highest return, assuming that events turn out in the best way possible. The maximax decision rule is a decision rule for the risk seeker.

- **Maximin decision rule**. The decision-maker will select the course of action with the highest expected return under the worst possible conditions. This decision rule might be associated with a risk averse decision maker.

- **Minimax regret decision rule**. The decision-maker selects the course of action with the lowest possible 'regret'. 'Regret' is the opportunity cost of having made the wrong decision, given the actual conditions that apply in the future.

Example

A business entity has to decide which of three projects to select for investment. The three projects are mutually exclusive, and only one of them can be selected.

The expected profits from investing in each of the projects will depend on the state of the market. The following estimates of net present value have been prepared:

State of market	Diminishing	Static	Expanding
	$000	$000	$000
Project 1	100	200	950
Project 2	0	500	600
Project 3	180	190	200

Which options would be selected?

(a) under the maximax decision rule

(b) under the minimax decision rule

(c) under the minimax regret decision rule?

Answer

(a) **Maximax decision rule**. The most favourable outcome is an expanding market. Project 1 offers the highest return in an expanding market; therefore project 1 will be selected.

(b) **Maximin decision rule**. The least favourable outcome is a diminishing market. The most favourable outcome in a diminishing market is project 3; therefore project 3 will be selected.

(c) **Minimax regret decision rule**. To establish the decision under the minimax regret decision rule, we must first prepare a pay-off table showing the regret the decision-maker would have choosing option 1, option 2 or option 3, and the actual market conditions turn out diminishing, static or expanding.

The regret with each course of action is shown in the pay-off table below. The right-hand column of the table shows the maximum regret.

State of market	Diminishing	Static	Expanding	Maximum regret
	$000	$000	$000	
Project 1	80	300	0	300
Project 2	180	0	350	350
Project 3	0	310	750	750

If you are not sure how regret is calculated, the following notes might be helpful:

- If project 1 is selected and the market condition turns out to be diminishing, the regret will be not having chosen option 3, because the NPV with option 1 would be 100 and with option 3 it would be 180. The regret is therefore 180 – 100 = 80.

- If project 1 is selected and the market condition turns out to be static, the regret will be not having chosen option 2, because the NPV with option 1 would be 200 and with option 2 it would be 500. The regret is therefore 500 – 200 = 300.

- If project 1 is selected and the market condition turns out to be expanding, there is no regret because the best possible option has been chosen.

- The maximum regret with option 1 is the highest of 180, 300 and 0. This is 300.

The minimum 'maximum regret' is 300 with option 1. Option 1 would therefore be selected if the minimax regret rule is applied.

> **Using probabilities**
>
> - Expected values
> - Simulation

3 Using probabilities

3.1 Expected values

Expected values can be used to analyse information where risk can be assessed. Where probabilities are assigned to different outcomes, we can evaluate the worth of a decision as the expected value or weighted average of these outcomes.

Expected value (EV) = weighted average of possible outcomes.

The weighted average value is calculated by applying the probability of each possible outcome to the value of the outcome.

$$EV = \sum px$$

Where
p = the probability of each outcome and
x = the value of each outcome

An EV is a measurement of **weighted average value**.

A decision might be based on selecting the course of action that offers the highest EV of profit, or the lowest EV of cost. In other words, the 'decision rule' is to select the course of action with the highest EV of profit or the lowest EV of cost.

The main advantage of using EVs to make a decision, compared to the decision rules explained earlier, is that it takes into consideration the probability or likelihood of each different possible outcome.

 Example

A business entity has to decide which of three projects to select for investment. The three projects are mutually exclusive, and only one of them can be selected.

The expected profits from investing in each of the projects will depend on the state of the market. The following estimates of net present value have been prepared:

State of market	Diminishing	Static	Expanding
Probability	0.4	0.3	0.3
	$000	$000	$000
Project 1	100	200	900
Project 2	0	500	600
Project 3	180	190	200

(**Note**: This type of table is called a 'pay-off table' or a 'pay-off matrix'. It shows all the possible 'pay-offs' or results – NPV, profit and so on – from different possible decisions or strategies).

Required

Identify which project would be selected if the decision is to choose the project with the highest expected value of NPV.

Answer

State of market	Probability	Project 1		Project 2		Project 3	
		NPV	EV of NPV	NPV	EV of NPV	NPV	EV of NPV
		$000	$000	$000	$000	$000	$000
Diminishing	0.4	100	40	0	0	180	72
Static	0.3	200	60	500	150	190	57
Expanding	0.3	900	270	600	180	200	60
			370		330		189

Based on expected values, project 1 should be selected.

Advantages of using expected values

Using EVs to make a decision has some advantages.

■ An EV is a weighted average value, that is based on all the different possible outcomes and the probability that each will occur.

■ It recognises the risk in decisions, based on the probabilities of different possible results or outcomes.

■ It expresses risk in a single figure.

Disadvantages of using expected values

Using EVs to make a decision also has some disadvantages.

■ The probabilities of the different possible outcomes may be difficult to estimate.

■ The EV is unlikely to be an actual outcome that could occur. In the example above, the EVs for projects 1, 2 and 3 (370, 330 and 189) are not expected to occur. They are simply weighted average values).

■ Unless the same decision has to be made many times, the average will not be achieved. It is therefore not a valid way of making a decision about the future when the outcome will happen only once.

■ An EV is an average value. It gives no indication of the range or spread of possible outcomes. It is therefore an inadequate measurement of risk.

3.2 Simulation

Simulation modelling is used when a plan or budget is represented by a mathematical model. The model will contain a large number of inter-related variables (sales volumes of each product, sales prices of each product, availability of constraining resources, resources per unit of product, costs of materials and labour, and so on).

The model is then used to calculate the value of the outcome or result, for a given set of values for each variable. It is then used to produce the expected outcome or result again, with a different set of values for each variable. The model is used to prepare a large number of different possible outcomes, each time with different combinations of values for all the variables.

As a result, the model will produce a range of many different possible results or outcomes that can be analysed statistically, by putting the possible outcomes into a probability distribution.

Simulation modelling therefore leads on to further statistical analysis of risk.

One example of simulation is a mathematical model which could be approached using the 'Monte Carlo' method. With Monte Carlo simulation, a probability distribution for the possible different values for each variable is used to allocate random numbers to each possible value. Random number allocations are given to all the different possible values for every input variable in the model. (The random number allocation should reflect the probability distribution).

A special computer program can be used to generate random numbers, and the random numbers generated by the program are used to give a value to each variable in the model. These values are then used to calculate the result or outcome that would occur.

Repeating the simulation many times produces a probability distribution of the possible outcomes.

Advantage of the Monte Carlo method

The advantages of Monte Carlo simulation modelling are as follows:

■ It gives more information about the possible outcomes and their relative probabilities.

■ It is useful for problems which cannot be solved analytically.

Limitation of the Monte Carlo method

It is not a technique for making a decision, only for getting more information about the risk and the probability of different possible outcomes.

> ### Sensitivity analysis
>
> - Sensitivity analysis
> - Changing the decision.

4 Sensitivity analysis

4.1 Sensitivity analysis

Sensitivity analysis is a method of risk or uncertainty analysis in which the effect on the expected outcome of changes in the values of key 'variables' or key factors are tested. For example, in budget planning, the effect on budgeted profit might be tested for changes in the budgeted sales volume, or the budgeted rate of inflation, or budgeted materials costs, and so on.

There are several ways of using sensitivity analysis.

- We can estimate by how much an item of cost or revenue would need to differ from their estimated values before the decision would change.

- We can estimate whether a decision would change if estimated sales were x% lower than estimated, or estimated costs were y% higher than estimated. (This is called 'what if...?' analysis: for example: 'What if sales volume is 5% below the expected amount)?

The starting point for sensitivity analysis is the original plan or estimates, giving an expected profit or value. Key variables are identified (such as sales price, sales volume material cost, labour cost, completion time, and so on). The value of the selected key variable is then altered by a percentage amount (typically a reasonable estimate of possible variations in the value of this variable) and the expected profit or value is re-calculated.

In this way, the sensitivity of a decision or plan to changes in the value of the key items or key factors can be measured.

An advantage of sensitivity analysis is that if a **spreadsheet model** is used for analysing the original plan or decision, sensitivity analysis can be carried out quickly and easily, by changing one value at a time in the spreadsheet model. Cash budgets are used extensively with what-if analysis to analyse the cash position in a business.

4.2 Changing the decision

Sensitivity analysis can be used to calculate by how much a variable must change before the decision is changed. In this way attention can be focused on the most sensitive variables.

Example

A company is considering launching a new product in the market. Profit estimates are as follows:

	£	£
Sales (10,000 units)		50,000
Variable costs		
Material	20,000	
Labour	5,000	
		25,000
Contribution		25,000
Fixed costs		20,000
Profit		5,000

Calculate the sensitivity of the project.

Solution

Profit can fall by £5,000 before the project become unviable. This represents:

- a change in sales revenue of 10%
- a change in material costs of 25%
- a change in labour costs of 100%
- a change in fixed costs of 25%

Management may therefore focus attention on the sales forecast to verify that the volume projections are valid at the price chosen.

CHAPTER

6

Budgeting principles and preparation

Contents
1   The planning and budgeting process
2   Functional budgets
3   Cash budgets
4   Fixed and flexed budgets
5   Budgetary systems

- Planning framework
- Purposes of budgeting
- Budgeting: planning and co-ordination
- Budgetary control
- Preparing the budget
- Stages in the budget process

1 The planning and budgeting process

1.1 Planning framework

A business entity should plan over the long-term, medium-term and short-term.

- Long-term planning, or strategic planning, focuses on how to achieve the entity's long-term objectives.
- Medium-term or tactical planning focuses on the next year or two.
- Short-term or operational planning focuses on day-to-day and week-to-week plans.

Budgets are medium-term plans for the business, expressed in financial terms. A typical budget is prepared annually, and the overall budget is divided into control periods for the purpose of control reporting. The stages in the planning and control process are set out below.

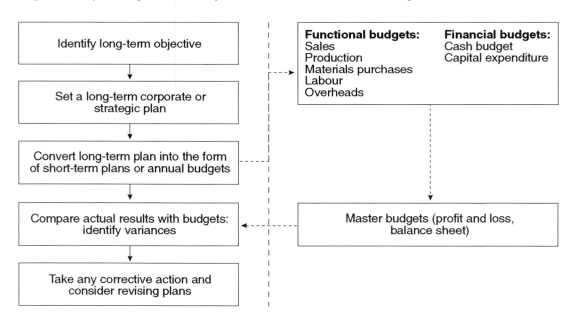

Stages in the planning and control process   Budget elements

1.2　Purposes of budgeting

Budgets have several purposes. These are:

- to convert long-term plans into more detailed shorter-term plans
- to ensure that planning is linked to the long-term objectives of the organisation
- to co-ordinate the actions of all the different parts of the organisation – so that they work towards the same goals (this is known as 'goal congruence')
- to communicate the company's plans to the individuals who have to implement them
- to motivate managers and employees, by setting targets for achievement, and possibly motivating them with the incentive of bonuses or other rewards if the targets are met
- to authorise expenditure and to identify areas of responsibility
- to provide a benchmark against which actual performance can be measured
- to provide the basis of an information system for management control (through budgetary control).

1.3　Budgeting: planning and co-ordination

Budgeting can be described as planning at the 'tactical' management level. As annual plans, they must be consistent with the longer-term strategic plans of the organisation. They can also provide a useful benchmark for setting shorter-term operational targets, such as monthly sales volumes and output volumes, efficiency targets, capacity utilisation targets, and so on.

Budgets can also be an effective method of co-ordinating activities throughout an organisation, because:

- targets for all activities are set within the budget, and the targets for all managers should therefore be consistent with each other
- as indicated above, budgets provide a co-ordinating link between longer-term strategic plans and shorter-term operational targets and plans.

1.4　Budgetary control

Budgets are used for control.

- The budget may be divided into control periods, typically periods of one month. Actual results for a control period are then compared with the budget, and differences reported as variances. Budgeting and variance reporting (and standard costing and variance reporting) are examples of a **feedback control system**.
    - When actual results are worse than budget, there is an adverse variance. If the variance is significant, and the cause of the variance is controllable, the manager responsible may be expected to take control action to bring actual results back towards the budgeted performance level. Adverse variances are an example of **negative feedback**, where control action is needed to correct weaknesses or inefficiencies.

- When actual results are better than budget, there is a favourable variance. If the variance is significant, and the cause of the variance is controllable, the manager responsible may be expected to take control action to continue the favourable results in the future. Favourable variances are an example of **positive feedback**, where control action is expected to take actual results even further away from the budget or target.

■ Another method of control reporting is to prepare an up-to-date forecast of the results for the budget period. An up-to-date forecast is compared with the budget. The comparison may show that actual results for the year may be better or worse than originally budgeted. The control information provided by comparisons of current forecasts with the budget is an example of **feedforward control**.

A combination of feedback and feedforward control information can be used to keep management informed about performance.

■ An advantage of feedforward control is that it is forward-looking. Managers can act to alter future results, but cannot change what has already happened. Looking forward is therefore practical. However, up-to-date forecasts might not be entirely reliable, and when forecasts are uncertain or unreliable, the value of feedforward control information is limited.

■ An advantage of feedback information is that it uses historical information for comparison with the budget or standard costs. The differences between actual results and the budget should therefore be a useful measurement of actual performance.

1.5 Preparing the budget

Medium-sized and large companies should have a well-defined budget process, because a large number of individuals have to co-ordinate their efforts to prepare the budget plans. The budget process may take several months, from beginning to eventual approval by the board of directors.

The budget process might be supervised and controlled by a special committee (the **budget committee**), consisting of senior managers from all the main areas of the business. This committee will co-ordinate the various functional budgets submitted to it for review, and give instructions for changes to be made when the draft budgets are unsatisfactory or the functional budgets are not consistent with each other.

Although the budget committee manages the budget process, the functional budgets are usually prepared by the managers with responsibility for the particular aspect of operations covered by that functional budget.

Budget manual

To guide everyone involved in the budgeting process, there should be a budget manual or budget handbook, setting out:

■ the key objectives that the budget should plan towards

- the planning procedures and the timetables to follow when preparing the budget

- instructions about the budget details to be submitted to the budget committee in the functional budgets

- responsibilities for the functional budgets (sales budget, production budget, purchases budget, direct labour budget, overhead expenditure budgets, etcetera)

- details of the budget approval process.

1.6   Stages in the budget process

The stages in setting the budget might be as follows:

- **Stage 1**: Identify the key budget factor (or principal budget factor). This is the factor that will set a limit on all other activities in the budget. The key budget factor is normally sales volume. However, if there is a shortage of key skilled staff, the availability of skilled labour could be the principal budget factor.

- All the functional budgets should be prepared within the limitation of the key budget factor. For example, even if the company has the capacity to produce more output, it should not produce more than it can profitably sell. In such a situation, the production budget will be limited by the sales budget.

- **Stage 2**: Prepare the functional budget or plan for the key budget factor. Usually, this means that the first functional budget to prepare is the sales budget.

- **Stage 3**: Prepare the other functional budgets, in logical sequence where necessary. When the sales budget has been prepared, a manufacturing organisation can then prepare budgets for inventories, a production budget, direct labour budgets and materials purchasing budgets. Expenditure budgets should also be prepared for overhead costs (production overheads, administration overheads and sales and distribution overheads).

- **Stage 4**: Submit the functional budgets to the budget committee for review and approval. The functional budgets are co-ordinated by the budget committee, which must make sure that they are both realistic and consistent with each other.

- **Stage 5**: Prepare the 'master budget'. This is the budget statement that summarises the plans for the budget period. The master budget might be presented in the form of:

  - a budgeted income statement for the next financial year

  - a budgeted balance sheet as at the end of the next financial year

  - a cash budget or cash flow forecast for the next financial year.

- It should be possible to prepare the master budget statements from the functional budgets.

- **Stage 6**: The master budget and the supporting functional budgets should be submitted to board of directors for approval. The board approves and authorises the budget.

- **Stage 7**: The detailed budgets are communicated to the managers responsible for their implementation.

- **Stage 8**: Control process. Actual results for the period should be recorded and reported to management. Actual results should be compared with the budget, and significant differences should be investigated. The reasons for the differences or variances should be discovered, and where appropriate, control measures should be taken. Comparing actual results with the budget therefore provides a system of control. The managers responsible for activities where actual results differ significantly from the budget will be held responsible and accountable.

> ## Functional budgets
>
> - The master budget
> - The sales budget
> - The production budget
> - The direct materials usage budget
> - The direct labour budget
> - The purchases budget
> - Budgeted income statement

2   Functional budgets

2.1   The master budget

A 'master budget' is the budget for an entire organisation, and consists of functional budgets, together with:

- a budgeted income statement for the financial year
- a cash budget
- a budgeted balance sheet as at the year end
- possibly, a capital expenditure budget (covering more than one financial year, but updated on a 'rolling' basis each year).

This chapter describes the logical approach that can normally be used to prepare budgets for a manufacturing organisation. (The mathematics of budgeting for service industry organisations are usually easier).

It is assumed here that the key budget factor is sales demand, and the initial functional budget to prepare is the sales budget.

The following example will be used to illustrate the preparation of the functional budgets.

In practice, budgets are usually prepared with computer models, such as a **spreadsheet model**.

 Example

Entity Yellow makes and sells two products, Product P and Product Q. The direct production costs of these products are as follows:

	Product P	$	Product Q	$
Direct materials				
Material A	(2 kg × $0.80)	1.60	(0.5 kg × $0.80)	0.40
Material B	(0.5 kg × $2)	1.00	(3 kg × $2)	6.00
Material C	(1 kg × $4)	4.00		-
		6.60		6.40
Direct labour				
Grade X	(0.25 hrs × $10)	2.50	(0.5 hrs × $10)	5.00
Grade Y	(0.25 hrs × $8)	2.00	(0.75 hrs × $8)	6.00
		4.50		11.00
Total direct cost		11.10		17.40

The sales price and expected sales volume for each product next year are as follows:

	Product P	Product Q
Sales price per unit	$20	$30
Budgeted sales volume	20,000 units	30,000 units

Budgeted overhead costs are as follows:

Production overheads	$80,000	including deprec'n charges of $20,000
Administration overheads	$120,000	including deprec'n charges of $10,000
Selling and distribution overheads	$190,000	including deprec'n charges of $10,000

Bad debts are expected to be 2% of sales, and should be provided for. Bad debts are actually written off at the end of the second month following the sale. The costs of bad debts and allowances for doubtful debts are not included in the overhead costs above.

Inventories of raw materials at the beginning of January, and planned closing inventories at the end of January, are as follows:

Direct material	Inventory	
	At beginning of January	At end of January
	kilos	kilos
Material A	5,000	6,000
Material B	5,500	4,000
Material C	1,000	2,500

No further changes in inventory levels are planned during the year.

2.2 The sales budget

The sales budget is prepared for each product individually, and for sales revenue in total.

Product	Sales quantity	Sales price	Sales revenue
	units	$	$
P	20,000	20	400,000
Q	30,000	30	900,000
Total			1,300,000

2.3 The production budget

The production budget is calculated initially in units, although a production cost budget can be prepared later. The production budget in units is prepared for each product, as follows:

	Units
Sales budget in units	S
Plus budgeted closing inventory	C
Minus opening inventory	(O)
Production budget	(S+C-O)

In other words, the production budget for each product in units is the sales budget in units plus any planned increase in finished goods inventories (and work-in-progress inventories) minus the opening inventories of finished goods (and work in progress).

In the example, there are no planned changes in finished goods inventories; therefore the production budget in units is the same as the sales budget.

2.4 The direct materials usage budget

The direct materials usage budget is a statement of the quantities of direct materials required for production, and their cost. The budget is prepared for each item of material separately, but a total usage cost can also be shown.

	Material A	Material B	Material C	Total
	kilos	kilos	kilos	
To make 20,000 P	40,000	10,000	20,000	
To make 30,000 Q	15,000	90,000	0	
Total quantities	55,000	100,000	20,000	
Price per kilo	$0.80	$2	$4	
Total cost	$44,000	$200,000	$80,000	$324,000

2.5 The direct labour budget

The direct labour budget is similar to the direct materials usage budget. It is a statement of the quantities of direct labour required for production, and its cost. The budget is prepared for each grade of labour separately, but a total direct labour cost can also be shown.

	Grade X	Grade Y	Total
	hours	hours	
To make 20,000 P	5,000	5,000	
To make 30,000 Q	15,000	22,500	
Total hours	20,000	27,500	
Cost per hour	$10	$8	
Total cost	$200,000	$220,000	$420,000

2.6   The purchases budget

The purchases budget is the budget for materials purchases. The purchases budget might be prepared for all materials, direct and indirect, or for direct materials only. The purchases budget differs from the materials usage budget by the amount of the planned increase or decrease in inventory levels of materials in the budget period.

The purchase quantities are calculated first, and these are converted into a purchases cost at the budgeted price for each material item. Purchase quantities are calculated as follows:

	Units
Material usage budget in units	S
Plus budgeted closing inventory	C
Minus opening inventory	(O)
Purchases budget, in units	(S+C-O)

The purchases budget in our example is as follows:

	Material A	Material B	Material C	Total
	kilos	kilos	kilos	
Usage budget	55,000	100,000	20,000	
Closing inventory	6,000	4,000	2,500	
	61,000	104,000	22,500	
Opening inventory	(5,000)	(5,500)	(1,000)	
Budgeted purchases	56,000	98,500	21,500	
Price per kilo	$0.80	$2	$4	
Purchases budget in $	$44,800	$197,000	$86,000	$327,800

2.7   Budgeted income statement

The functional budgets, together with budgets for the overhead costs and any other items of cost, should be sufficient to prepare a budgeted income statement for the period.

In our example, we need to remember that the bad and doubtful debt provisions for the year are expected to be 2% × $1,300,000 = $26,000
The budgeted income statement below is presented using marginal costing.

	Product P	Product Q	Total
	$	$	$
Sales	400,000	900,000	1,300,000
Variable cost of sales			
Direct materials	132,000	192,000	324,000
Direct labour	90,000	330,000	420,000
Total variable costs	222,000	522,000	744,000
Contribution	178,000	378,000	556,000
		$	
Production overheads		80,000	
Administration overheads		120,000	
Sales and distribution overheads		190,000	
Bad and doubtful debts		26,000	
			416,000
Budgeted profit			140,000

> **Cash budgets**
>
> ■ Format of a cash budget
>
> ■ Bank overdraft interest
>
> ■ Receipts from credit sales
>
> ■ Payments to suppliers and payments for running costs (overheads)

3 Cash budget

3.1 Format of a cash budget

A cash budget is a budget of cash receipts and cash payments during each control period of the budget. Cash budgets might be prepared on a month-by-month basis. However, cash budgets might be prepared on a week-by-week basis, or even a day-by-day basis if required for short-term planning.

A recommended format for a monthly cash budget is as follows. Illustrative figures are included for January and February.

	January	February	and so on
	$	$	$
Cash receipts			
Cash sales	15,000	10,000	
Cash from trade receivables	80,000	85,000	
Other cash income	2,000	0	
Total cash receipts	97,000	95,000	
Cash payments			
To suppliers	40,000	28,000	
Wages and salaries	35,000	35,000	
Other running costs	12,000	12,000	
Capital purchases	70,000	0	
Other cash payments	1,000	2,000	
Total cash payments	158,000	77,000	
Cash receipts minus cash payments	(61,000)	18,000	
Cash at beginning of month	50,000	(11,000)	7,000
Cash at end of month	(11,000)	7,000	

The cash budget should show all cash items of receipt or payment, including:

■ cash from issuing shares

■ interest or dividends received from investments

■ interest payments, but only in the months that interest is actually paid

■ taxation payments but only in the months that tax is actually paid

■ dividend payments.

Receipts and payments must be recorded in the month when they are expected to occur. Non-cash expenditures, such as depreciation of non-current assets, must not be included.

3.2   Bank overdraft interest

In an examination question, you might be required to calculate bank overdraft interest. For example, you might be told that the bank overdraft is calculated at the end of the month on any opening negative bank balance at the beginning of the month.

You should include a line in the cash payments section for the overdraft interest each month, but you cannot work out the interest cost until you know what the bank balance is at the beginning of the month. It is therefore one of the last items you can enter in the cash budget.

3.3   Receipts from credit sales

One of the more difficult calculations in a cash budget is the cash receipts from trade receivables. When sales are on credit, payments will not be received until a later month. There might also be bad debts to allow for.

We recommend that you should prepare a table for your workings for cash received from credit sales.

 Example

The previous example will be continued. Suppose the sales of the company were as follows:

	Product P	Product Q
	units	units
November	1,500	2,000
December	2,000	3,000
January	1,000	2,000
February	2,000	3,000
March	3,000	4,000

All sales are on credit. 20% of total sales are paid for in the month of sale, and 40% in the following month. The rest, excluding bad debts, are paid at the end of the second month. Bad debts are 2% of total sales and are written off at the end of the second month following sale.

Required

Calculate the budgeted cash receipts from sales, for inclusion in the cash budget for January, February and March.

Answer

The total sales in each month must be calculated.

	Product P ($20)		Product Q ($30)		Total
	units	$	units	$	$
November	1,500	30,000	2,000	60,000	90,000
December	2,000	40,000	3,000	90,000	130,000
January	1,000	20,000	2,000	60,000	80,000
February	2,000	40,000	3,000	90,000	130,000
March	3,000	60,000	4,000	120,000	180,000

The pattern of payments must be established. Here, the pattern is:

20% in the month of sale
40% one month after sale
38% two months after sale
Bad debts = 2%

A table of workings for cash receipts can now be prepared, as follows:

	Sales in month	Received in		
		January	February	March
Month of sale	$	$	$	$
November	90,000	34,200	-	-
December	130,000	52,000	49,400	-
January	80,000	16,000	32,000	30,400
February	130,000	-	26,000	52,000
March	180,000	-	-	36,000
Total cash receipts		102,200	107,400	118,400

3.4 Payments to suppliers and payments for running costs (overheads)

Payments to suppliers

Payments to suppliers can be calculated in a similar way to cash receipts from credit sales. The starting point for calculating payments in each month should be the material purchases in each month. Having established total purchases, you can then work out when the payments will be made.

There will be no bad debts to worry about, because all purchases will be paid for.

Payments for running costs (overheads)

To work out the cash payments for running costs or overhead expenses:

■ exclude any non-cash costs such as depreciation from the total of running costs

■ if any specific payments are made in a particular month, deduct these from the total costs, and enter them in the cash budget in the month when the cash payment will be made

It is usual to assume that all other cash payments for running costs will be an equal amount in every month, so the remaining costs can be divided by 12, and the monthly amount entered in the cash budget as payments in each month.

Example

In the example used earlier, the budgeted annual overhead costs were as follows:

Production overheads	$80,000	including deprec'n charges of $20,000
Administration overheads	$120,000	including deprec'n charges of $10,000
Selling and distribution overheads	$190,000	including deprec'n charges of $10,000

Suppose that the administration overheads include office rental of $20,000 for the year, payable in February, and the selling and distribution overheads include annual bonuses for salesmen of $30,000, payable in December.

The budgeted cash payments for overheads in January, February and March would be calculated as follows:

	Production	Administration	Sales and distribution
	$	$	$
Total annual costs	80,000	120,000	190,000
Depreciation	(20,000)	(10,000)	(10,000)
Annual cash expenses	60,000	110,000	180,000
Rent	-	(20,000)	-
Sales bonuses	-	-	(30,000)
Other cash expenses	60,000	90,000	150,000
Regular monthly payments	5,000	7,500	12,500

The January to March cash budget for overhead costs is as follows:

		Payments in	
	January	February	March
	$	$	$
Rent	-	20,000	-
Production overheads	5,000	5,000	5,000
Administration overheads	7,500	7,500	7,500
Selling/distribution overheads	12,500	12,500	12,500
Total	25,000	45,000	25,000

> ## Fixed and flexed budgets
>
> - The nature of fixed and flexed budgets
> - Flexed budgets using marginal costing
> - Flexed budgets using absorption costing

4 Fixed and flexed budgets

4.1 The nature of fixed and flexed budgets

In a budgetary control system, there is a fixed budget at the beginning of the budget period. Flexible budgets are then prepared in each control period, and compared with the flexed budget, to provide control information in the form of variances.

- A fixed budget is a budget for the planned volume of output and sales (the planned level of activity).

- A flexible budget is prepared at the beginning of the budget period, as a supplement to the fixed budget. A flexed budget is used to estimate what costs, revenue and profit will be if the actual volume of activity is different from the volume in the fixed budget.

- A fixed budget might be divided into several shorter control periods. For example, a fixed annual budget might be divided into fixed budgets for each month of the year.

- Actual results are measured and recorded in each control period.

- A flexed budget is prepared for the control period, stating what the budget should be at the actual level of activity in the period. (A flexed budget is prepared at the **end** of a control period. Note that a flexed budget is not the same as a flexible budget. A flexible budget is forward-looking, whereas a flexed budget looks back at what costs, revenues and profits should have been.)

- Comparing actual results for a control period with the flexed budget provides information about sales price variances and cost variances.

- Comparing the fixed budget with the flexed budget provides information about sales volume variances.

Fixed and flexed budgets therefore provide the framework for a system of budgetary control through variance analysis.

4.2 Flexed budgets using marginal costing

The logical approach to preparing flexed budgets is to prepare the fixed and the flexed budget using marginal costing. The following example shows the fixed budget for a month, the actual results for the month and a flexed budget, based on marginal costing.

Example

	Original budget	Flexed budget	Actual results	Variance
Sales units	10,000	15,000	15,000	
	$	$	$	$
Sales revenue	200,000	300,000	286,000	
Sales price variance				14,000 (A)
Variable costs				
Direct materials	60,000	90,000	94,000	
Direct materials cost variance				4,000 (A)
Direct labour	70,000	105,000	97,000	
Direct materials cost variance				8,000 (F)
Variable overheads	20,000	30,000	23,000	
Variable overhead cost variance				7,000 (F)
Total variable costs	150,000	225,000	214,000	
Contribution	50,000	75,000	72,000	
Fixed costs	40,000	40,000	55,000	
Fixed overhead expenditure var.				15,000 (A)
Profit	10,000	35,000	17,000	

The sales volume variance is the difference in the fixed budget profit and the flexed budget profit. Here, there is a favourable sales volume variance of $25,000, because the flexed budget profit (and contribution) is $25,000 higher than the profit expected in the fixed budget, and this is due to the fact that actual sales volume has exceeded budget.

Operating statement summary, marginal costing

	$	
Budgeted profit	10,000	
Sales volume variance	25,000	(F)
Sales price variance	14,000	(A)
	21,000	
Cost variances		
Direct materials	4,000	(A)
Direct labour	8,000	(F)
Variable overheads	7,000	(F)
Fixed overhead expenditure	15,000	(A)
Actual profit	17,000	

4.3 Flexed budget using absorption costing

A similar approach to preparing flexed budgets can be used when a system of absorption costing is operated.

Example

In this example, there is a fixed production overhead cost (absorption rate) of $4 per unit. It is assumed that all costs are production costs.

	Original Budget	Flexed budget	Actual results	Variance
Sales units	10,000	15,000	15,000	
	$	$	$	
Sales revenue	200,000	300,000	286,000	Sales price variance $14,000(A)
Variable costs				
Direct materials	60,000	90,000	94,000	Direct materials cost variance $4,000 (A)
Direct labour	70,000	105,000	97,000	Direct labour cost variance $8,000 (F)
Variable overheads	20,000	30,000	23,000	Variable overhead cost variance $7,000(F)
	150,000	225,000	214,000	
Contribution	50,000	75,000	72,000	
Fixed costs	40,000	60,000	55,000	Fixed overh'd variances $5,000 (F)
Profit	10,000	15,000	17,000	

The fixed overhead total cost variance is the over-absorbed or under-absorbed overhead. Here there is over-absorbed overhead of $5,000, and the total fixed overhead cost variance is therefore $5,000(F).

(Absorbed fixed overheads = $60,000 at $4 per unit; actual fixed overheads = $55,000; therefore over-absorbed = $5,000).

This total fixed overhead variance can be analysed into an expenditure variance and a volume variance. The variances are calculated in the same way as for standard costing.

- There is an expenditure variance, which is the difference between the budgeted fixed overhead expenditure ($40,000) and the actual fixed overhead expenditure ($55,000), giving an expenditure variance of $15,000(A).

  The volume variance is the difference between the budgeted production volume (10,000 units) and the actual production volume (15,000 units). This is 5,000 units (Favourable), and at an absorption rate of $4 per unit, the fixed overhead volume variance is $20,000 (F) [= 5,000(F) × $4].

- The sales volume variance is measured at the standard profit of $1 per unit (budgeted profit = $10,000, budgeted sales = 10,000 units). It is favourable, because actual sales volume exceeded the budget by 5,000 units. The sales volume variance in the table above is shown as the difference between the fixed budget profit and the flexed budget profit.

Operating statement summary, absorption costing

	$	
Budgeted profit	10,000	
Sales volume variance	5,000	(F)
Sales price variance	14,000	(A)
	1,000	
Cost variances		
Direct materials	4,000	(A)
Direct labour	8,000	(F)
Variable overheads	7,000	(F)
Fixed overhead volume	20,000	(F)
Fixed overhead expenditure	15,000	(A)
Total variances	16,000	(F)
Actual profit	17,000	

(Note: Since there are no changes in the inventory level, and sales volume equals production volume, the profit reported by marginal costing is the same as the profit reported by absorption costing).

Budgetary systems

- Periodic and rolling budgets (continuous budgets)
- Incremental budgeting and zero based budgeting (ZBB)
- Activity based budgeting

5 Budgetary systems

5.1 Periodic and rolling budgets (continuous budgets)

A **periodic budget** is a budget for a particular time period. Typically, this time period is the financial year. The budget is not changed or revised during the year, and it is the fixed budget for the period. A company might therefore prepare a periodic budget for its financial year 2007, which will then be replaced the next year by the periodic budget for 2008, which will then be replaced the year afterwards by the periodic budget for 2009, and so on.

In some situations, there are major disadvantages with using a fixed budget for planning purposes, particularly when events change rapidly, and plans must be continually revised. In these situations, it might be advisable for the organisation to prepare budgets more frequently.

A **rolling budget**, also called a **continuous budget**, is a budget that is continuously being updated - for example as one quarter of a 12-month budget is finished, a new quarter is added to the budget – so that there is a new 12-month budget every three months.

A rolling budget can therefore be defined as 'a budget continuously updated by adding a further period, say a month or a quarter, and deducting the earliest period'.

Rolling budgets are most useful where future costs or activities cannot be forecast reliably, so that it makes much more sense for planning purposes to review the budget regularly, but to plan ahead for a full planning period each time.

Rolling budgets might be particularly useful for cash budgeting. An organisation must ensure that it will always have sufficient cash to meet its requirements, but actual cash flows often differ considerably from the budget. It might therefore be appropriate to prepare a new annual cash budget every month, and so have 12 rolling cash budgets every year.

The main disadvantage of rolling budgets is the time and cost required to prepare new budgets at frequent intervals throughout each financial year.

5.2   Incremental budgeting and zero based budgeting (ZBB)

Incremental budgets and zero based budgeting are two different approaches to estimating budgeted expenditure. The difference between them is most obvious in budgeting for administrative activities (and other overhead activities) and overhead costs.

With **incremental budgeting**, the budgeted expenditure for the next financial period is estimated by taking expenditure in the current period as a starting point. An incremental amount is then added for:

■ inflation in costs next year, and

■ possibly, the cost of additional activities that will be carried out next year.

In its simplest form, incremental budgets for a financial period are prepared by taking the expenditure in the current year, and adding a percentage to allow for inflation next year.

Zero based budgeting (ZBB)

Zero based budgeting (ZBB) has a completely different approach. It aims to eliminate all wasteful spending ('budget slack') and only to budget for activities that are worth carrying out and that the organisation can afford. Planning starts from 'zero' and all spending must be justified.

It can be particularly useful in budgeting for activities that are prone to budget slack and wasteful spending, such as bureaucracy. ZBB might be usefully applied, for example, to the budgets of government departments.

The approach used in ZBB is as follows:

■ The minimum level of operations in the department or the budget centre is identified. These are the essential things that the department will have to do. A budget is prepared for this minimum essential level.

■ All other activities are optional additional activities that need to be justified, in terms of the benefits obtained in return for the costs. Each additional activity is called a **decision package**.

A decision package is a program of activity that will achieve a specific purpose. Each decision package must have a clearly-stated purpose that contributes to the goals and objectives of the entity.
There are two types of decision package.

■ **Decision packages for a minimum level of operation**. For example, there may be a minimum acceptable level of training for a group of employees. There may be several alternative decision packages for providing the training – internal courses, external courses, or computer-based training programmes. An expenditure estimate should be prepared for each alternative basic decision package.

■ **Incremental decision packages**. These are programmes for conducting a more extensive operation than the minimum acceptable level. For example, there may be incremental decision packages for providing some employees with more training, or for having more extensive supervision, or more extensive quality control checks. For incremental decision packages, an estimate should be made of the cost of the incremental operation, and the expected benefits.

For each decision package, the following should be considered:

■ Purpose of the activity

■ The likely results and benefits from the activity

■ The resources required for the activity, and their cost

■ Alternative ways of achieving the same purpose, but perhaps at a lower cost

■ A comparison of the costs and benefits of the activity.

A zero based budget is then prepared as follows:

■ A decision must be taken to provide for a minimum level of operation. This means deciding for each basic operation:

- whether or not to perform the operation at all – do the benefits justify the costs?

- If the operation is performed at a basic level, which of the alternative basic decision packages should be selected?

■ Having decided on as basic level of operations, a basic expenditure budget can be prepared.

■ The next step is to consider each incremental decision package, and decide whether this additional operation, or additional level of operations, is justified. An incremental decision package is justified if the expected benefits exceed the estimated costs.

■ A budget can then be prepared consisting of all the selected basic decision packages and incremental decision packages.

■ If the total expenditure budget is too high, when all these decision packages are included, some incremental decision packages should be eliminated from the budget. One method of doing this is to rank the incremental decision packages in an order of priority (typically in order of net expected benefits, which are the expected benefits minus the estimated incremental costs). The decision packages at the bottom of the priority list can then be eliminated from the budget, until total budgeted expenditure comes within the maximum permitted spending limit.

Extensive use of value judgements by managers will be needed to rank decision packages in a priority order. This is because the expected benefits from incremental activities or incremental programmes are often based on guesswork and opinion, or on forecasts that might be difficult to justify.

The advantages of zero based budgeting

■ All activities are reviewed and evaluated.

■ Inefficiency in using resources and inefficiency in spending should be identified and eliminated.

■ A ZBB approach helps managers to question the reason for doing things rather than simply accepting the current position.

- When total expenditure has to be reduced, ZBB provides a priority list for activities.

- ZBB encourages greater involvement by managers and might motivate them to eliminate wasteful spending.

The disadvantages of zero based budgeting

- ZBB is very time consuming, particularly if undertaken annually.

- It is also costly, because it takes more time.

- Planners need to understand the principles of relevant costing and decision-making, in order to compare properly the incremental costs and incremental benefits of activities.

- ZBB might be seen as a threat, to cut back expenditure allowances in the next budget year.

- When incremental decision packages are ranked in priority order, there may be disputes between managers of different decision units (budget cost centres), as each tries to protect his own spending levels and argue that budget cuts should fall on other cost centres.

In view of the large amount of management time that is required to prepare a zero based budget, an entity may decide to produce a zero based budget periodically, say every three years, and to prepare incremental budgets in the intervening years.
In order to maintain the support of budget cost centre managers for a system of ZBB, it is also necessary to make sure that any system of performance-based rewards (such as annual bonuses for keeping spending within budget limits) is not affected by the use of ZBB. If managers feel that their rewards will be threatened – for example because it will be difficult to keep spending within the ZBB limits – they are unlikely to give their support to the ZBB system.

ZBB and performance monitoring

A successful system of ZBB requires methods for monitoring actual performance and comparing actual performance with the budget.

- Each decision package must therefore have one or more measurable performance objectives. The package must specify the objective or objectives, and the activities or operations that will be required to achieve those objectives.

- Actual performance should be measured and compared with the objectives. Management must be informed whether or not the performance objectives are achieved.

5.3 Activity based budgeting

Activity based budgeting applies the principles of ABC to the preparation of budgets

- Activities drive costs. By identifying cost drivers, costs can be more accurately forecast and monitored

- In service cost centres and non-production departments many costs are likely to be caused by activities outside of the control of the department. By identifying cost drivers, activity levels are more visible. For example, maintenance requirements may be a function of the age of the machinery and level of usage. The maintenance manager will require estimates from the production manager to enable a budget to be produced.

- By identifying cost drivers, non value-adding activities can be highlighted.

 Example

The costs of a marketing department are found to be driven by the number of new products launched each period plus the number of existing products, which generally have a lower level of marketing. The remaining costs are departmental administration costs.

£000	Total	New Products	Existing products	Departmental administration
Salaries	150	75	67	8
Materials	85	52	31	2
Other costs	62	40	20	2
	297	167	118	12
Volume		8	16	
Cost per cost driver		£20,875	£7,375	

If the actual number of new or existing products is different from the budget level, the budget can now be flexed to provide a more realistic measure of expected costs.

CHAPTER

7

Quantitative aids to budgeting

Contents
1   High low method
2   Linear regression analysis
3   Time series analysis
4   The learning curve
5   Uncertainty in budgeting

> ## High low method
>
> - Using quantitative aids in budgeting
> - Estimating fixed and variable costs: high low method
> - Using the high low method

1 High low method

1.1 Using quantitative aids in budgeting

Some quantitative methods might be used in budgeting. These include quantitative methods for:

- analysing fixed costs and variable costs per unit, and
- preparing forecasts, on the assumption that the future will continue on in the same trend as in the past.

1.2 Estimating fixed and variable costs: high low method

Organisations that budget their expenditure using a marginal costing approach must be able to estimate the fixed costs and the variable costs per unit in the budget period.

Direct materials costs and direct labour costs are usually treated as variable costs, and fairly accurate estimates of these direct costs can often be prepared. However, it is often much more difficult to analyse overhead costs, for production, administration and selling and distribution, into fixed and variable overheads.

One assumption is that the fixed costs in each period and the variable cost per unit will continue to be the same as in the past, costs can be analysed into fixed and variable components using:

- the high low method, or
- linear regression analysis.

1.3 Using the high low method

The high low method is a basic method to estimate the formula for a line:

$y = a + bx$

When estimating fixed and variable costs:

y = total costs

a = fixed costs in the period

b = variable cost per unit (or variable cost per \$1 of sales)

x = number of units produced/sold (or total sales)

The high low estimate is obtained by taking two historical records of total costs and the associated total number of units. The two records used for the estimate are the costs for the highest volume of activity (output or sales) and the costs for the lowest volume of activity (output or sales) from amongst the records available.

- It is then assumed that these records of cost for the highest and lowest volumes of activity are representative of costs at all levels of activity.

- The difference between the total cost at the high volume of activity and the total cost at the low volume of activity must consist entirely of variable costs, because the fixed costs are the same at both volumes of activity.

- The difference between the total costs at the two levels of activity, divided by the difference in activity level, gives us an estimate of the variable cost per unit.

- Having calculated a variable cost per unit, we can use either the high volume or the low volume of activity and the total costs at that activity level to estimate the total fixed costs

Example

A company is trying to estimate its fixed and variable production overhead costs in each month. It has the following historical data of costs in the previous five months:

Production volume	Total cost
000 units	$000
8	25
6	22
6	19
9	24
5	16

Required

Use this data to estimate fixed costs each month and the variable cost per unit, using the high low method.

What should be the estimated costs for production overheads next month if the expected volume of production is 8,000 units?

Answer

With the high low method, the total cost for the highest volume of production and the total cost for the lowest volume of production are used. These are the costs for 9,000 units and 5,000 units.

Since fixed costs are the same at both volumes of activity, the difference in total cost between the high and the low volumes must be the variable costs of the difference in output.

	$
Total cost of 9,000 units	24,000
Total cost of 5,000 units	16,000
Therefore variable cost of 4,000 units	8,000

The variable cost per unit is therefore $8,000/4,000 units = $2 per unit.

This variable cost can be used, with either the high cost or the low cost, to estimate the fixed costs for the period.

	$
Total cost of 9,000 units	24,000
Variable cost of 9,000 units (× $2)	18,000
Therefore fixed costs each month	6,000

The estimate of costs using the high low method is therefore:

- fixed costs = $6,000
- variable cost = $2 per unit.

If estimated output is 8,000 units, the estimated total costs for the month are: $6,000 + (8,000 × $2) = $22,000.

> ## Linear regression analysis
>
> - The formulae
> - Using the formulae
> - Correlation
> - The correlation coefficient r
> - Linear regression analysis and forecasting

2 Linear regression analysis

2.1 The formulae

Linear regression analysis is a more accurate forecasting method than the high low method. Like the high low method, it assumes that there is a straight-line formula y = a + bx. It also uses historical data to produce an estimate for the values of a and b.

However, unlike the high low method, it uses any number of historical data items, not just two (the high and the low data items).

The formulae for estimating fixed costs and variable costs with linear regression analysis are given to you in the examination. You do not need to remember them, but you might be required to use them.

The formulae are, for y = a + bx:

$$a = \frac{\sum y}{n} - \frac{b \sum x}{n}$$

$$b = \frac{n \sum xy - \sum x \times \sum y}{n \sum x^2 - (\sum x)^2}$$

Where:

n = the number of data items used.

To calculate the value of a, you must first know the value of b. The estimated value for b must therefore be calculated first.

2.2 Using the formulae

Using the formula is probably best explained with an example. The following example is the same as the example used earlier to demonstrate the high low method.

Example

A company is trying to estimate its fixed and variable production overhead costs in each month. It has the following historical data of costs in the previous five months.

Production volume	Total cost
000 units	**$000**
8	25
6	22
6	19
9	24
5	16

Required

Use this data to estimate fixed costs each month and the variable cost per unit, using the linear regression formulae.

What should be the estimated costs for production overheads next month if the expected volume of production is 8,000 units?

Answer

The number of items of data: n = 5

The other values for the formulae are calculated as follows:

Production volume	Total cost		
x	**y**	**xy**	**x^2**
8	25	200	64
6	22	132	36
6	19	114	36
9	24	216	81
5	16	80	25
34	106	742	242

The values for y are the total costs and the values for x are the activity/output volumes.

$\Sigma x = 34$

$\Sigma y = 106$

$\Sigma xy = 742$

$\Sigma x^2 = 242$

$n = 5$

The formulae can now be used to establish a value for b and then a.

$$b = \frac{5(742) - (34)(106)}{5(242) - (34)^2}$$

$$= \frac{3,710 - 3,604}{1,210 - 1,156} = \frac{106}{54}$$

b=1.96

$$a = \frac{106}{5} - \frac{1.96(34)}{5}$$

a=21.2-13.3=7.9

The estimate of costs is therefore = 7,900 + 1.96x.

When output x = 8,000 units, the estimated total costs will be:

Total costs = \$7,900 + (8,000 × \$1.96) = \$23,580, say \$23,600.

2.3 Correlation

The linear regression formulae can be applied to any data, where there are pairs of data for x and y.

They do not indicate, however, how reliable the estimates might be. The values for a and b that are estimated from linear regression analysis might not be reliable at all. On the other hand, they might be very reliable.

Correlation refers to the extent to which values for y can be predicted from any given value for x, using the values for a and b obtained from linear regression analysis.

■ A high degree of correlation indicates that values for y can be estimated with a reasonable degree of confidence from values of x.

■ A low degree of correlation indicates that values for y estimated from any given value of x will not be particularly reliable.

The extent of correlation between values of x and values of y can be measured by a correlation coefficient, r.

2.4 The correlation coefficient r

The correlation coefficient is calculated using the following formula:

$$r = \frac{n \sum xy - \sum x \sum y}{\sqrt{\left[n \sum x^2 - (\sum x)^2\right]\left[n \sum y^2 - (\sum y)^2\right]}}$$

This formula is given to you in the examination. You do not have to learn it, but you might be required to use it.

If you look at the formula carefully, you should notice that most of the values in the formula are the same as the values used to calculate b in the linear regression analysis formula. The only additional values you need are for $n \sum y^2$ and $(\sum y)^2$.

The value of r

The value of r produced by this formula must always be within the range – 1 to + 1.

■ When r is close to + 1, there is a high degree of positive correlation. When r = + 1, there is perfect positive correlation, and all the pairs of data for x and y that have been used to estimate the values for a and b lie on a straight line, y = a + bx, when drawn graphically.

■ When r is close to - 1, there is a high degree of negative correlation. When r = - 1, there is perfect negative correlation, and all the pairs of data for x and y that have been used to estimate the values for a and b lie on a straight line, y = a - bx, when drawn graphically.

■ When r is 0, there is no correlation at all between the values of x and the values of y, and the linear regression formula would be completely unreliable. Correlation probably needs to be at the very least between 0.80 and 1.00 or between – 0.80 and – 1.00 to be considered of much significance.

Example

The correlation coefficient can be calculated for the previous example, as follows:

Production volume		Total cost		
x	y	xy	x^2	y^2
8	25	200	64	625
6	22	132	36	484
6	19	114	36	361
9	24	216	81	576
5	16	80	25	256
34	106	742	242	2,302

$$r = \frac{106}{\sqrt{[54][5(2,302)-(106)^2]}} = \frac{106}{\sqrt{(54)(274)}}$$

$$r = \frac{106}{121.6} = +0.87.$$

Here, there is a reasonably strong positive correlation between the values of x and the values of y that are estimated using the linear regression formula.

2.5 Linear regression analysis and forecasting

Linear regression analysis can also be used in forecasting, where it can be assumed that there has been a linear trend in the past, and this same linear trend will continue into the future.

Exactly the same method is used in forecasting as for estimating fixed and variable costs. The trend line is a formula y = a + bx, where x is the year or month.

To simplify the arithmetic, you should number the years 1, 2, 3, 4 and so on (or even start at year 0, and number the years 0, 1, 2, 3 and so on).

> **Time series analysis**
>
> - The nature of a time series
> - Moving averages
> - Seasonal variations with an additive model
> - Using the trend line and seasonal variations to make forecasts
> - Problems with seasonal variation analysis
> - Estimating seasonal variations with the proportional model

3 Time series analysis

3.1 The nature of a time series

A time series is a record of data over a period of time. A problem arises with forecasting when a time series fluctuates. If the fluctuation is regular then this can be included in forecasts to make these more accurate.

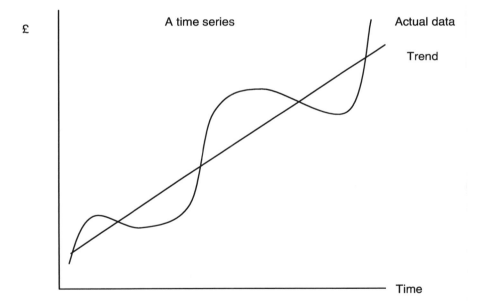

In time series analysis it is assumed that actual data is made up of four components:

- A trend (T) – This is the long term underlying movement of the data. If this is linear it can be forecast using the high low method, linear regression analysis, by plotting the data and estimating a line of best fit or by using moving averages which will be explained later in the chapter.

- A cyclical variation (C) – This is a long-term regular fluctuation around the trend and is caused by the economic cycle of boom, recession and recovery.

- A seasonal variation (S) – This is the short-term regular fluctuation around the trend. Examples include actual sales which vary by the quarter of the year (skiing holidays, ice cream sales), usage which varies by the time of the day (electricity, telephone), usage which varies by the days of the week (rail transport, hotel accommodation).

■ A random variation (R) – Unpredictable affects like strikes, adverse weather conditions or stock market crashes.

In time series analysis, cyclical variations are often ignored as they require too much data to analyse. Random variations are, by definition, unpredictable so the time series model concentrates on identifying the trend and seasonal variations which affect data. These can then be used to make forecasts.

There are two different models used;
■ The additive model

Actual data = T + S
■ The proportional model

Actual data = T × S

The additive model assumes that a seasonal variation is an absolute figure which can be added or subtracted to the trend each period to find the actual data. The proportional model assumes that the seasonal variation is an index or percentage which is multiplied by the trend to find the actual data. The proportional model is often considered to be more accurate when considering sales or production data when the trend is increasing.

3.2 Moving averages

Moving averages can be used to estimate help estimate the trend and seasonal variation. This is done as follows:

■ **Step 1**. Decide the length of the cycle. For example, the cycle will be seven days when historical data is collected daily for each day of the week. The cycle will be one year when data is collected monthly for each month of the year, or quarterly for each season.

■ **Step 2**. Use the historical data to calculate a series of moving averages. A moving average is the average of all the historical data in one cycle. For example, suppose that historical data is available for daily sales over a period Day 1 – Day 21, and there are seven days of selling each week. A moving average can be calculated for Day 1 – Day 7. Another moving average can be calculated for Day 2 – Day 8. Another moving average can be calculated for Day 3 – Day 9, and so on up to a moving average for Day 15 – Day 21.

■ **Step 3**. Match each moving average with an actual time period. The moving average should be matched with the middle time period of the cycle. For example a moving average for Day 1 – Day 7 is matched with Day 4, which is the middle of the period. Similarly, a moving average for Day 2 – Day 8 is matched with Day 5, and a moving average for Day 15 – Day 21 is matched with Day 18.

■ **Step 4**. Use the moving averages (and their associated time periods) to calculate a trend line, using simple averaging, high low method or linear regression analysis. It is also often useful to plot the data on a graph and extend a line of best fit.

Example

A company operates for five days each week. Sales data for the most recent three weeks are as follows:

Sales	Monday units	Tuesday units	Wednesday units	Thursday units	Friday units
Week 1	78	83	89	85	85
Week 2	88	93	99	95	95
Week 3	98	103	109	105	105

For convenience, it is assumed that Week 1 consists of Days 1 – 5, Week 2 consists of Days 6 – 10, and Week 3 consists of Days 11 – 15.

This sales data can be used to estimate a trend line. A weekly cycle in this example is 5 days, so we must calculate moving averages for five day periods, as follows:

Period	Middle day		Moving average
Days 1 – 5	Day 3	[78 + 83 + 89 + 85 + 85] /5	84
Days 2 – 6	Day 4	[83 + 89 + 85 + 85 + 88] /5	86
Days 3 – 7	Day 5	[89 + 85 + 85 + 88 + 93] /5	88
Days 4 – 8	Day 6	[85 + 85 + 88 + 93 + 99] /5	90
Days 5 – 9	Day 7	[85 + 88 + 93 + 99 + 95] /5	92
Days 6 – 10	Day 8	[88 + 93 + 99 + 95 + 95] /5	94
Days 7 – 11	Day 9	[93 + 99 + 95 + 95 + 98] /5	96
Days 8 – 12	Day 10	[99 + 95 + 95 + 98 + 103] /5	98
Days 9 – 13	Day 11	[95 + 95 + 98 + 103 + 109] /5	100
Days 10 – 14	Day 12	[95 + 98 + 103 + 109 + 105] /5	102
Days 11 – 15	Day 13	[98 + 103 + 109 + 105 + 105]/5	104

In this example, all the moving average figures lie on a perfect straight line. It can be seen that each day the trend increases by 2. If x = the day number, the formula for the trend can be calculated by taking any day, say day 12

$a + 2 \times 12 = 102$ so $a = 78$.

The formula is daily sales = $78 + 2x$.

This trend line can be used to calculate the seasonal variations. The approach will be slightly different depending on whether an additive or proportional model is being used.

3.3 Seasonal variations with an additive model

The trend line on its own is not sufficient to make forecasts for the future. We also need estimates of the size of the 'seasonal' variation for each of the different seasons. In the example above, we need an estimate of the amount of the expected daily variation in sales, for each day of the week.

For the purpose of forecasting, the seasonal variation (in the above example, the daily variation) is the difference between:

- the trend line value, and
- the forecast or expected value (allowing for the seasonal variation).

The size of the seasonal variations is estimated from the historical data. Seasonal variations for each quarter of the year or each day of the week can be estimated from the difference between:

- the actual historical value for each time period, and
- the moving average value for the same time period

The seasonal variation for each season (or daily variation for each day) is estimated as follows:

- Use the moving average values that have been calculated from the historical data, and the corresponding historical data. ('actual' data) for the same time period.
- Calculate the difference between the moving average value and the actual historical figure for each time period. This is a seasonal variation. You will now have a number of seasonal variations, covering several weekly or annual cycles.
- Group these seasonal variations into the different seasons of the year (or days of the week). You will now have several seasonal variations for each day of the week or season of the year.
- For each season (or day), calculate the average of these seasonal variations.
- This average seasonal variation for each day of the week or season of the year is used as the seasonal variation for the purpose of forecasting.

The seasonal variations can then be used, with the estimated trend line, to make forecasts for the future.

Example

Using the previous example, the seasonal variations are calculated as follows:

Middle day	Day of the week	Moving average value	Actual sales	Variation (Actual – moving average)
Day 3	Wednesday	84	89	+ 5
Day 4	Thursday	86	85	- 1
Day 5	Friday	88	85	- 3
Day 6	Monday	90	88	- 2
Day 7	Tuesday	92	93	+ 1
Day 8	Wednesday	94	99	+ 5
Day 9	Thursday	96	95	- 1
Day 10	Friday	98	95	- 3
Day 11	Monday	100	98	- 2
Day 12	Tuesday	102	103	+ 1
Day 13	Wednesday	104	109	+ 5

The seasonal variation (daily variation) is now calculated as the average seasonal variation for each day, as follows:

Variation	Monday units	Tuesday units	Wednesday units	Thursday units	Friday units
Week 1			+ 5	- 1	- 3
Week 2	- 2	+ 1	+ 5	- 1	- 3
Week 3	- 2	+ 1	+ 5		
Average	- 2	+ 1	+ 5	- 1	- 3

Points to note

(1) In this example, the average seasonal variation for each day of the week is exactly the same as the actual seasonal variations. This is because the historical data in this example produces a perfect trend line.

(2) The total of the seasonal variations for each day of the week is 0. (- 2 + 1 + 5 – 1 – 3 = 0.) When seasonal variations are applied to a straight-line trend line, they must always add up to zero. If the seasonal variations did not add up to 0, the trend line would not be straight. It would 'curve' up or down, depending on whether the sum of the seasonal variations is positive or negative.

3.4 Using the trend line and seasonal variations to make forecasts

When the trend line and seasonal variations have been estimated, we can make forecasts for the future. In the example above, suppose that we wanted to forecast sales in Week 4 (days 16 – 20). The trend line is 78 + 2x. The daily forecasts are as follows:

Day		Trend line value (78 + 2x)	Seasonal variation	Forecast
16	Monday	110	- 2	108
17	Tuesday	112	+ 1	113
18	Wednesday	114	+ 5	119
19	Thursday	116	- 1	115
20	Friday	118	- 3	115

3.5 Problems with seasonal variation analysis

There are two problems with using this technique to make forecasts with seasonal variations.

(1) The historical data will not provide a perfect trend line. The trend line that is estimated with the historical data is a 'best estimate', not a perfect estimate. The seasonal variations measured from historical data will not be a constant amount for each day of the week or season of the year. In practice, seasonal variations are estimated as average values from the historical data.

(2) The number of seasons in each cycle might be an even number (2, 4, 6 or 8). A moving average is an average for the middle time period in the cycle. When there is an even number of periods in one cycle, the moving average does not match any specific time period. For example, the moving average of Season 1 – Season 4 is for Season 2.5, which does not exist.

There are techniques to deal with each of these problems.

Historical data does not produce a perfect trend line

When historical data does not produce a perfect trend line, the same technique is used to prepare forecasts, with one difference.

The sum of the seasonal variations must be 0 for a straight trend line, but the actual seasonal variations calculated from the historical data will not add up to 0. They must therefore be adjusted so that they do add up to 0.

Example

Sales	Monday units	Tuesday units	Wednesday units	Thursday units	Friday units
Week 1	55	49	54	60	65
Week 2	70	65	65	76	80
Week 3	88	81	85	91	93

For convenience, it is assumed that Week 1 consists of Days 1 – 5, Week 2 consists of Days 6 – 10, and Week 3 consists of Days 11 – 15.

A trend line is calculated using linear regression analysis, giving the following forecast of daily sales:

Sales = 45 + 3x.

The actual sales and moving average values of sales are compared, to produce seasonal variations for each day, as follows:

Day	3	4	5	6	7	8	9	10	11	12	13
Moving average	56	59	62	64	68	71	75	78	82	85	88
Actual	54	60	65	70	65	65	76	80	88	81	85
Variation	- 2	+ 1	+ 3	+ 6	- 3	- 6	+ 1	+ 2	+ 6	- 4	- 3

The average variation for each day is now calculated, but they sum of the averages in not 0. It is 2.33. To reduce this total of seasonal variations to 0, we can reduce the average seasonal variation per day (for five days) by $2.33/5 = 0.466$, say 0.5. (Remember that minus a minus figure is 'plus'.)

Variation	Monday units	Tuesday units	Wednesday units	Thursday units	Friday units	Total
Week 1			- 2	+ 1	+ 3	
Week 2	+ 6	- 3	- 6	+ 1	+ 2	
Week 3	+ 6	- 4	- 3			
Average	+ 6	- 3.5	- 3.67	+ 1	+ 2.5	+ 2.33
Adjustment	- 0.5	- 0.5	- 0.5	- 0.5	- 0.5	
Seasonal variation	+ 5.5, say + 5	- 4	- 4.17, say - 4	+ 0.5, say + 1	+ 2	0

The estimated variations each day of the week are therefore:
Monday + 5, Tuesday – 4, Wednesday – 4, Thursday + 1 and Friday + 2.

These add up to zero, so can be used with the trend line to make forecasts of future sales based on an assumption that sales will rise in a straight line, with daily variations according to the day of the week.

An even number of seasons

When there is an even number of seasons in a cycle, and the moving averages do not correspond to an actual season, it is necessary to take moving averages of the moving averages. These will correspond to an actual season of the year.

Example

The following sales figures will be used to estimate a trend line for quarterly sales with seasonal variations:

Sales	Quarter 1 $000	Quarter 2 $000	Quarter 3 $000	Quarter 4 $000
Year 1	20	24	27	31
Year 2	35	39	44	47
Year 3	49	56	60	64

These quarters for the three years will be called quarter 1 – Quarter 12. There are four seasons in the annual cycle, so moving average values for each quarter are calculated as follows:

Period	Middle quarter	Moving average	Moving average of moving average (average of 2)
Quarters 1 – 4	Quarter 2.5	25.50	
	Quarter 3		27.375
Quarters 2 – 5	Quarter 3.5	29.25	
	Quarter 4		31.125
Quarters 3 – 6	Quarter 4.5	33.00	
	Quarter 5		35.125
Quarters 4 – 7	Quarter 5.5	37.25	
	Quarter 6		39.250
Quarters 5 – 8	Quarter 6.5	41.25	
	Quarter 7		43.000
Quarters 6 – 9	Quarter 7.5	44.75	
	Quarter 8		46.875
Quarters 7 – 10	Quarter 8.5	49.00	
	Quarter 9		51.000
Quarters 8 – 11	Quarter 9.5	53.00	
	Quarter 10		55.125
Quarters 9 – 12	Quarter 10.5	57.25	

The moving averages in the right hand column correspond with an actual season. These moving averages are used to estimate the trend line and the seasonal variations.

3.6 Estimating seasonal variations with the proportional model

A proportional time series model uses the same approach as the additive model to find the trend. The seasonal variation is then calculated by dividing the actual data by the trend. (Since $A = T \times S$, then $S = A/T$)

 Example

A company has used sales records for each quarter of the year for the past few years to prepare an estimate of the trend in sales each quarter.

The straight-line trend in quarterly sales is
$y = 150,000 + 10,000x$

where
x = the quarter in the time series, where 0 = the sales in the first quarter of 20X1.

The actual and trend sales in each quarter are shown in the table below. The seasonal variation is found by dividing the actual sales by the trend.

Time period	Actual sales	Estimated sales, using trend line y = 150,000 + 10,000x	Seasonal variation = A/T
	$	$	$
Quarter 1, 20X1	119,200	150,000	0.79
Quarter 2, 20X1	167,500	160,000	1.05
Quarter 3, 20X1	219,200	170,000	1.29
Quarter 4, 20X1	151,500	180,000	0.84
Quarter 1, 20X2	162,000	190,000	0.85
Quarter 2, 20X2	203,700	200,000	1.02
Quarter 3, 20X2	258,400	210,000	1.23
Quarter 4, 20X2	199,700	220,000	0.91
Quarter 1, 20X3	200,400	230,000	0.87
Quarter 2, 20X3	248,000	240,000	1.03
Quarter 3, 20X3	296,200	250,000	1.18
Quarter 4, 20X3	237,200	260,000	0.91
Quarter 1, 20X4	242,000	270,000	0.90
Quarter 2, 20X4	284,800	280,000	1.02
Quarter 3, 20X4	341,200	290,000	1.18
Quarter 4, 20X4	276,400	300,000	0.92

These figures can be used to calculate an average seasonal variation for each quarter of the year.

However, the total seasonal variations must add up to 4, otherwise a straight-line trend does not exist. If the average does not sum to 4 an adjustment must be made to the average.

Seasonal variations	Quarter 1	Quarter 2	Quarter 3	Quarter 4	Total
	$	$	$	$	$
20X1	0.79	1.05	1.29	0.84	
20X2	0.85	1.02	1.23	0.91	
20X3	0.87	1.03	1.18	0.91	
20X4	0.9	1.02	1.18	0.92	
Total	3.41	4.12	4.88	3.58	
Average	0.85	1.03	1.22	0.9	4

The trend and seasonal variations can now be used to forecast future sales.

Sales forecast for 20X5

Time period	Estimated sales, using trend line y = 150,000 + 10,000x	Seasonal variation	Sales forecast T x S
	$	$	$
Quarter 1, 20X5 (x = 16)	310,000	0.85	263,500
Quarter 2, 20X5 (x = 17)	320,000	1.03	329,600
Quarter 3, 20X5 (x = 18)	330,000	1.22	402,600
Quarter 4, 20X5 (x = 19)	340,000	0.9	306,000

The reliability of forecasts of trends and seasonal variations

Forecasts using estimated trends and seasonal variations are based on the assumptions that the past is a reliable guide to the future. This assumption may be incorrect. However, forecasts must be made; otherwise it is impossible to make plans beyond the very short term.

> ## The learning curve
>
> - Learning curve theory
> - The learning curve model
> - Graph of the learning curve
> - Formula for the learning curve
> - Conditions for the learning curve to apply

4 The learning curve

4.1 Learning curve theory

When a workforce begins a task for the first time, and the task then becomes repetitive, it will probably do the job more quickly as it learns. It will find quicker ways of performing tasks, and will become more efficient as knowledge and understanding increase.

When a task is well-established, the learning effect wears out, and the time to complete the task becomes the same every time the task is carried out.
However, during the learning period, the time to complete each subsequent task can fall by a very large amount.

The learning curve effect was first discovered in the US during the 1940s, in aircraft manufacture. Aircraft manufacture is a highly-skilled task, where:

- the skill of the work force is important, and
- the labour time is a significant element in production resources and production costs.

The time taken to produce the first unit of a new model of an aeroplane might take a long time, but the time to produce the next unit is much less, and the time to produce the third is even less, and so on. Labour times per extra unit therefore fall.

This has important implications for:

- budgeting/forecasting production requirements and production costs
- pricing: prices calculated on a 'cost plus' basis can allow for future cost savings.

4.2 The learning curve model

The effect of the learning curve can be predicted mathematically, using a learning curve model. This model was developed from actual observations and analysis in the US aircraft industry.

The learning curve is measured as a percentage learning curve effect. For example, for a particular task, there might be an 80% learning curve effect, or a 90% learning curve effect, and so on.

When there is an 80% learning curve, the cumulative average time to produce units of an item is 80% of what it was before, every time that output doubles.

■ The **cumulative average time per unit** is the average time for all the units made so far, from the first unit onwards.

■ This means, for example, that if an 80% learning curve applies, the average time for the first two units is 80% of the average time for the first unit. Similarly, the average time for the first four units is 80% of the average time for the first two units.

Example

The time to make a new model of a sailing boat is 100 days. It has been established that in the boat-building industry, there is an 80% learning curve.

Required

Calculate:

(a)   the cumulative average time per unit for the first 2 units, first 4 units, first 8 units and first 16 units of the boat

(b)   the total time required to make the first 2 units, the first 4 units, the first 8 units and the first 16 units

(c)   the additional time required to make the second unit, the 3rd and 4th units, units 5 – 8 and units 9 – 16.

Answer

Total units (cumulative)	Cumulative average time per unit	Total time for all units	Incremental time for additional units	Average time for additional units
	days	days	days	days
1	100	100	100	
2	80	160	60	60
4	64	256	96	48
8	51.2	409.6	153.6	38.4
16	40.96	655.36	245.76	30.72

Example

The first unit of a new model of machine took 1,600 hours to make. A 90% learning curve applies. How much time would it take to make the first 32 units of this machine?

Answer

Average time for the first 32 units = 1,600 hours × 90% × 90% × 90% × 90% × 90% = 944.784 hours

Total time for the first 32 units = 32 × 944.784 hours = 30,233 hours.

4.3 Graph of the learning curve

The learning curve can be shown as a graph. There are two graphs following:

The left-hand graph shows the cumulative average time per unit. This falls rapidly at first, but the learning effect eventually ends and the average time for each additional unit becomes constant (a standard time). This is known as the steady state.

The right hand graph shows how total costs increase. The total cost line is a curved line initially, because of the learning effect.

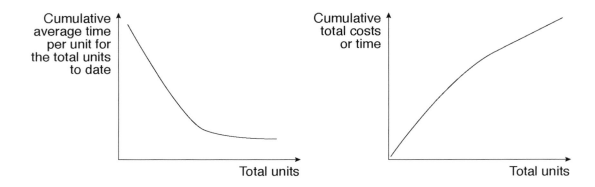

4.4 Formula for the learning curve

The learning curve is represented by the following formula (mathematical model):

Learning curve: $y = ax^b$

Where
y = the cumulative average time per unit for all units made
x = the number of units made so far (cumulative number of units)
a = the time for the first unit
b = the learning factor.

$$\text{The learning factor b} = \frac{\text{Logarithm of learning rate}}{\text{Logarithm of 2}}$$

The learning rate is expressed as a decimal, so if the learning curve is 80%, the learning factor is: (logarithm 0.80/logarithm 2)

To use this formula you must be able to calculate logarithms. Make sure that you know how to use the logarithms function on your calculator.

Example

If there is an 80% learning curve, the learning factor is calculated as follows:

$$\frac{\text{Logarithm} \quad 0.80}{\text{Logarithm} \quad 2} = \frac{-0.09691}{0.30103} = -0.32193$$

The learning curve formula is therefore: $y = ax^{-0.32193}$

It might help to remember that $x^{-0.32913}$ is another way of writing $\frac{1}{x^{0.32193}}$

Going back to the previous example, the cumulative average time to produce 8 units can therefore be calculated as:

$$y = 100 \times \frac{1}{8^{0.32193}}$$

$$= 100\,(0.512)$$

$$= 51.20$$

 Example

It will take 500 hours to complete the first unit of a new product. There is a 95 % learning curve effect.

Calculate how long it will take to produce the 7th unit.

 Answer

The time to produce the seventh unit is the difference between:

- the total time to produce the first 6 units, and
- the total time to produce the first 7 units.

(1) **Learning factor**

$$\frac{\text{Logarithm} \quad 0.95}{\text{Logarithm} \quad 2} = \frac{-0.02227639}{0.30103} = -0.074$$

(2) **Average time to produce the first 6 units**

$$y = 500 \times \frac{1}{6^{0.074}}$$

$$= 500\,(0.8758239)$$

$$= 437.9 \text{ hours per unit}$$

(3) **Average time to produce the first 7 units**

$$y = 500 \times \frac{1}{7^{0.074}}$$

= 500 (0.86589)

= 432.9 hours per unit

(4) **Time to produce the 7th unit**

	Hours
Total time for the first 7 units (7 × 432.9)	3,030.3
Total time for the first 6 units (6 × 437.9)	2,627.4
Time for the 7th unit	402.9

4.5 Conditions for the learning curve to apply

The learning curve effect will only apply in the following conditions:

■ There must be stable conditions for the work, so that learning can take place. For example, labour turnover must not be high; otherwise the learning effect is lost. The time between making each subsequent unit must not be long; otherwise the learning effect is lost because employees will forget what they did before.

■ The activity must be labour-intensive, so that learning will affect the time to complete the work.

■ There must be no change in production techniques, which would require the learning process to start again from the beginning.

■ Employees must be motivated to learn.

In practice, the learning curve effect is not used extensively for budgeting or estimating costs (or calculating sales prices on a cost plus basis). In a modern manufacturing environment production is highly mechanised and therefore the learning curve effect does not apply.

Uncertainty in budgeting
■ The nature of uncertainty in budgeting
■ Flexible budgets
■ Probabilities and expected values
■ Spreadsheets and 'what if' analysis

5 Uncertainty in budgeting

5.1 The nature of uncertainty in budgeting

Uncertainty arises when there is a lack of reliable information. In budgeting, there is uncertainty because estimates and forecasts may be unreliable. Information is almost never 100% reliable (or 'perfect'), and some uncertainty in budgeting is therefore inevitable.

Risk arises in business because actual events may turn out better or worse than expected. For example, actual sales volume may be higher or lower than forecast. The amount of risk in business operations varies with the nature of the operations. Some operations are more predictable than others. The existence of risk means that forecasts and estimates in the budget, which are based on expected results, may not be accurate.

Both risk and uncertainty mean that estimates and forecasts in a budget are likely to be wrong.

Management should be aware of risk and uncertainty when preparing budgets and when monitoring performance.

■ When preparing budgets, it may be appropriate to look at several different forecasts and estimates, to assess the possible variations that might occur. In other words, managers should think about how much better or how much worse actual results may be, compared with the budget.

■ When monitoring actual performance, managers should recognise that adverse or favourable variances might be caused by weaknesses in the original forecasts, rather than by good or bad performance.

Several approaches may be used for analysing risk and uncertainty in budgets. These include:

■ flexible budgets

■ using probabilities and expected values

■ using spreadsheet models and 'what if' analysis (sensitivity analysis).

5.2 Flexible budgets

Flexible budgets may be prepared during the budget-setting process. A flexible budget is a budget based on an assumption of a different volume of output and sales than the volume in the master budget or 'fixed budget'.

For example, a company might prepare its master budget on the basis of estimated sales of $100 million. Flexible budgets might be prepared on the basis that sales will be higher or lower – say $80 million, $90 million, $110 million and $120 million. Each flexible budget will be prepared on the basis of assumptions about fixed and variable costs, such as increases or decreases in fixed costs if sales rise above or fall below a certain amount, or changes in variable unit costs above a certain volume of sales.

During the financial year covered by the budget, it may become apparent that actual sales and production volume will be higher or lower than the fixed budget forecast. In such an event, actual performance can be compared with a suitable flexible budget.

Flexible budgets can be useful, because they allow for the possibility that actual activity levels may be higher or lower than forecast in the master budget. The main disadvantage of flexible budgets could be the time and effort needed to prepare them. The cost of preparing them could exceed the benefits of having the information that they provide.

5.3 Probabilities and expected values

Estimates and forecasts in budgeting may be prepared using probabilities and expected values. An expected value is a weighted average value calculated with probabilities.

Example

A company is preparing a sales budget. The budget planners believe that the volume of sales next year will depend on the state of the economy.

State of the economy	Sales for the year
	$ million
No growth	40
Low growth	50
Higher growth	70

It has been estimated that there is a 60% probability of no growth, a 30% probability of low growth and a 10% probability of higher growth.

The expected value (EV) of sales next year could be calculated as follows:

State of the economy	Sales for the year	Probability	EV of sales
	$ million		$ million
No growth	40	0.6	24
Low growth	50	0.3	15
Higher growth	70	0.1	7
EV of sales			46

The company might decide to prepare a sales budget on the assumption that annual sales will be $46 million.

The problems with using probabilities and expected values

There are two problems that might exist with the use of probabilities and expected values:

- The estimates of probability might be subjective, and based on the judgement or opinion of a forecaster. Subjective probabilities might be no better than educated guesses. Probabilities should have a rational basis.

- An expected value is most useful when it is a weighted average value for an outcome that will happen many times in the planning period. If the forecast event happens many times in the planning period, weighted average values are suitable for forecasting. However, if an outcome will only happen once, it is doubtful whether an expected value has much practical value for planning purposes.

This point can be illustrated with the previous example of the EV of annual sales. The forecast is that sales will be $40 million (0.60 probability), $50 million (0.30 probability) or $70 million (0.10 probability). The EV of sales is $46 million.

- The total annual sales for the year is an outcome that occurs only once. It is doubtful whether it would be appropriate to use $46 million as the budgeted sales for the year. A sales total of $46 million is not expected to happen.

- It might be more appropriate to prepare a fixed budget on the basis that sales will be $40 million (the most likely outcome) and prepare flexible budgets for sales of $50 million and $70 million.

When the forecast outcome happens many times in the planning period, an EV might be appropriate. For example, suppose that the forecast of weekly sales of a product is as follows:

Weekly sales	Probability	EV of weekly sales
$		$
7,000	0.5	3,500
9,000	0.3	2,700
12,000	0.2	2,400
		8,600

Since there are 52 weeks in a year, it would be appropriate to assume that weekly sales will be a weighted average amount, or EV. The budget for annual sales would be (52 × $8,600) = $447,200. If the probability estimates are fairly reliable, this estimate of annual sales should be acceptable as the annual sales budget.

5.4 Spreadsheets and 'what if' analysis

Preparing budgets is largely a 'number crunching' exercise, involving large amounts of calculations. This aspect of budgeting was made much easier, simpler and quicker with IT and the development of computer-based models for budgeting. Spreadsheet models, or similar planning models, are now widely used to prepare budgets.

A feature of computer-based budget models is that once the model has been constructed, it becomes a relatively simple process to prepare a budget. Values are input for the key variables, and the model produces a complete budget.

Amendments to a budget can be made quickly. A new budget can be produced simply by changing the value of one or more input variables in the budget model.

This ability to prepare new budgets quickly by changing a small number of values in the model also creates opportunities for **sensitivity analysis** and **stress testing**. The budget planner can test how the budget will be affected if forecasts and estimates are changed, by asking 'what if' questions. For example:

■ What if sales volume is 5% below the budget forecast?

■ What if the sales mix of products is different?

■ What if the introduction of the new production system or the new IT system is delayed by six months?

■ What if interest rates go up by 2% more than expected?

■ What if the fixed costs are 5% higher and variable costs per unit are 3% higher?

The answers to 'what if' questions can help budget planners to understand more about the risk and uncertainty in the budget, and the extent to which actual results might differ from the expected outcome in the master budget. This can provide valuable information for risk management, and management can assess the 'sensitivity' of their budget to particular estimates and assumptions.

CHAPTER

8

Other aspects of budgeting

Contents

1	The behavioural aspects of budgeting
2	Beyond budgeting

> **The behavioural aspects of budgeting**
>
> - Participative versus imposed budgets
> - Behavioural problems in budgeting
> - Budgeting as a bargaining process
> - Management styles and budgetary control
> - The contingency theory of management accounting

1 The behavioural aspects of budgeting

The effectiveness of budgeting and budgetary control depends largely on the behaviour and attitudes of managers and (possibly) other employees.

- Budgets provide performance targets for individual managers. If managers are rewarded for achieving or exceeding their target, budgets could provide them with an incentive and a motivation to perform well.

- It has also been suggested that budgets can motivate individuals if they are able to participate in the planning process. Individuals who feel a part of the planning and decision-making process are more likely to identify with the plans that are eventually decided. By identifying with the targets, they might have a powerful motivation to succeed in achieving them.

1.1 Participative versus imposed budgets

Participative budgets or bottom up budgets are when line managers prepare a budget for their own responsibility centre which is then submitted to head office for approval. An imposed budget, or top down budget, is when the budget is prepared by the senior management team and given to line managers as a target for the year.

Advantages and disadvantages of participation

The **advantages** of participative budgeting are as follows:

- Better motivation, because individuals are involved in setting the targets
- There should be much better communication of goals and budget targets to the individuals involved
- Involvement by junior managers in budgeting provides excellent experience for personal development
- Better decisions – participation might lead to better planning decisions, because 'local' managers often have a much better detailed knowledge of operations and local conditions than senior managers.

However, there are significant **disadvantages** with participation.

- It might be difficult for junior managers to understand the overall objectives of the organisation that budgets should be designed to meet.

- The quality of planning with participation depends on the skills, knowledge and experience of the individuals involved. Participation is not necessarily beneficial in all circumstances.

- There might be a danger that budget targets will be set at a level that is not ambitious. Participation on its own is not necessarily a sufficient incentive to raise standards and targets for achievement.

- Senior managers might pretend to be encouraging participation, but in practice they might disregard all the proposals and ideas of their subordinates. To be effective, participation must be 'real'.

- It is generally considered that participation is a good thing, but it needs to be strictly managed by senior management to make sure optimum decisions are taken that are in line with the company's goals.

Advantages and disadvantages of imposed budgets

Imposed budgets have certain advantages:

- Less time consuming. Line managers are not distracted from the task of running the business.

- Senior managers may have a greater appreciation of constraints faced by the business, eg cash, profit expectations

- It may be easier to co-ordinate departmental budgets if they are prepared together.

- It may be easier to plan the effective use of resources centrally.

However the disadvantages of imposed budgets are that:

- Targets may be unachievable and lead to demotivation

- Opportunities for exploiting line managers' specialist knowledge may be lost.

1.2   Behavioural problems in budgeting

When budgeting helps to create motivation in individuals, the human aspect of budgeting is positive and good for the organisation.

Unfortunately, in practice, human behaviour in the budgeting process has a negative effect. There are several possible reasons why behavioural factors can be harmful:

- Misunderstanding and worries about cost-cutting.

- Opposition to unfair targets set by senior management

- Sub-optimisation

- Lack of goal congruence

- Budget slack or budget bias

Misunderstanding and worries about cost-cutting

Budgeting is often considered by the managers affected to be an excuse for cutting back on expenditure and finding ways to reduce costs. Individuals often resent having to reduce their spending, and so have a hostile attitude to the entire budgeting process. This fear and hostility can exist even when senior management do not have a cost-cutting strategy.

Opposition to unfair targets set by senior management.

When senior managers use the budgeting process to set unrealistic and unfair targets for the year, their subordinates may unite in opposition to what the senior managers are trying to achieve. Senior managers should communicate and consult with the individuals affected by target-setting, and try to win their agreement to the targets they are trying to set. Targets need to be reasonable.

A distinction can be made between:

- **aspirational budgets**, which are budgets based on performance levels and targets that senior managers would like to achieve, and
- **expectational budgets**, which are budgets based on performance levels and targets that senior managers would realistically expect to achieve.

Aspirational budgets might be considered unfair, especially if the individuals affected have not been consulted. Expectational budgets, based on current performance levels, do not provide for any improvements in performance.

Ideally perhaps, budgets might be set with realistic targets that provide for some improvements in performance.

Sub-optimisation

There may be a risk that the planning targets for individual managers are not in the best interests of the organisation as a whole. For example, a production manager might try to budget for production targets that fully utilise production capacity. However, working at full capacity is not in the best interests of the company as a whole if sales demand is lower. It would result in a build-up of unwanted finished goods inventories. The planning process must be co-ordinated in order to avoid sub-optimal planning. In practice, however, effective co-ordination is not always achieved.

Lack of goal congruence

The behavioural problems with budgeting arise because the corporate aims of an organisation are usually not the same as the aspirations of the individuals who work for it. This is known as lack of goal congruence and leads to dysfunctional behaviour. For example, the aim of a company might be to maximise shareholder wealth, but there is no reason at all why this should be the aim of the company's employees and managers. Individuals have their own aims and ambitions, that working might (or might not) satisfy.

The potential conflict between corporate objective and the aspirations of the company's employees can become apparent in the budgeting process, when an organisation sets its targets for the next year.

The accepted wisdom is that there is a potential conflict between corporate and individual aspirations. Individuals will be inclined to do what they want for themselves, regardless of whether this is good for the organisation.

The solution to the problem should be to bring the aspirations of individual managers and other employees as closely as possible into line with the objectives of the organisation. This is the rationale for measures to motivate individuals, such as reward schemes and motivation through participation

Budget slack (budget bias)

Budget slack has been defined as 'the intentional overestimation of expenses and/or underestimation of revenue in the budgeting process' (CIMA *Official Terminology*). Managers who prepare budgets may try to overestimate costs so that it will be much easier to keep actual spending within the budget limit. Similarly, managers may try to underestimate revenue in their budget so that it will be easier for them to achieve their budget revenue targets. As a result of slack, budget targets are lower than they should be.

When managers are rewarded for achieving their budget targets, the motivation to include some slack in the budget is even stronger.

An additional problem with budget slack is that when a manager has slack in his spending budget, he may try to make sure that actual spending is up to the budget limit. There are two reasons for this:

■ If there is significant under-spending, the manager responsible might be required to explain why.

■ Actual spending needs to be close to the budget limit in order to keep the budget slack in the budget for the next year.

The problem of budget slack is particularly associated with spending on 'overhead' activities and **incremental budgeting**. One of the advantages of **zero based budgeting** is that it should eliminate a large amount of slack from budgets.

In some cases, budget bias operates the other way. Some managers might prepare budgets that are too optimistic. For example, a sales manager might budget for sales in the next financial year that are unrealistic and unachievable, simply to win the approval of senior management.

1.3   Budgeting as a bargaining process

Budgeting should be a process where an organisation prepares short-term plans that are consistent with its objectives and strategies. In practice, however, planning often involves compromises, and balancing the requirements of different long-term and short-term objectives.

As a result, budgeting can become a bargaining process between managers. The managers with the greatest power and influence are the most likely to get what they want. In many cases, managers will make 'deals' and reach compromises on what should be included in the budget.

The bargaining process is evident perhaps in the annual round of budgeting in central government, when spending departments (health, education, social services, defence and so on) argue and negotiate with each other and with the treasury department. They try to reach agreement through bargaining on spending allowances for the next financial year.

In companies, managers might also use the budgeting process to bargain, giving way on some demands in order to get what they want in other matters.

1.4 Management styles and budgetary control

In the 1970s, research was carried out by Anthony Hopwood into performance evaluation by managers, and how the performance of managers with cost centre responsibility is judged. He identified three types of management style:

■ A **budget-constrained style**. With this style of management, the performance of managers is based on their ability to meet budget targets in the short-term. With this style of performance evaluation, the focus is mainly on budgeted costs, actual costs and variances. Managers are under considerable pressure to meet their short-term budget targets. Stress in the job is high. Managers might be tempted to manipulate accounting data to make actual performance seem better in comparison with the budget.

■ A **profit-conscious style**. The performance of managers is evaluated on the basis of their ability to increase the general effectiveness of the operations under their management. Increasing general effectiveness means being more successful in achieving the longer-term aims of the organisation. For example, success in reducing costs in the long-term would be considered an increase in general effectiveness.

With a profit-conscious style, budgets and variances are not ignored, but they are budgetary control information which is treated with caution, and variances are not given the same importance as with a budget-constrained style.

Hopwood found that with this style of management evaluation, costs remain important, but there is much less pressure and stress in the job. As a consequence, there was a good working relationship between managers and their subordinates. In addition, there was less manipulation of accounting data than with a budget-constrained style.

■ A **non-accounting style**. With this style, budgetary control information plays a much less important part in the evaluation of managers' performance. Other (non-accounting) measures of performance were given greater prominence.

Hopwood appeared to suggest that a profit-conscious style of evaluation was the most effective of the three.

This conclusion has been challenged by David Otley. His research into profit centre managers in the UK coal mining industry (1978) found that there was a fairly close link between good performance and a budget-constrained style of management evaluation. Managers whose performance was judged on success in meeting budget targets were generally more successful in actually meeting their targets.

The differing conclusions between the research of Hopwood and Otley suggest that the most appropriate approach to the evaluation of performance depends on the circumstances and conditions in which the organisations and their managers operate. This conclusion is consistent with the contingency theory of management accounting.

1.5   The contingency theory of management accounting

Contingency theory is a theory that the most appropriate solution or system in a particular situation is dependent upon ('contingent' upon) the circumstances of the case. A contingency theory has been developed for management accounting, by writers such as Otley, to suggest what management accounting methods are most appropriate in any particular set of circumstances.

This approach may be relevant when an organisation chooses a budgeting system. Factors which may impact on the choice of budgeting system include
- the environment
    - technology
    - size and complexity of the organisation
    - strategy
    - culture
- other information systems within the organisation

Thus a large, centralised company operating in a stable environment may choose an imposed, incremental budget. A decentralised company operating in a competitive environment may choose a participative rolling budget.

> ## Beyond budgeting
>
> - Weaknesses of traditional budgeting systems
> - The beyond budgeting model

2 Beyond budgeting

The concept of 'beyond budgeting' has been described by writers such as Hope and Fraser to describe the inadequacies of the traditional budgeting system for the needs of modern businesses. They argue that in a continually-changing business world, traditional budgeting systems can have the effect of making business organisations fixed and rigid in their thinking, and unable to adapt. As a result, business organisations may be much too slow and inflexible in reacting to business developments.

The budgeting system establishes 'last year's reality' as the framework for the current year's activities. When the business environment is changing rapidly, this approach is inadequate. Managers should respond quickly to changes in the environment, but traditional budgeting and budgetary control systems act as a restraint on innovation and initiative.

Consequences of the inadequacy of the traditional budgeting system are that:

- operational managers regard the budgeting process as a waste of their time and resent having to prepare and then continually revise budget plans

- management accountants are involved in the budgetary planning and control system, but their work adds little or no value to the business. As a result, it may be difficult to justify the existence of the management accounting function.

2.1 Weaknesses of traditional budgeting systems

The traditional budgeting and budgetary control system has several weaknesses.

- Traditional budgeting adds little value and uses up valuable management time that could be better used in other ways.

- Managers concentrate on achieving 'agreed' budget targets, which may not be in the best interests of the organisation as a whole, particularly when circumstances change after the budget has been agreed.

- Traditional budgeting is seen as a method of imposing financial control, by comparing actual results with budget. Budgeting should be a system for communicating corporate goals – setting objectives and improving performance.

- In many cases, budget plans are not the result of a rational decision-making process. Often, budgets are a political compromise between different departments and managers, and budgeted spending limits for each manager are the outcome of a bargaining process.

- Traditional budgetary control encourages managers to achieve fixed budget targets, but does not encourage continuous improvement. Managers will be reluctant to exceed their budgeted spending limits, even though extra spending would be necessary to react to events, possibly because spending above budget will put their bonus at risk. In a dynamic business environment, business organisations should be seeking continuous improvement and innovation.

■ The traditional budgeting process focuses too much on internal matters and not enough on external factors and the business environment.

■ Traditional budgeting shows the costs of departments and functions, but not the costs of activities that are performed by employees. The traditional budget figures do not give managers information about the cost drivers in their business. In addition, traditional budgets do not help managers to identify costs that do not add value.

2.2 The beyond budgeting model

A solution to the lack of flexibility in traditional budgeting may be **continuous rolling forecasting** (or even continuous budgets), so that the business organisation can adapt much more quickly to changes in its environment and to new events.

Responsibility should be delegated to operational managers, who should be empowered to take decisions in response to changing circumstances, that the managers believe would be in the best interests of the organisation.

■ Goals should be agreed by reference to external benchmarks (such as increasing market share, or beating the competition in other ways) and targets should not be fixed and internally-negotiated.

■ Operational managers should be motivated by the challenges they are given and by the delegation of responsibility.

■ Operational managers can use their direct knowledge of operations to adapt much more quickly to changing circumstances and new events.

■ Operational managers may be expected to work within agreed parameters, but they are not restricted in their spending by detailed line-by-line budgets.

■ Delegated decision-making should encourage more transparent and open communication systems within the organisation. Managers need continuous rolling forecasts to make decisions and apply control. Efficient IT systems are therefore an important element in the 'beyond budgeting' model.

It has been argued that the 'beyond budgeting' model is much more easily applied in the private sector than in the public sector. Government activity is managed through expenditure budgets and spending controls, and there is accountability for spending to politicians (government ministers and elected representatives) and to the general public. There may also be uncertainty about the objectives of particular government activities or departments. In such circumstances, it is difficult to apply a flexible system of decision-making or to devolve decision-making to lower levels of management.

CHAPTER

9

Standard costing - principles

Contents
1   Standard costs
2   Types of standard

Standard costs

- Standard units of product or service
- Standard cost defined
- Standard costing
- The uses of standard costing
- Establishing a standard cost

1 Standard costs

1.1 Standard units of product or service

A standard costing system might be used when an organisation produces standard units of product or service that are identical to all other similar units produced. Standard costing is usually associated with standard products, but can be applied to standard services too (for example, standard costs of MacDonalds burgers and other items).

A standard unit should have exactly the same input resources (direct materials, direct labour time) as all other similar units, and these resources should cost exactly the same. Standard units should therefore have the same cost.

1.2 Standard cost defined

A **standard cost is a predetermined unit cost** based on expected direct materials quantities and expected direct labour time, and priced at a predetermined rate per unit of direct materials and rate per direct labour hour and rate per hour of overhead.

- Standard costs are usually restricted to production costs only, not administration and selling and distribution overheads.
- Overheads are normally absorbed into cost at a rate per direct labour hour.

 Example

The standard cost of Product XYZ might be:

	£	£
Direct materials:		
Material A: 2 litres at £4.50 per litre	9.00	
Material B: 3 kilos at £2 per kilo	6.00	
		15.00
Direct labour		
Grade 1 labour: 0.5 hours at £10 per hour	5.00	
Grade 2 labour: 0.75 hours at £8 per hour	6.00	
		11.00
Variable production overheads: 1.25 hours at £4 per hour		5.00
Fixed production overheads: 1.25 hours at £20 per hour		25.00
Standard (production) cost per unit		56.00

Who sets standard costs?

Standard costs are set by managers with the expertise to assess what the standard prices and rates should be. Standard costs are normally reviewed regularly, typically once a year as part of the annual budgeting process.

■ Standard prices for direct materials should be set by managers with expertise in the purchase costs of materials. This is likely to be a senior manager in the purchasing department (buying department).

■ Standard rates for direct labour should be set by managers with expertise in labour rates. This is likely to be a senior manager in the human resources department (personnel department).

■ Standard usage rates for direct materials and standard efficiency rates for direct labour should be set by managers with expertise in operational activities. This may be a senior manager in the production or operations department, or a manager in the technical department.

■ Standard overhead rates should be identified by a senior management accountant, from budgeted overhead costs and budgeted activity levels that have been agreed in the annual budgeting process.

1.3 Standard costing

Standard costing is a system of costing in which:

■ all units of product (or service) are recorded in the cost accounts at their standard cost, and

■ the value of stock is based on standard production cost.

Differences between actual costs and standard costs are recorded as variances.

Standard costing may be used with either a system of absorption costing or a system of marginal costing. The only difference is in the valuation of stock and the calculation of variances for fixed overheads.

1.4 The uses of standard costing

Standard costing has three main uses:

■ It is an alternative system of cost accounting. In a standard costing system, all units produced are recorded at their standard cost of production.

■ It is a system of performance measurement. The differences between standard costs (expected costs) and actual costs can be measured as variances. Variances can be reported regularly to management, in order to identify areas of good performance or poor performance.

■ It is also a system of control reporting. When differences between actual results and expected results (the budget and standard costs) are large, this could indicate that operational performance is not as it should be, and that the causes of the variance should be investigated. Management can therefore use variance reports to identify whether control measures might be needed, to improve poor performance or continue with good performances.

When there are large adverse variances, this might indicate that actual performance is poor, and control action is needed to deal with the weaknesses.

When there are large favourable variances, and actual results are much better than expected, management should investigate to find out why this has happened, and whether any action is needed to ensure that the favourable results continue in the future.

1.5 Establishing a standard cost

A standard variable cost is established by building up the standard materials, labour and variable overhead costs for each standard unit.

In a standard absorption costing system, the standard fixed overhead cost is a standard cost per unit, based on budgeted data about fixed costs and the budgeted production volume.

 Example

A company manufactures two products, X and Y. In Year 1 it budgets to make 2,000 units of Product X and 1,000 units of Product Y. Budgeted resources per unit and costs are as follows:

	Product X	Product Y
Direct materials per unit:		
Material A	2 units of material	1.5 units of material
Material B	1 unit of material	3 units of material
Direct labour hours per unit	1.5 hours	2 hours

Costs	
Direct material A	£4 per unit
Direct material B	£3 per unit
Direct labour	£10 per hour
Variable production overhead	£2 per direct labour hour

Fixed production overheads per unit are calculated by applying a direct labour hour absorption rate to the standard labour hours per unit, using the budgeted fixed production overhead costs of £60,000 for the year.

Required

Calculate the standard full production cost per unit of:

(a) Product X, and
(b) Product Y

Solution

First calculate the budgeted overhead absorption rate.

Budgeted direct labour hours	hours
Product X: (2,000 units × 1.5 hours)	3,000
Product Y (1,000 units × 2 hours)	2,000
	5,000
Budgeted fixed production overheads	£60,000
Fixed overhead absorption rate/hour	£12

	Product X		Product Y	
		£		£
Direct materials				
Material A	(2 units × £4)	8	(1.5 units × £4)	6
Material B	(1 unit × £3)	3	(3 units × £3)	9
Direct labour	(1.5 hours × £10)	15	(2 hours × £10)	20
Variable production overhead	(1.5 hours × £2)	3	(2 hours × £2)	4
Standard variable prod'n cost		29		39
Fixed production overhead	(1.5 hours × £12)	18	(2 hours × £12)	24
Standard full production cost		47		63

Types of standard

- Setting standards
- Behavioural impact
- Reviewing standards
- Standards and the modern manufacturing environment

2 Types of standard

2.1 Setting standards

Standards are predetermined estimates of unit costs but how is the level of efficiency inherent in the estimate determined? Should it assume perfect operating conditions or should it incorporate an allowance for waste and idle time? The standard set will be a performance target and if it seen as unattainable this may have a detrimental impact on staff motivation. If the standard set is too easy to attain there may be no incentive to find improvements.

There are four types of standard:
- Ideal standards. These assume perfect operating conditions. No allowance is made for wastage, inefficiencies and machine breakdowns.

- Attainable standards. These assume efficient but not perfect operating conditions. An allowance is made for waste and inefficiencies but this will be challenging to achieve.

- Current standards. These are based on current working conditions. They do not provide any incentive to make improvements

- Basic standards. These are standards which remain unchanged over a long period of time and can be used to show trends.

Standard costs are normally set assuming attainable conditions and you should assume this unless there are clear indications that this is not the case.

 Example

A company produces sandwiches. Each sandwich requires two slices of bread and a loaf of bread contains 24 slices. Each loaf costs 50p. It is estimated that currently 20% of bread is wasted. Management would like to reduce this wastage to 10%.

Calculate a standard material cost for a sandwich based on
a) Ideal conditions
b) Current conditions
c) Attainable conditions

Solution

a) $2/24 \times 50p = 0.042p$

b) With 20% wastage each loaf has 80% × 24 = 19.2 usable slices

$2/19.2 \times 50p = 0.052p$

c) with 10% wastage each loaf has 90% × 24 = 21.6 usable slices

$2/21.6 \times 50p = 0.046p$

2.2   Behavioural impact

One of the purposes of standard costing is to motivate employees to strive to improve performance. The level of standard set can impact on this.

- Ideal standards are unlikely to be achieved. They may be very useful as long term targets and may provide senior managers with an indication of the potential for savings in a process but generally there will be an adverse variance. This may lead to employees becoming demotivated as they know that the standard is unachievable.

- Current standards may be useful for producing budgets as they are based on current levels of efficiency and may therefore give a realistic guide to resources required in the production process. They are unlikely to motivate employees to improve current performance unless they are linked to a reward system which gives bonuses for improvements.

- Basic standards will not motivate employees as they are based on achievable conditions at some time in the past. They are also not useful for budgeting and are the least common type of standard.

- Attainable standards are the most likely to motivate employees to improve performance as they are based on challenging but attainable targets. It is for this reason that standards are usually based on attainable conditions.

2.3   Reviewing standards

How often should standards be revised?

Some argue that standards should be revised regularly.

- Regular revision leads to standards which are meaningful targets and employees must strive to achieve

- Variance analysis is more meaningful.

- But it is costly to revise all standards frequently and some changes may be short in nature and average out over time.

Others argue that standards should be revised less frequently, perhaps once a year.

- Standards by their nature are long-term averages and therefore some variation is expected over time.

- Changing targets too frequently may be demotivating if employees feel that 'the goalposts are moving'

- Revising the standards annually may fit in with the budgeting cycle and be less time consuming and costly.

In practise, standards may be generally revised each year but individual standards may be changed if there are known long term changes to processes.

2.4 Standards and the modern manufacturing environment

There has been much debate concerning the usefulness of standard costing in a modern manufacturing environment. Many criticisms relate to the usefulness of individual variances which you will meet in the next chapter but there are also criticisms of the approach.

- Standard costing is best used in a repetitive stable environment where a long-term average cost can be calculated. The modern manufacturing environment is very competitive and many products have short lives.

- Modern manufacturing techniques such as Just in Time and Total Quality Management advocate zero defects, continuous improvement and cost reduction programmes. Attainable standards incorporate an acceptable allowance for waste and efficiency and there is no incentive to improve on the standard set.

- Calculating standard cost variances is normally carried out on a monthly basis in conjunction with a monthly management reporting cycle. It is argued that this is too infrequent to be successful as a control tool. Operating managers need real time control systems which give immediate feedback if a system is out of control so that action can be taken immediately.

- Standard cost variances may motivate managers to take the wrong actions to improve performance. For example, in a JIT environment material is likely to cost a premium as it must be of high quality and be available for delivery at short notice. In a standard costing system there may be pressure on a purchasing manager to find the cheapest sources of material.

- Variance analysis is often used in conjunction with responsibility accounting and managers are given responsibility for individual variances under their control. This is different to the approach of many modern manufacturing approaches where there is a culture of group responsibility to cost reduction. For example target costing emphasises that all functions are responsible for achieving cost targets.

Standard costing may still be a useful approach in a modern manufacturing environment but it may need some small adjustment to the traditional approach.

- Standards could be set at ideal levels. This would reflect 100% quality and no wastage in the process.

- Employees could be rewarded for finding methods of closing the gap between current standards and ideal standards

- Standards could be revised frequently to reflect continuous improvement.

- Standards could be produced frequently to provide more relevant feedback. This would give employees more information as the impact of any variation of performance could be assessed in terms of cost and impact on profit.

- Overhead variances be could analysed in more detail by using activity based costing.

CHAPTER

10

Variance analysis

Contents

> ## Standard costs and cost variances
>
> - Cost variances: favourable and adverse variances
> - Variances and performance reporting
> - The total cost variance for a variable cost item

1 Standard costs and cost variances

1.1 Cost variances: favourable and adverse variances

In a standard costing system, all units of output are valued at their standard cost. Cost of production and cost of sales are therefore valued at standard cost.

Actual costs will differ from standard costs. A cost variance is the difference between an actual cost and a standard cost.

- When actual cost is higher than standard cost, the cost variance is adverse [(A)] variance or unfavourable [(U)].
- When actual cost is less than standard cost, the cost variance is favourable [(F)].

Several different variances are calculated, relating to direct materials, direct labour, variable production overhead and fixed production overhead. (There are also some sales variances).

In a cost accounting system, cost variances are adjustments to the profit in an accounting period.

- Favourable variances adjust the profit upwards.
- Adverse variances adjust the profit down.

1.2 Variances and performance reporting

Variance reports are produced at the end of each control period (say, at the end of each month).

- Large adverse variances indicate poor performance and the need for control action by management.
- Large favourable variances indicate unexpected good performance. Management might wish to consider how this good performance can be maintained in the future.

The method of calculating cost variances is similar for all variable production cost items (direct materials, direct labour, variable production overhead).

A different method of calculating cost variances is required for fixed production overhead.

1.3   The total cost variance for a variable cost item

The total cost variance for the variable cost item is the difference between the actual variable cost of production and the standard variable cost of producing the items. However, the total cost variance is not usually calculated. Instead, the total variance is calculated in two parts, that add up to the total cost variance:

- **Price variance/rate variance/expenditure per hour variance**. This compares the actual cost of the material resources used or the actual hours worked with the standard price of the materials or the standard rate per hour.

- **Usage/efficiency variance**. This measures the difference in cost between the actual materials used and the standard usage quantity, or the actual hours worked and the standard hours for the work.

Total variable cost variance

X units actually produced:

	$
X units of output should cost (× Standard cost per unit)	
X units of output did cost	
Total cost variance for the variable cost item	(F) or (A)

Example

A unit of Product P123 has a standard cost of five litres of Material A at $3 per litre. The standard direct material cost per unit of Product 123 is therefore $15.

In a particular month, 2,000 units of Product 123 were manufactured. These used 10,400 litres of Material A, which cost $33,600.

The total direct material cost variance is calculated as follows:

	$	
2,000 units of output should cost (× $15)	30,000	
They did cost	33,600	
Total direct materials cost variance	3,600	(A)

The variance is adverse, because actual costs were higher than the standard cost.

Direct materials: price and usage variances

- Direct materials price variance
- Direct materials usage variance

2 Direct materials: price and usage variances

The direct materials total cost variance can be analysed into a price variance and a usage variance.

2.1 Direct materials price variance

A materials price variance is the difference between:

- the actual cost of the materials purchased (or used) and
- what they should have cost (the actual materials purchased or used at their standard price).

The calculation of a materials price variance can be set out in a table, as follows:

Materials price variance	$	
Units of materials purchased should cost (actual materials purchased × standard price per unit)	X	
They did cost	Y	
Material price variance	X - Y	(F) or (A)

The variance is:

- favourable if the actual cost was less than the expected cost of the materials, and
- adverse if the actual cost was more than the expected cost.

Example

A unit of Product P123 has a standard cost of five litres of Material A at $3 per litre. The standard direct material cost per unit of Product 123 is therefore $15. In a particular month, 2,000 units of Product 123 were manufactured. These used 10,400 litres of Material A, which cost $33,600.

The total direct material cost variance is $3,600 (A), as calculated earlier, in the previous example.

The materials price variance is calculated as follows:

	$	
10,400 litres of materials should cost (× $3)	31,200	
They did cost	33,600	
Material price variance	2,400	(A)

The price variance is adverse because the materials cost more to purchase than they should have.

2.2 Direct materials usage variance

A materials usage variance is the difference between:

- the actual materials used and
- the amount of materials that should have been used for the quantity of units produced (the actual units of output produced × standard usage quantity per unit).

This variance is converted into a money value at the standard price per unit of materials.

The calculation of a materials usage variance can be set out in a table, as follows:

Materials usage variance	Units of material	
Units produced should use (× standard material usage per unit)	X	
They did use	Y	
Material usage variance in quantities	X-Y	(F) or (A)
× Standard price per unit of material	$P	
Material price variance in $	(X-Y) × $P	(F) or (A)

Example

Using the same example above that was used to illustrate the material price variance, the usage variance should be calculated as follows:

	kilos	
2,000 units of Product P123 should use (× 5 kilos)	10,000	
They did use	10,400	
Material usage variance in kilos	400	(A)
Standard price per kilo of Material A	$3	
Material usage variance in $	$1,200	(A)

The usage variance is adverse because more materials were used than expected, which has added to costs.

> ## Direct labour: rate and efficiency variances
>
> - Total direct labour cost variance
> - Direct labour rate variance
> - Direct labour efficiency variance
> - Direct labour: idle time variance
> - Direct labour: the impact of the learning curve

3 Direct labour: rate and efficiency variances

3.1 Total direct labour cost variance

The total cost variance for direct labour is the difference between the standard and actual direct labour cost for the units produced.

Example

Product P123 has a standard direct labour cost per unit of:

1.5 hours × $12 per direct labour hour = $18 per unit.

During a particular month, 2,000 units of Product 123 were manufactured. These took 2,780 hours to make and the direct labour cost was $35,700.

Required

Calculate the total direct labour cost variance.

Answer

	$
2,000 units of output should cost (× $18)	36,000
They did cost	35,700
Total direct labour cost variance	300 (F)

The variance is favourable, because actual costs were less than the standard cost.

The direct labour total cost variance can be analysed into a rate variance and an efficiency variance. The calculations are similar to the calculations for the materials price and usage variances.

3.2 Direct labour rate variance

A direct labour rate variance is the difference between:

- the actual cost of the direct labour (hours paid for) and
- what the hours should have cost (the actual hours paid for at their standard rate).

The calculation of a direct labour rate variance can be set out in a table, as follows:

Direct labour rate variance	$
The hours worked should cost (actual hours worked × standard rate per hour)	X
They did cost	Y
Direct labour rate variance	X - Y (F) or (A)

The variance is:

■ favourable if the actual cost was less than the expected cost of the hours worked, and

■ adverse if the actual cost was more than the expected cost.

Example

Using the same example that was used previously to calculate the total labour cost variance, calculate the direct labour rate variance.

Answer

	$
2,780 hours should cost (× $12)	33,360
They did cost	35,700
Direct labour rate variance	2,340 (A)

The rate variance is adverse because the labour hours worked cost more than they should have.

3.3 Direct labour efficiency variance

A direct labour efficiency variance is the difference between:

■ the actual hours worked and

■ the hours that should have been required to make the quantity of units produced (the actual units of output produced × standard hours per unit).

This variance is converted into a money value at the standard labour rate per hour.

The calculation of a labour efficiency variance can be set out in a table, as follows:

Direct labour efficiency variance	hours
Actual units produced should take (× standard hours per unit)	X
They did take	Y
Direct labour efficiency variance in hours	X-Y (F) or (A)
× Standard rate per hour	$R
Direct labour efficiency variance in $	(X-Y) × $R (F) or (A)

Example

Using the same example above that was used to illustrate the total direct labour cost variance and the direct labour rate variance, the efficiency variance should be calculated as follows:

	hours	
2,000 units of Product P123 should take (× 1.5 hours)	3,000	
They did take	2,780	
Efficiency variance in hours	220	(F)
Standard direct labour rate per hour	$12	
Direct labour efficiency variance in $	$2,640	(F)

The efficiency variance is favourable because production took less time than expected, which has reduced costs.

Labour cost variances: summary	$	
Labour rate variance	2,340	(A)
Labour efficiency variance	2,640	(F)
Total direct labour cost variance	300	(F)

3.4 Direct labour: idle time variance

On occasion, some of the time of the direct labour work force might be wasted due to idle time. Idle time is a particular case of inefficiency. When it occurs, it might be useful, for the purpose of providing control reports to management, to separate the idle time variance from the efficiency variance in the hours actually worked.

Example

In a particular month, a company made 8,000 units of output, which have a standard production time of 0.2 hours per unit. The standard rate per hour is $10. The direct labour force was paid $18,000 for 1,800 hours of work. Of this total paid time, 260 hours were recorded as idle time.

Idle time variance = 260 hours (A) × $10 = $2,600 (A). Idle time variances should always be adverse, because they represent wasted spending.

Direct labour efficiency variance in hours actually worked	hours	
8,000 units should take (× 0.2 hours)	1,600	
They did take (1,800 – 260)	1,540	
Efficiency variance in hours	60	(F)
Standard direct labour rate per hour	$10	
Direct labour efficiency variance in $	$600	(F)
Labour efficiency variances: summary	$	
Idle time variance	2,600	(A)
Labour efficiency variance (in hours actually worked)	600	(F)
Total direct labour efficiency variance	2,000	(A)

3.5   Direct labour: the impact of the learning curve

The learning curve effect refers to the reduction in time taken to produce labour intensive, complex products as production is repeated. If the learning curve applies to a product then this will have an impact on the setting of standard labour costs. It may also impact on the setting of standard variable overhead and fixed overhead absorption rates if overhead is absorbed on the basis of labour hours.

The time taken to produce the first units of product will be much greater than subsequent units. If standards are based on these initial estimates of labour hours required, then labour efficiency, variable overhead efficiency and fixed overhead volume variances are all likely to be favourable. It may be preferable to set standards based on the labour hours that will be required once the learning curve effect reaches its steady state.

> **Variable production overheads: expenditure and efficiency variances**
>
> ■ Total variable production overhead cost variance
> ■ Variable production overhead expenditure variance
> ■ Variable production overhead efficiency variance

4 Variable production overheads: expenditure and efficiency variances

4.1 Total variable production overhead cost variance

The total cost variance for variable production overhead is the difference between the standard and actual variable production overhead cost for the units produced.

Example

Product P123 has a standard variable production overhead cost per unit of:

1.5 hours × $2 per direct labour hour = $3 per unit. During a particular month, 2,000 units of Product 123 were manufactured. These took 2,780 hours to make and the variable production overhead cost was $6,550.

Required

Calculate for the month the total variable production overhead cost variance.

(Note: This same example will be used to illustrate the expenditure and efficiency variances.)

Answer

	$	
2,000 units of output should cost (× $3)	6,000	
They did cost	6,550	
Total variable production overhead cost variance	550	(A)

The variance is adverse, because actual costs were more than the standard cost.

4.2 Variable production overhead expenditure variance

Variable production overheads are assumed to vary with the direct labour hours worked.

A variable production overhead expenditure variance is the difference between:

■ the actual variable production overhead cost of the hours worked and
■ what the hours worked should have cost (the actual hours paid for at their standard rate of expenditure).

The calculation of a variable production overhead expenditure variance can be set out in a table, as follows:

Variable production overhead expenditure variance	$
The hours worked should cost (actual hours worked × standard expenditure per hour)	X
They did cost	Y
Variable production overhead expenditure variance	X - Y (F) or (A)

The variance is:

■ favourable if the actual cost was less than the expected cost of the hours worked, and

■ adverse if the actual cost was more than the expected cost.

Example

Using the same example that was used previously to calculate the total variable production overhead cost variance, calculate the variable production overhead expenditure variance.

Answer

	$
2,780 hours should cost (× $2)	5,560
They did cost	6,550
Variable production overhead expenditure variance	990 (A)

The expenditure variance is adverse because the expenditure on variable overhead in the hours worked was more than it should have been.

4.3 Variable production overhead efficiency variance

A variable production overhead efficiency variance is the difference between:

■ the actual hours worked and

■ the hours that should have been required to make the quantity of units produced (the actual units of output produced × standard hours per unit).

This is the same variance in hours as the direct labour efficiency variance (excluding any hours of idle time variance, because it is assumed that variable overhead expenditure is not incurred during idle time). This variance in hours is converted into a money value at the standard expenditure rate per hour.

The calculation of a variable production overhead efficiency variance can be set out in a table, as follows:

Variable production overhead efficiency variance	hours	
Units produced should take (× standard hours per unit)	X	
They did take	Y	
Variable production overhead efficiency variance in hours	X-Y	(F) or (A)
× Standard expenditure rate per hour	$R	
Variable production overhead efficiency variance in $	(X-Y) × $R (F) or (A)	

Example

Using the same example that was used previously to calculate the total variable production overhead cost variance and the variable production overhead expenditure variance, calculate the variable production overhead efficiency variance.

Answer

	hours	
2,000 units of Product P123 should take (× 1.5 hours)	3,000	
They did take	2,780	
Efficiency variance in hours	220	(F)
Standard variable production overhead rate per hour	$2	
Variable production overhead efficiency variance in	$440	(F)

The efficiency variance is favourable because production took less time than expected, which has reduced costs.

Variable production overhead variances cost variances: summary	$	
Variable production overhead expenditure variance	990	(A)
Variable production overhead efficiency variance	440	(F)
Total variable production overhead cost variance	550	(A)

> **Fixed production overhead cost variances: absorption costing**
>
> - The structure of fixed overhead variances
> - Total fixed overhead cost variance
> - Fixed overhead expenditure and volume variances
> - Fixed overhead efficiency and capacity variances
> - ABC based variances

5 Fixed production overhead cost variances: absorption costing

5.1 The structure of fixed overhead variances

With standard absorption costing, the standard cost per unit is a full production cost, including an amount for absorbed fixed production overhead. Every unit produced is valued at standard cost.

This means that production overheads are absorbed into production costs at a standard cost per unit produced.

However, this standard fixed cost per unit is derived from a standard number of direct labour hours per unit and a fixed overhead rate per hour.

Fixed overhead variances are as follows:

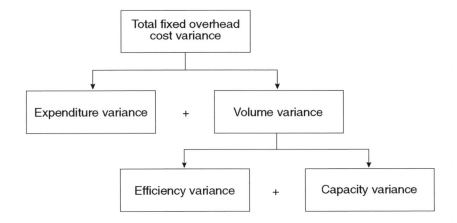

5.2 Total fixed overhead cost variance

The total fixed overhead cost variance is rarely calculated, because it is more usual to calculate the expenditure and volume variances.

However, the total fixed overhead cost variance is the amount of under-absorbed fixed production overhead (adverse variance) or over-absorbed fixed production overhead (favourable variance).

	$	
Standard fixed overhead cost of units produced (units produced × standard fixed cost per unit)	X	
Actual fixed overhead costs	Y	
Total fixed production overhead cost variance (fixed overheads over- or under-absorbed)	X - Y	(F) or (A)

The variance is favourable when actual costs are less than standard costs, and there is over-absorption of overheads.

The variance is adverse when actual costs are higher than standard costs, and there is under-absorption of overheads.

5.3 Fixed overhead expenditure and volume variances

The total fixed overhead cost variance is usually analysed into an expenditure variance and a volume variance.

Fixed production overhead expenditure variance	$	
Budgeted fixed overheads	X	
Actual fixed overheads	Y	
Fixed production overhead expenditure variance	X - Y	(F) or (A)

Fixed overhead expenditure should be the same in total at any volume of output. If actual fixed overhead costs differ from expected fixed costs (budgeted fixed costs), the difference is an expenditure variance.

■ The expenditure variance is favourable if actual fixed overhead costs are less than budgeted.

■ The expenditure variance is adverse if actual fixed overhead costs are more than budgeted.

Fixed production overhead volume variance	units
Actual production volume	X
Budgeted production volume	Y
Fixed production overhead volume variance in units	X-Y
× Standard fixed overhead cost per unit	$C
Fixed production overhead volume variance in $	(X-Y) × $C (F) or (A)

Higher production volume results in greater overhead absorption so when actual volume exceeds budgeted volume the variance is favourable.

Example

A company budgeted to make 5,000 units of a single standard product in Year 1. Budgeted direct labour hours are 10,000 hours. Budgeted fixed production overhead is $40,000. Actual production in Year 1 was 5,200 units and fixed production overhead was $40,500.

Required

Calculate for Year 1:

- the fixed overhead total cost variance
- the fixed overhead expenditure variance
- the fixed overhead volume variance

 Answer

Standard fixed overhead cost per unit = $8 (2 hours per unit × $4 per hour).

Fixed production overhead total cost variance	$	
5,200 units: standard fixed cost (× $8) = fixed overhead absorbed	41,600	
Actual fixed overhead cost expenditure	40,500	
Fixed production overhead total cost variance	1,100	(F)

The variance is favourable, because fixed overhead costs have been over-absorbed.

Fixed overhead expenditure variance	$	
Budgeted fixed production overhead expenditure	40,000	
Actual fixed production overhead expenditure	40,500	
Fixed overhead expenditure variance	500	(A)

This variance is adverse because actual expenditure exceeds the budgeted expenditure.

Fixed overhead volume variance	units of production	
Budgeted production volume in units	5,000	
Actual production volume in units	5,200	
Fixed overhead volume variance in units	200	(F)
Standard fixed production overhead cost per unit	$8	
Fixed overhead volume variance in $	$1,600	(F)

This variance is favourable because actual production volume exceeded the budgeted volume.

Summary	$	
Fixed overhead expenditure variance	500	(A)
Fixed overhead volume variance	1,600	(F)
Fixed overhead total cost variance	1,100	(F)

5.4 Fixed overhead efficiency and capacity variances

The fixed overhead volume variance can be analysed into an efficiency variance and a capacity variance. Together, efficiency and capacity variances explain why actual production volume in units was more or less than the budgeted production volume.

These variances are calculated as follows:

Fixed production overhead efficiency variance	hours	
Actual units produced should take (× standard hours per unit)	X	
They did take	Y	
Fixed production overhead efficiency variance in hours	X-Y	(F) or (A)
× Standard fixed overhead rate per hour	$R	
Fixed production overhead efficiency variance in $	(X-Y) × $R (F) or (A)	

Fixed production overhead capacity variance	hours	
Budgeted hours of work	X	
Actual hours of work	Y	
Capacity variance in hours	X-Y	(F) or (A)
× Standard fixed overhead rate per hour	$R	
Fixed overhead capacity variance in $	(X-Y) × $R (F) or (A)	

If actual hours are greater than budgeted, this is an increase in capacity. More products can be produced and this will increase profit. This is a favourable variance.

The **efficiency variance** is the same in hours as the efficiency variance for direct labour and variable production overheads. It is priced, however, at the fixed production overhead rate per hour.

The **capacity variance** is an hours worked variance. It is the difference between the budgeted hours and the actual hours worked, and is priced at the fixed production overhead rate per hour.

Example

A company budgeted to make 5,000 units of a single standard product in Year 1. Budgeted direct labour hours are 10,000 hours. Budgeted fixed production overhead is $40,000. Actual production in Year 1 was 5,200 units in 10,250 hours of work, and fixed production overhead was $40,500.

Required

The fixed production overhead volume variance is $1,600 (F), calculated earlier. Calculate for Year 1:

- the fixed overhead efficiency variance
- the fixed overhead capacity variance.

Answer

Fixed production overhead efficiency variance	hours	
5,200 units produced should take (× 2 hours per unit)	10,400	
They did take	10,250	
Fixed production overhead efficiency variance in hours	150	(F)
× Standard fixed overhead rate per hour	$4	
Fixed production overhead efficiency variance in $	$600	(F)

Fixed production overhead capacity variance	hours	
Budgeted hours of work	10,000	
Actual hours of work	10,250	
Capacity variance in hours	250	(F)
× Standard fixed overhead rate per hour	$4	
Fixed overhead capacity variance in $	$1,000	(F)

The capacity variance is favourable because actual hours worked exceeded the budgeted hours (therefore more units should have been produced).

Summary	$	
Fixed overhead efficiency variance	600	(F)
Fixed overhead capacity variance	1,000	(F)
Fixed overhead volume variance	1,600	(F)

5.5 ABC based variances

In organisations which use ABC, overhead variances can be calculated in a similar way to variable overhead variances.

 Example

Entity Blue makes and sells two products, X and Y. The budget is to produce 1,000 units of X per month and 1,600 units of Y per month.

An analysis of budgeted costs suggests that setups are one of the drivers that cause overhead expenditure. Budgeted costs were as follows:

Activity	Total cost	Cost driver	Total number	Product X	Product Y
	$				
Batch setup	100,000	Number of setups	20	10	10

Actual overhead costs in a period were:

Activity	Total cost	Cost driver	Total number	Product X	Product Y
	$				
Batch setup	96,000	Number of setups	18	10	8

There were 1,200 units of X and 1,400 units of Y produced.

Required

Calculate the overhead efficiency and expenditure variances for each category of overhead.

Answer

Activity	Total cost	Cost driver	
	$		$
Batch setup	100,000	Cost/setup	5,000

	Product X	Product Y
Standard overhead cost per unit	$	$
Batch setup	50	31.25

Efficiency variance
Product X

1,200 units should use 10/1,000 × 1,200	12 set ups
did use	10 set ups
	2 set ups F
Value at standard cost per setup (× $5,000)	$10,000 F

Product Y

1,400 units should use 10/1,600 x 1,400	8.75 set ups
did use	8 set ups
	.75 set ups F
Value at standard cost per set up (× $5,000)	$3,750 F

Expenditure variance

18 set ups should cost (× $5,000)	90,000
did cost	96,000
	6,000 A

Total batch setup variance

1,200 units of X should cost (× $50)	60,000
1,400 units of Y should cost (× $50)	43,750
	103,750
Did cost	96,000
	7,750 F

Reconciling the variances
Efficiency variance

Product X	10,000 F
Product Y	3,750 F
Expenditure variance	6,000 A
	7,750 F

It can be seen that the lower number of setups used than expected led to a favourable efficiency variance. The products may have been produced in larger batches than expected. The cost per set up was higher than expected leading to an adverse expenditure variance.

Sales variances: sales price and sales volume variances
■ Sales price variance
■ Sales volume variance: units method
■ Sales volume variance: standard selling price method

6 Sales variances: sales price and sales volume variances

Sales variances, unlike cost variances, are not recorded in a standard costing system of cost accounts. However, sales variances are included in variance reports to management.

- They help to reconcile actual profit with budgeted profit.
- They indicate to management to assess performance.

There are two sales variances:

- a sales price variance, and
- a sales volume variance.

These are calculated as shown below, when a standard absorption costing system is used.

6.1 Sales price variance

The sales price variance is the difference between:

- the actual sales revenue from the units sold, and
- the expected sales revenue from the units sold.

The sales price variance is calculated as follows:

	$
Actual units sold should sell for (× standard sales price/unit)	X
They did sell for (actual sales revenue)	Y
Sales price variance	X – Y (F) or (A)

6.2 Sales volume variance: units method

The sales volume variance, in standard absorption costing, explains:

- the difference between budgeted and actual profit
- that was caused by actual sales volume being different from the budgeted sales volume.

The sales volume variance can be calculated in units, as follows, and then converted into a monetary amount at the standard profit per unit.

	Units of sales
Budgeted sales volume (units)	X
Actual sales volume (units)	Y
Sales volume variance in units	X – Y (F) or (A)
x Standard profit per unit	× $P
Sales volume variance in $	(X – Y) × $P (F) or (A)

6.3 Sales volume variance: standard selling price method

There is an alternative method of calculating the sales volume variance, which produces exactly the same figure for the variance. This is shown below.

Sales volume variance: alternative method of calculation	$
Actual sales at standard selling price	X
Budgeted sales	Y
Sales volume variance in $ revenue	(X – Y) (F) or (A)
Standard profit/sales price ratio	P%
Sales volume variance (profit variance)	(X – Y) x P% (F) or (A)

Example

A company budgets to sell 7,000 units of Product P456. The standard sales price of Product P456 is $50 per unit and the standard cost per unit is $42.

Actual sales were 7,200 units, which sold for $351,400.

The sales price variance and sales volume variance would be calculated as follows:

Sales price variance	$
7,200 units should sell for (x $50)	360,000
They did sell for	351,400
Sales price variance	8,600 (A)

The sales price variance is adverse because actual sales revenue from the units sold was less than expected.

Sales volume variance: usual method of calculation	units
Actual sales volume (units)	7,200
Budgeted sales volume (units)	7,000
Sales volume variance in units	200 (F)
Standard profit per unit ($50 – $42 = $8)	$8
Sales volume variance (profit variance)	$1,600 (F)

The sales volume variance is favourable because actual sales exceeded budgeted sales.

Sales volume variance: alternative method of calculation	$	
Actual sales at standard selling price (5,200 × $50)	260,000	
Budgeted sales (5,000 units × $50)	250,000	
Sales volume variance in $ revenue	10,000	(F)
Standard profit/sales price ratio ($8/$50)	16%	
Sales volume variance (profit variance)	$1,600	(F)

Both methods of calculating the sales volume variance produce the same answer.

- Purpose of an operating statement
- Format of an operating statement

7 Reconciling budgeted and actual profit: standard absorption costing

7.1 Purpose of an operating statement

A management report called an operating statement might be prepared, showing how the difference between budgeted and actual profit is explained by the sales variances and cost variances.

The purpose of an operating statement is to enable management to assess actual performance, and identify aspects of performance where investigation or control action might be appropriate.

7.2 Format of an operating statement

In a standard absorption costing system, an operating statement can be set out as follows:

Operating statement (standard absorption costing)

	(F)	(A)	£	
Budgeted profit			BP	
Sales price variance			X	(F) or (A)
Sales volume variance			X	(F) or (A)
			X	
Cost variances	(F)	(A)		
	£	£		
Direct materials price	X			
Direct materials usage		X		
Direct labour rate		X		
Direct labour efficiency	X			
Variable production o'head expenditure	X			
Variable production o'head efficiency	X			
Fixed production overhead expenditure		X		
Fixed production overhead efficiency	X			
Fixed production overhead capacity		X		
Other overhead expenditure variances		X		
Total cost variances	Totals		X	(F) or (A)
Actual profit			AP	

Other overhead expenditure variances, assuming administration overheads and selling and distribution overheads are all fixed costs, are the difference between:

- budgeted other overheads expenditure, and
- actual other overheads expenditure.

> ## Standard marginal costing
>
> - Standard marginal costing and standard absorption costing compared
> - Fixed production overhead variances in standard marginal costing
> - Sales volume variance in standard marginal costing
> - Standard marginal costing operating statement

8   Standard marginal costing

8.1   Standard marginal costing and standard absorption costing compared

When a company uses standard marginal costing rather than standard absorption costing:

- finished goods stock is valued at the standard variable production cost, not the standard full production cost
- variances are calculated and presented in the same way as for standard absorption costing, but with two important differences:
  - fixed production overhead variances
  - sales volume variances.

8.2   Fixed production overhead variances in standard marginal costing

In standard marginal costing, there is a fixed production overhead expenditure variance, but no fixed production overhead volume variance.

The fixed production overhead expenditure variance is calculated in the way already described and is the same amount in a standard marginal costing system as in a standard absorption costing system.

8.3   Sales volume variance in standard marginal costing

In standard marginal costing, the sales volume variance is calculated using standard contribution, as follows:

Sales volume variance: usual method of calculation

	units	
Actual sales volume (units)	X	
Budgeted sales volume (units)	Y	
Sales volume variance in units	X - Y	(F) or (A)
Standard contribution per unit	£C	
Sales volume variance (contribution variance)	(X – Y) x £C	(F) or (A)

Sales volume variance: alternative method of calculation

	£	
Actual sales at standard selling price	X	
Budgeted sales	Y	
Sales volume variance in £ revenue	(X – Y)	(F) or (A)
Standard contribution /sales ratio	C%	
Sales volume variance (contribution variance)	£(X – Y) x C%	(F) or (A)

Both methods of calculating the sales volume variance produce the same answer.

8.4 Standard marginal costing operating statement

An operating statement is presented in a different way. Budgeted contribution can be reconciled with actual contribution, by means of the sales price variance, sales volume variance and variable cost variances. Fixed cost expenditure variances should be presented in a separate part of the operating statement.

Operating statement: standard marginal costing

	(F)	(A)	£	
Budgeted profit			BP	
Add budgeted fixed costs			BF	
Budgeted contribution (BP + BF)			BC	
Sales price variance			X	(F) or (A)
Sales volume variance			X	(F) or (A)
Sales less standard variable cost of sales			X	
Variable cost variances	(F)	(A)		
	£	£		
Direct materials price	X			
Direct materials usage		X		
Direct labour rate		X		
Direct labour efficiency	X			
Variable production overhead rate	X			
Variable production o'head efficiency	X			
Total variable cost variances	Totals		X	(F) or (A)
Actual contribution			AC	
Budgeted fixed overhead expenditure	BF			
Fixed overhead expenditure variance	X	(F) or (A)		
Actual fixed production overheads			AF	
Actual profit (AC – AF)			AP	

CHAPTER

11

Advanced variance analysis

Contents
1   Material mix and yield variances
2   Planning and operational variances

> ## Materials mix and yield variances
>
> - Definition of materials mix and yield variances
> - Calculating a direct materials mix variance
> - Calculating a direct materials yield variance
> - Changing the mix

1 Materials mix and yield variances

1.1 Definition of materials mix and yield variances

When standard costing is used, and when there are two or more materials in the manufactured product, the materials usage variance can be analysed into a materials mix and a materials yield variance.

- The **total direct materials usage variance** is calculated by taking each item of direct material in turn, and calculating a materials usage variance in the normal way. The total direct material usage variance is the sum of the direct materials usage variance for each of the individual materials.

- The **materials mix variance** measures how much of this total variance is attributable to the fact that the actual combination or mixture of materials that was used was more expensive or less expensive than the standard mixture for the materials.

- The **materials yield variance** is a total usage variance for all the materials taken together, assuming that the materials are in the standard proportions or mix. It is calculated as a single figure, using the weighted average standard price per unit of material for the calculation of the variance.

The mix component of the usage variance therefore indicates the effect on costs of changing the combination (or mix or proportions) of material inputs in the production process.

The yield component indicates the effect on costs of the total materials inputs yielding more or less output than expected.

There is possible value for management, for control purposes, in calculating a mix variance and a yield variance, but only if they are in a position to control the mixture or proportions of the materials in the manufactured item.

1.2 Calculating a direct materials mix variance

There are two methods of calculating the mix variance. Both should provide exactly the same variance. You should use the method that you find easier to understand.

Method 1

- Take the total quantities of materials used.

- Compare the actual quantities of each individual material that were used, and the standard quantities that would have been used (the standard mix) if the total usage had been in the standard proportions or standard mix.

- For each material, take the difference between the quantity in the actual mix used and the standard quantity. If actual usage is higher than standard usage, the variance is adverse. If actual usage is less than standard usage, the variance is favourable. The total mix variance *in material quantities* is always zero.

- Convert the mix variance for each individual material into a money value by multiplying by the standard price per unit of the material. Add the total mix variances for each material (money values) to obtain the total mix variance.

- If the actual mix used is more expensive than the standard mix, the total mix variance is adverse. If the actual mix used is cheaper than the standard mix, the total mix variance is adverse.

Method 2

- Take the total quantities of materials used.

- Compare the actual quantities of each individual material that were used, and the standard quantities that would have been used (the standard mix) if the total usage had been in the standard proportions or standard mix.

- For each material, take the difference between the quantity in the actual mix used and the standard quantity. Note for each material whether there is more of the material in the actual mix than in the standard mix. However, do not decide yet whether the variance is adverse or favourable for each material.

- Next, calculate the weighted average price per unit of materials in the mix. This is calculated as [the total direct materials cost per unit divided by the total number of units of materials in one unit of finished product].

- For each material, calculate the difference between the standard price for the material and the weighted average standard price.

- Next, for each material in the mix, multiply the mix variance in quantities by the difference between its standard price and the weighted average standard price.

  - If there is more of a cheap material in the actual mix than in the standard mix, the variance for the material is favourable.

  - If there is less of a cheap material in the actual mix than in the standard mix, the variance for the material is adverse.

  - If there is more of an expensive material in the actual mix than in the standard mix, the variance for the material is adverse.

  - If there is less of an expensive material in the actual mix than in the standard mix, the variance for the material is favourable.

- The total mix variance is calculated by adding the mix variance for each individual material.

Notes

(a)   A cheap material is a material whose standard price is lower than the weighted average standard price for materials in the mix.

(b)   An expensive material is a material whose standard price is higher than the weighted average standard price for materials in the mix.

1.3   Calculating a direct materials yield variance

The direct materials yield variance is a total usage variance for all items of direct materials.

■   A materials usage variance is calculated for each item of materials individually.

■   A yield variance is calculated for all materials in total. It is converted into a money value at the weighted average standard price per unit of materials.

A yield variance is calculated as follows:

		Material quantities	
Actual quantity of units produced	should use	X	
	did use	Y	
Yield variance in quantities		(X – Y)	(F) or (A)
× Weighted average standard price per unit of material		$P	
Yield variance in money value		P x (X – Y)	(F) or (A)

Example

Product N is produced from three direct materials that are mixed together in a process, material materials A, B and C. The standard cost card for product N is as follows:

Material	Quantity	Standard price per kilo	Standard cost
	kilos	$	$
A	1	20	20
B	1	22	22
C	8	6	48
	10		90

Actual output during month 6 amounted to 200 units of product N in total. Actual usage of each material was as follows:

Material	kilos
A	160
B	180
C	1,760
	2,100

Required

Calculate the direct materials mix and yield variances for month 6, and prove that the mix and yield variances add up to the total usage variance.

Answer

Working

The weighted average standard cost per kilo of material = $\dfrac{\$90}{10}$ kilos = \$9 per kilo.

Materials mix variance

Method 1

Material	Actual mix		Standard mix	Mix variance in quantities		Standard price per kilo	Mix variance in value	
	kilos		kilos	kilos		\$	\$	
A	160	(1)	210	50	(F)	20	1,000	(F)
B	180	(1)	210	30	(F)	22	660	(F)
C	1,760	(8)	1,680	80	(A)	6	480	(A)
	2,100		2,100	0			1,180	(F)

The mix variance is favourable because the actual mix of materials used is cheaper than the standard mix.

Method 2

Material	Actual mix		Standard mix	Mix variance in quantities	Standard price per kilo minus weighted average standard price	Mix variance in value	
	kilos		kilos	kilos	\$	\$	
A	160	(1)	210	50	(20 – 9 =) 11	550	(F)
B	180	(1)	210	30	(22 – 9 =) 13	390	(F)
C	1,760	(8)	1,680	80	(6 – 9 =) 3	240	(F)
	2,100		2,100			1,180	(F)

Materials yield variance

		kilos	
200 units of N	should use (× 10 kilos)	2,000	
	did use	2,100	
Yield variance in quantities		100	(A)
× Weighted average standard price per unit of material = \$9			
Yield variance in money value		= \$900	(A)

Materials usage variance

Material	To make 200 units of N		Variance Kg	Standard price per kilo	Usage variance	
	Did use kilos	Should use kilos	kilos	$	$	
A	160	200	40 (F)	20	800	(F)
B	180	200	20 (F)	22	440	(F)
C	1,760	1,600	160 (A)	6	960	(A)
					280	(F)

Summary

	$	
Mix variance	1,180	(F)
Yield variance	900	(A)
Usage variance	280	(F)

1.4 Changing the mix

Analysis of the material usage variance into the mix and yield components is worthwhile if management have control of the proportion of each material used. Management will seek to find the optimum mix for the product and ensure that the process operates as near to this optimum as possible.

Identification of the optimum mix involves consideration of several factors:

■ Cost. The cheapest mix may not be the most cost effective. Often a favourable mix variance is offset by an adverse yield variance and the total cost per unit may increase.

■ Quality. Using a cheaper mix may result in a lower quality product and the customer may not be prepared to pay the same price. A cheaper product may also result in higher returns and loss of repeat business.

Planning and operational variances

- The reasons for planning and operational variances
- Ex ante and ex post standards or budgets
- Using ex post standards (or ex post budgets) to calculate planning and operational variances
- Calculating planning and operational variances
- Comparing planning and operational variances with traditional variances
- More than one difference between the ex ante and ex post standard costs
- Market size and share variances
- Advantages and disadvantages of using planning and operational variances

2 Planning and operational variances

2.1 The reasons for planning and operational variances

The purpose of variances and variance reporting is to inform management of any differences between budgeted and actual results, or between standard costs and actual costs. Managers can use information about variances to identify problems that should be investigated, and where appropriate:

- take control action to correct adverse results or
- take measures to exploit favourable results.

The effectiveness of variance reporting, and the effectiveness of control management based on variance reports, depends on reliable budgets and standards. It is essential that the budget or standard cost must be reasonable, because they are used for comparison with actual results for calculating the variances.

If the budget or standard is unreliable, the variance reports will also be unreliable – and so useless for management.

2.2 Ex ante and ex post standards or budgets

If management decide that the standard cost is unreliable and invalid, they can prepare a more realistic or accurate standard cost. (Similarly, if the original budget is invalid, a more realistic budget can be prepared).

- The original standard cost is known as the **ex ante standard**.
- The revised and more realistic standard cost is known as the **ex post standard**.

(Similarly, if required, an ex post budget can be prepared as a realistic new budget. The original unreliable budget would be the ex ante budget).

2.3 Using ex post standards (or ex post budgets) to calculate planning and operational variances

Ex post standards can be used to calculate variances, as an alternative to the 'normal' method of calculating variances.

- Actual results are compared with the ex post standard (or ex post budget) and variances are calculated using the ex post standard. These variances are the **operational variances.**

- The ex post standard cost (or ex post budget) is compared with the ex ante standard cost (or ex ante budget) and the difference between them is the **planning variance.**

The planning variance is therefore a measurement of the amount by which an unreliable standard cost (or unreliable budget) – in other words, weak or poor planning – is the cause of the difference between actual results and the original ex ante standard cost or ex ante budget. **Planning variances are uncontrollable,** in the sense that control action by management will not eliminate a weakness in planning.

The operational variances, by comparing actual results with a realistic standard cost, provide useful control information for management. **Operational variances may be controllable variances**.

2.4 Calculating planning and operational variances

Planning and operational variances can be calculated for any aspect of a standard cost or budget: for example, an ex post standard cost can be calculated for the direct materials cost per unit, or the direct materials usage per unit, or the direct materials price per unit, or the direct labour cost per unit, the direct labour hours per unit, and so on.

Similarly, an ex post budget can be prepared with revised figures for sales volumes or sales prices.

The following example will be used to illustrate the basic method of calculating planning and operational variances.

 Example

Product Z has a standard labour cost of 3 hours per unit at $8 per hour = $24 per unit.

During the first month of the current year, 500 units of Product Z were manufactured. These took 1,960 hours to make, at a labour cost of $16,500.

Using **traditional variances**, the labour variances for the month would be as follows:

Labour rate variance	$
1,960 hours should cost (× $8)	15,680
But they did cost	16,500
	820 (A)

Labour efficiency variance	hours	
500 units of product Z should take (× 3 hours)	1,500	
But they did take	1,960	
Efficiency variance in hours	460	(A)
Standard labour rate per hour	$8	
Efficiency variance in $	$3,680	(A)

The **total labour cost variance** is $820 (A) + $3,680 (A) = $4,500 (A).

Suppose, however, that it is discovered early during the month that the planned improvements in efficiency that were expected from introducing new equipment could not be achieved, because the new equipment had suffered a major breakdown and had been returned to the supplier for repair.

It is decided that a more appropriate labour cost for each unit of Product Z should be:

4 hours × $8 per hour = $32.

This is accepted as a **new ex post standard cost** for direct labour cost.

A planning variance compares the difference between:

■ the original standard cost or budget (the ex ante standard cost or ex ante budget), and

■ the revised standard cost or budget (the ex post standard cost or ex post budget).

The planning variance is reported as the effect that this difference has had on reported profit or cost.

In this example, the planning variance applies to the labour hours per unit, but it can be calculated either on a labour cost per unit basis or a labour hours basis.

Since direct labour is a variable cost, the planning variance is calculated as the difference between:

■ the standard labour cost with the ex ante standard, and

■ the standard labour cost with the ex post standard.

Method 1

Total labour cost for 500 units of Z	$	
Ex ante standard cost (× $24)	12,000	
Ex post standard cost (× $32)	16,000	
Planning variance	4,000	(A)

The planning variance is adverse because the ex post standard cost is less favourable (is more costly) than the ex ante standard cost.

Method 2

Since the planning error is in the labour hours per unit, the planning variance can be calculated in labour hours:

Labour hours: time required to make 500 units of product Z	Hours
Ex ante standard (× 3 hours)	1,500
Ex post standard (× 4 hours)	2,000
Planning variance in standard hours	500 (A)
Standard labour rate per hour	$8
Planning variance in $	$4,000 (A)

Operating variances are calculated in the same way as traditional variances, except that the ex post standard cost (or ex post budget) is used, not the ex ante standard cost.

In this example, only the labour efficiency variance is affected by the change. The labour rate variance remains at $820 (A). The operating variance for labour efficiency is calculated as follows:

Labour efficiency (operating) variance	Hours
500 units of product Z should take (× 4 hours)	2,000
But they did take	1,960
Efficiency variance in hours	40 (F)
Standard labour rate per hour	$8
Efficiency variance in $ (operating variance)	$320 (F)

2.5 Comparing planning and operational variances with traditional variances

The planning and operating variances in the previous example can be summarised as follows:

	$		$	
Planning variance:				
Labour efficiency			4,000	(A)
Operating variances				
Labour rate	820	(A)		
Labour efficiency	320	(F)		
			500	(A)
Total direct labour variances			4,500	(A)

This compares with the traditional variances, which are:

	$	
Labour efficiency	3,680	(A)
Labour rate	820	(A)
Total direct labour variances	4,500	(A)

The total variances come to the same amount.

However, it can be argued that planning and operational variances provide much more useful control information to management than the traditional variances, because the original (ex ante) standard cost is unreliable and incorrect.

2.6 More than one difference between the ex ante and ex post standard costs

A situation could arise where there are planning errors in two parts of the ex ante standard cost, and the errors both relate to:

- direct materials cost – with a planning variance in the standard material price and another planning variance in the standard material usage per unit.

- direct labour cost – with a planning variance in the standard labour rate per hour and another planning variance in the standard labour hours per unit.

In these circumstances, the planning variance can be analysed to show the effect of each separate planning variance.

The principle to apply in calculating the planning and operating variances is the same as if there is just one planning error in the standard cost.

- The planning variance in total is the difference between the ex ante standard cost and the ex post standard cost.

- The operating variances are calculated using the ex post standard cost.

The only difference is that if the total planning variance is caused by two factors, it should be possible to analyse the total planning variance into its different causes.

 Example

Entity Green manufactures product G, which has a standard direct material cost per unit of:

5 kilos at $6 per kilo = $30.

Actual output during a month is 4,000 units of product G, and the materials actually used in production were 16,500 kilos at a cost of $119,000.

The operations manager of Entity Green persuades his colleagues that the standard cost for direct materials is incorrect, and a more realistic standard cost is:

4 kilos at $7 per kilo = $28.

Total planning variance

The planning variance is caused by two factors, an incorrect price per kilo and an incorrect usage quantity per unit of output. However, the total planning variance is calculated in the same way as shown previously (method 1).

Total material cost for 4,000 units of G	$	
Ex ante standard cost (× $30)	120,000	
Ex post standard cost (× $28)	112,000	
Planning variance	8,000	(F)

The planning variance is favourable because the ex post standard cost is more favourable (is less costly) than the ex ante standard cost.

Further analysis

The planning variance can be analysed into a planning variance caused by an error in the standard for materials price and an error in the standard for materials usage.

The two standard costs that we are comparing are as follows:

Ex ante standard	4,000 units × 5 kilos × $6	$120,000
Ex post standard	4,000 units × 4 kilos × $7	$112,000

Planning variance caused by the material price difference

If there had been no planning variance for material usage, the standard usage for 400 units of product G would have been 4,000 units × 5 kilos = 20,000 kilos. The planning variance for price is $7 – $6 = $1 (A). It is adverse because the ex post standard cost is less favourable than the ex ante standard cost (the cost is higher in the ex post standard).

The planning variance attributable to the material price is therefore 20,000 kilos × $1 (A) = $20,000 (A).

Planning variance caused by the material usage difference

The planning variance for usage is the difference between the ex ante standard of 20,000 kilos (4,000 units x 5 kilos) and the ex post standard of 16,000 kilos (4,000 units x 4 kilos). The planning usage variance is therefore 4,000 kilos (F). It is favourable because the ex post standard cost is more favourable than the ex ante standard cost (the cost is lower in the ex post standard).

It might seem logical to price this planning variance at the ex ante standard price for materials, $6. However, to make the total of the planning price variance and the planning usage variance add up to the total planning variance of $8,000(F), we have to use the ex post standard price of materials, $7.

The planning variance attributable to the material usage is therefore 4,000 kilos (F) × $7 = $28,000 (F)

Note

When a planning variance is analysed into two component parts, such as a planning price and a planning usage variance, one of these variances has to be valued using the ex ante standard cost and the other has to be valued using an ex post standard cost. Here, the planning price variance has been valued using the ex ante standard cost for usage, and the planning usage variance has been calculated using the ex post standard cost for material price.

Confusingly, it would also be possible to calculate a planning price variance using the ex post standard usage (which here is 4 kilos per unit or 16,000 kilos for 4,000 units of product) and the ex ante material price (which here is $6). This approach would give a planning price variance of $16,000 (A) and a planning usage variance of $24,000 (F), with a total planning variance of $8,000 (A).

The variance analysis is completed by calculating the operating variances using the ex post standard cost.

Material price (operating) variance	$	
16,500 kilos of material should cost (× $7)	115,500	
But they did cost	119,000	
Price variance	3,500	(A)

Material usage (operating) variance	kilos	
4,000 units of product G should use (× 4 kilos)	16,000	
But they did use	16,500	
Usage variance in kilos	500	(A)
Standard material price per kilo (ex post)	$7	
Usage variance in $	$3,500	(A)

Summary

	$		$	
Planning variances:				
Material price			20,000	(A)
Material usage			28,000	(F)
			8,000	(F)
Operating variances				
Material price	3,500	(A)		
Material usage	3,500	(A)		
			7,000	(A)
Total direct material variances			1,000	(F)

2.7 Market size and share variances

Just as standard cost variances can be analysed into planning and operational variances by preparing an ex post standard cost, sales volume variances can be analysed into planning and operational variances by producing an ex post sales budget.

However, with sales volume:

■ the planning variance is called a **market size variance** and

■ the operational variance is called the **market share variance**.

Example

Entity Red has set the following sales budget:

Sales of Product Y = 43,000 units
Contribution per unit = $25
Entity Red estimates that it has a market share of 10%.

Actual sales results for the period were as follows:

Sales for Entity Red = 50,000 units
Total market sales = 645,000 units

In retrospect, it is accepted that the budget should have been based on a total market share of 645,000 units.

Required

Calculate:

(a)   the traditional sales volume variance and

(b)   planning and operational variances (market size variance and market share variance)

Answer

Traditional sales volume variance	units	
Budgeted sales volume	43,000	
Actual sales volume	50,000	
Sales volume variance (units)	7,000	(F)
Standard contribution per unit	$25	
Sales volume variance in $	$175,000	(F)

Planning and operational variances for sales volume

The ex post sales budget is 10% × 645,000 units = 64,500 units.

Planning variance = market size variance	units	
Ex ante budgeted sales volume	43,000	
Ex post budgeted sales volume	64,500	
Market size variance (units)	21,500	(F)
Standard contribution per unit	$25	
Market size variance in $	537,500	(F)

Operational variance = market share variance	units	
Ex post budgeted sales volume	64,500	
Actual sales volume	50,000	
Market share variance (units)	14,500	(A)
Standard contribution per unit	$25	
Market share variance in $	362,500	(A)

Summary

	$	
Market size variance	537,500	(F)
Market share variance	362,500	(A)
Total sales volume variance	175,000	(F)

2.8 Advantages and disadvantages of using planning and operational variances

Advantages

- They identify variances due to poor planning and put a realistic value to variances resulting from operations.

- Planning variances can be used to update standard costs and budgets.

- Large operational variances can be investigated, with a view to taking control action to correct adverse variances or sustain favourable variances.

- The performance of managers is assessed on 'realistic' variance calculations, using ex post standard costs that are more realistic than ex ante standard costs.

Disadvantages

- They are based on the assumption that planning will be inaccurate or unrealistic. This should occur only occasionally, not regularly.

- It takes time and effort to prepare ex post standard costs.

- Managers might try to blame poor results on poor planning and not on their operational performance.

CHAPTER

12

Variances: causes and investigation

Contents

1	Causes of variances
2	Investigating variances

> ## Causes of variances
>
> - Three broad reasons for reported variances
> - Operational reasons for variances
> - Interdependence between variances

1 Causes of variances

1.1 Three broad reasons for reported variances

When variances are reported, the reason for the variance could be caused by any of the following:

- Poor budgeting and standard-setting. The standard cost or budget is unrealistic, and actual results are therefore different. Variances will be reported as a consequence. For example, if the budget includes a large amount of 'budget slack' for overhead spending, there should be favourable overhead expenditure variances in every month.

- Inaccurate measurement and recording of results. There could be errors in the recording of actual costs and sales. If so, variances will be reported because of the measurement errors.

- Operational factors. The main reason for reporting variances is to identify aspects of operational performance that are unusually poor or unusually good, so that control measures can be taken if appropriate. However, the operational reasons for a variance could be either:

  - controllable, so that control action by the manager responsible should improve operations in the future: for example, an adverse labour efficiency variance might be caused by inefficient working, and control action could be taken to improve procedures and the efficiency of operations

  - uncontrollable, which means that control action could not have any effect. For example, an adverse labour rate variance might be caused by a recent increase in wages. This would be a variance outside management control.

1.2 Operational reasons for variances

Variances might be reported for a variety of operational reasons. Some possible reasons for variances are set out in the table below.

Materials price variance	- Materials ordered in bulk quantities to obtain a price discount (favourable variance)
	- New supplier for materials, charging different prices
	- Inefficient buying; Buying without asking two or more suppliers to quote a price.
	- Ordering an emergency delivery of materials, and having to pay a higher price for the speed.

- Buying material of a different quality from the quality assumed in the standard cost

- Buying a different, substitute material from the material in the standard cost

Materials usage variance

- Inefficient materials handling in production (adverse variance)

- Problems with operating machinery, resulting in higher-than-usual materials wastage (adverse variance)

- Buying a higher quality material, with the effect that there is lower wastage in production (favourable variance)

- Better quality control in the production process (favourable variance)

- A change in the specification of the product, so that actual usage is no longer the same as the standard usage

Materials mix variance

- Using a cheaper mix of materials in production, with more of the cheaper materials and less of the more expensive materials

- Using a more expensive mix in production.

Labour rate variance

- The grade or level of labour actually used was different from the grade of labour in the standard cost

- Wage rates have been altered (usually, raised)

Labour efficiency variance

- Efficient working by the work force

- Inefficient working and poor supervision of the work force

- Better working conditions, leading to more efficient working

- Effective supervision

- The effect of a new incentive scheme, which has been an improvement in efficiency

- The skills level of the labour used is different from the assumed skills level in the standard cost

Sales price variance

- Unexpected price rises/falls

- Offering customers price discounts to encourage them to buy

Sales volume variance

- Changes in market size

- Changes in market share

- Poor sales effort or a good sales effort

- The effect of advertising or a sales promotion campaign has been better or worse than anticipated.

Identifying the reasons for overhead variances is often difficult, because overhead expenditure can arise in many different departments, and is the responsibility of many different managers. The basic approach to investigating overhead variances should be:

- for expenditure variances, to identify the cause or causes of the adverse or favourable spending

- for variable overhead efficiency variances, it can usually be assumed that the reasons for this variance are similar to the reasons for the direct labour efficiency variances

1.3 Interdependence between variances

It is important to realise that in many cases, individual variances cannot be considered in isolation. The cause of one variance might be connected to the cause of another variance. For example:

- An adverse materials usage variance might be caused by purchasing cheaper-than-normal materials (favourable price variance)

- An adverse direct labour rate variance might be due to using skilled and experienced workers who are paid a higher rate, but they might do the work more efficiently and more quickly (so there would be a favourable efficiency variance for labour and variable overheads)

- A favourable sales volume variance might be the result of cutting prices (adverse sales price variance).

Investigating variances

- Factors to consider
- Statistical control charts
- Cost-benefit analysis for variance investigation

---

2 Investigating variances

When a variance is reported, the manager responsible must decide whether it should be investigated:

- to find out the cause or causes of the variance.

- to decide whether any control action should be taken to deal with the cause of the variance.

Investigating the cause of a variance takes management time and can be costly. Management should not spend time and money on an investigation if the expected benefits are unlikely to exceed the costs.

2.1 Factors to consider

Before making a decision whether to investigate a variance, the following factors should be considered:

- Size of the variance. As a general rule, the cause of a variance is more likely to be significant when the variance is large. The larger the variance, the greater the potential benefit from investigation and control measures.

- Favourable or adverse. Favourable variances should be investigated as well as adverse variances. However, more significance might be given to adverse variances than to favourable variances. Whereas a fairly small adverse variance might be investigated, a favourable variance of the same amount might not be investigated.

- Probability that the cause of the variance will be controllable. A production manager might therefore be more willing to investigate a labour efficiency variance than a labour rate variance.

- Costs and benefits of control action. The manager might carry out an assessment of the likely costs involved in investigation, and the probability of gaining benefits from control action. A variance will not be investigated if the expected costs exceed the expected value of benefits.

- Random variation. Management might take the view that a favourable or adverse variance in one month is due to random factors that will not recur next month. A decision might therefore be taken to do nothing in the current month about the variance, but to wait and see whether the same variance occurs again next month. If the variance is due to random factors, it should not happen again next month, and management can probably ignore it without risk.

- Reliability of budgets and measurement systems. Management might have a view about whether the variance is caused by poor planning and poor measurement systems, rather than by operating factors. If so, investigating the

---

variance would be a waste of time and would be unlikely to lead to any cost savings.

2.2 Statistical control charts

Statistical control charts might be used for the assessment variance.

- A statistical assessment might be made of the probability distribution of a particular variance.

- Control limits might then be set to the variance, so that only variances that are an unusual size, and exceed the control limit, should be investigated.

- This could be plotted on a statistical control chart, with the control limits shown as 'trigger limits' for control action. The control limit for investigating a favourable variance could be a different size to the control limit for an adverse variance.

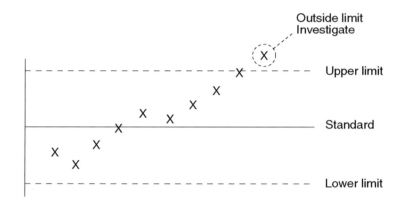

This statistical control chart shows reported variances over time. The variances recorded on the chart could be:

- The variance in each individual control period

- A cumulative total of variances, for example a 12-month rolling total for the variance. The variance should only be investigated if the cumulative total for the past 12 months exceeds the upper or lower control limit.

2.3 Cost-benefit analysis for variance investigation

The decision about whether or not to investigate a variance might be based on an assessment of:

- the costs of investigating the variance

- the probability that the cause of the variance will be a controllable factor

- the costs of control action if the cause is controllable

- the expected benefits from control action if the cause is controllable.

This method weighs up the costs and benefits of investigating a variance using the following relationship:

The decision rule can be expressed as a formula.

The variance should be investigated if:

I + pC < pB

Where:
I = the cost of investigating the variance
C = the cost of correcting the cause of the variance, if the cause is found to be controllable
p = the probability that the cause of the variance will be controllable
B = the expected benefits from control action, if the cause of the variance is found to be controllable

 Example

An adverse material usage variance of $1,400 has been reported.

The cost of investigating the cause of a material usage variance is estimated as $800.

It is also estimated that if the cause of the variance is found, after investigation, to be controllable, the cost of taking control action would be $650.

The estimated benefits from control action, if the cause of the variance is found to be controllable, are $2,500.

The probability that the variance will be caused by a controllable factor is 60%.

Should the variance be investigated?

 Answer

EV of costs of investigation = I + pC = $800 + 0.60 ($650) = $1,190.

EV of benefits from investigation and control = pB = 0.6 × $2,500 = $1,500.

The EV of benefits exceed the EV of costs; therefore the variance should be investigated.

CHAPTER

13

Performance measurement

Contents
1   Measuring performance
2   Ratio analysis
3   Profitability ratios
4   Working capital efficiency ratios
5   Liquidity ratios
6   Debt ratios
7   The limitations of financial ratios
8   Balanced scorecard approach
9   Performance pyramid
10   Performance measurement in service industries
11   Behavioural aspects of performance reporting: reward systems

> ## Measuring performance
>
> - Reasons for measuring performance
> - Responsibility and controllability
> - Long-term, medium-term and short-term performance
> - Financial and non-financial performance measures
> - Benchmarking

1 Measuring performance

1.1 Reasons for measuring performance

Performance in business is measured and reported back to:

- the individuals most directly responsible for the performance
- the managers to whom these individuals report.

The purpose of measuring performance is to:

- inform individuals and their managers as to whether planning targets or standards are being met
- indicate the risk that targets will not be met, so that action to correct the situation can be considered
- indicate poor performance, so that individuals and their managers can take whatever corrective action seems appropriate
- reward the successful achievement of targets or standards.

A business entity must have management information systems that are capable of providing reliable and relevant information about performance.

1.2 Responsibility and controllability

Two essential features of an effective performance reporting system are:

- **Responsibility**. Performance reports should be provided to the individuals (and their managers) who are actually responsible for the performance. Performance reports are irrelevant if they are sent to individuals with no responsibility.
- **Controllability**. Performance reports should distinguish between aspects of performance that should be controllable by the responsible individual, and aspects of performance that are outside the individual's control.

1.3 Long-term, medium-term and short-term performance

Performance measurement should cover the long-term, medium-term and short-term.

Long-term performance

Long-term performance measures should be linked to the long-term objectives and the strategies of the organisation. The most significant long-term objectives might be called **critical success factors** or **CSFs**. In order to achieve its long-term and strategic objectives, the critical success factors must be achieved.

For each critical success factor, there should be a way of measuring performance, in order to check whether the CSF targets are being met. Performance measurements for CSFs might be called **key performance indicators (KPIs)** or possibly **key risk indicators** (KRIs).

Medium-term performance

Medium-term performance measurement is perhaps most easily associated with the budget, and meeting budget targets. Targets, whether financial or non-financial, can be set for a planning period such as the financial year, and actual results should be compared against the planning targets.

Short-term performance

Short-term performance should be monitored by means of operational performance measures. For example, quality might be measured by the percentage of rejected units in production, or the rate of customer returns or customer complaints. Speed might be measured by the average time required to meet a customer order.

1.4 Financial and non-financial performance measures

Performance measures can be financial or non-financial. The performance of managers might be assessed on the basis of several performance measures, some financial and some non-financial.

Financial performance measures are linked to:

- costs: for example, keeping costs under control and avoiding large adverse cost variances
- costs, revenues and profits
- profits and capital investment: for example, measuring performance in terms of the returns made on capital invested.

Financial performance measures might be established for operational cost-effectiveness, such as measuring the cost per passenger mile in transport services, the cost per tonne-mile carried in road haulage services and the cost per patient-day in hospital services.

Non-financial performance measures at a strategic level might be linked to targets for:

- customer satisfaction
- work force skills and quality
- innovation.

Non-financial performance measures at an operational level might relate to:

- quality of products and services
- reliability or dependability of products, services and operations
- speed of service.

1.5 Benchmarking

Benchmarking is another way of measuring and assessing performance. Benchmarking involves comparing performance with the performance of another, similar organisation or operation. In other words, another organisation or department is used as a benchmark for comparison.

By making such comparisons, it should be possible to identify strengths and weaknesses in performance.

There are three main types of benchmarking.

- **Internal benchmarking**. An organisation might have many similar operations, such as regional or area branches that carry out similar operations in their geographical area. The best-performing branches or departments can be used as a benchmark, and the performance of other branches compared against it.

- **Competitive benchmarking**. This involves comparing the performance of the organisation against the performance of its most successful competitors. In this way, the areas of performance where the competitor is better can be identified, and measures can then be planned for reducing the gap in performance.

  The practical difficulty with competitive benchmarking is that the competitor will not willingly act as a benchmark, and allow its competitors to make a detailed study of its operations. Competitive benchmarking is therefore usually done without the competitor's knowledge. For example, a company might buy a product of a successful competitor and analyse its qualities and features in detail, perhaps by taking it apart in a laboratory and investigating its structure and components.

- **Operational benchmarking**. A company might use benchmarking to assess the performance of a particular aspect of its operations, such as customer order handling, handling e-commerce orders from the Internet, or warehousing and despatch operations. It might be able to identify a company in a completely different industry that carries out similar operations successfully. The other company might be prepared to act as a benchmark, and allow its operations to be studied and its staff interviewed. The benefit of this type of benchmarking is that a business is able to learn from world-class companies how to improve its operations and raise its performance levels.

> ## Ratio analysis
>
> - Obtaining information from the financial statements: financial ratios
> - Using ratios: comparisons
> - Categories of financial ratios

2 Ratio analysis

2.1 Obtaining information from the financial statements: financial ratios

A common method of analysing and measuring the financial performance of an organisation is by ratio analysis. Published financial statements contain information which can be analysed and interpreted by calculating financial ratios.

2.2 Using ratios: comparisons

Financial ratios can be used to make comparisons:

- Comparisons over a number of years. By looking at the ratios of a company over a number of years, it might be possible to detect improvements or a deterioration in the financial performance or financial position of the entity. Ratios can therefore be used to make comparisons over time, and to identify changes or trends
- Comparisons with the similar ratios of other, similar companies for the same period.
- In some cases, perhaps, comparisons with 'industry average' ratios.

Investors compare the performance of different companies using ratio analysis. Quoted companies will be keen to ensure that their own financial statements compare favourably with other similar companies. If performance is poor, the company will need to provide explanations to shareholders and have action plans in place to improve performance. Financial ratios may therefore become KPIs for businesses.

2.3 Categories of financial ratios

The main financial ratios relate to:

- financial performance: return on capital, profitability and use of assets
- working capital 'turnover' ratios
- liquidity ratios
- debt or risk ratios.

In addition there are some 'investor ratios' that monitor stock market performance and other measures of performance that are of interest to investors in shares and bonds.

> ### Profitability ratios
>
> - Return on capital employed
> - Analysing return: profitability and asset utilisation
> - Profit/sales ratio (and cost/sales ratios)
> - Sales/capital employed ratio
> - Percentage annual growth in sales

3 Profitability ratios

3.1 Return on capital employed

Profit-making companies should try to make a profit that is large enough in relation to the amount of money or capital invested in the business. The most important profitability ratio is return on capital employed or ROCE.

ROCE = Profit before interest and tax/Capital employed x 100%

Example

Sting Company achieved the following results in Year 1.

	1st January Year 1	31st December Year 1
	$	$
Share capital	200,000	200,000
Share premium	100,000	100,000
Accumulated profits	500,000	600,000
Bank loans	200,000	500,000

	$
Profit before taxation	210,000
Taxation	75,000
Profit after taxation	145,000

Interest charges on bank loans were $30,000. Sales during the year were $5,800,000.

Required

Calculate the return on capital employed for Year 1.

Answer

Capital employed at the beginning of the year = $1,000,000.

Capital employed at the end of the year = $1,400,000.

Average capital employed = [$1,000,000 + $1,400,000]/2 = $1,200,000.
Profit before interest and taxation = $210,000 + $30,000 = $240,000.

$$ROCE = \frac{240,000}{1,200,000} \times 100\% = 20\%$$

3.2 Analysing return: profitability and asset utilisation

The size of the return on capital employed depends on two factors:

■ the profitability of the goods or services that the entity has sold

■ the volume of sales that the entity has achieved with the capital and assets it has employed: this is known as asset utilisation or asset turnover.

3.3 Profit/sales ratio (and cost/sales ratios)

The profit/sales ratio is the ratio of the profit that has been achieved for every $1 of sales.

Profit/sales ratio = Profit/sales × 100%

Profit/sales ratios are commonly used by management to assess financial performance, and a variety of different figures for profit might be used.

The definition of profit can be any of the following:

■ Profit before interest and taxation

■ Gross profit (Sales minus the Cost of sales) = **'gross profit ratio'**

■ Net profit (Profit after taxation) = **'net profit ratio'**.

It is important to be consistent in the definition of profit, when comparing performance from one year to the next.

The gross profit ratio is often useful for comparisons between companies in the same industry, or for comparison with an industry average.

It is also useful to compare the net profit ratio with the gross profit ratio. A high gross profit ratio and a low net profit ratio indicates high overhead costs for administrative expenses and selling and distribution costs.

 Example

Using the figures in the previous example, profit/sales ratios can be calculated as follows:

■ If profit is defined as profit **before** interest and taxation, the profit/sales ratio = $240,000/$5,800,000 = 0.0414 = 4.14%

■ If profit is defined as profit **after** interest and taxation, the profit/sales ratio = $145,000/$5,800,000 = 0.025 = 2.5%

- It is also useful to monitor the ratio of costs to sales:
- Ratio of (Cost of sales/Sales) × 100%
- Ratio of (Administration costs/Sales) × 100%
- Ratio of (Selling and distribution costs/Sales) × 100%

3.4   Sales/capital employed ratio

The sales/capital employed ratio is also called the 'asset turnover ratio'. It measures the amount of sales achieved during the period for each $1 of investment in assets.

Asset turnover ratio = sales /capital employed

It is measured as 'x times a year'.

Example

Using the figures in the previous example, the asset turnover ratio = $5,800,000/$1,200,000 = 4.83 times.

Note that:

ROCE = Profit/sales ratio × Asset turnover ratio
(where profit is defined as profit before interest and taxation).

Using the figures in the previous example:

ROCE	=	Profit/sales	×	Sales/capital employed
$\dfrac{240,000}{1,200,000}$	=	$\dfrac{240,000}{5,800,000}$	×	$\dfrac{5,800,000}{1,200,000}$
20%	=	4.14%	×	4.83 times

3.5   Percentage annual growth in sales

It can be useful to measure the annual growth (or decline) in sales, measured as a percentage of sales in the previous year.

For example, if sales in the year just ended were $5,800,000 and sales in the previous year were $5,500,000, the annual growth in sales has been ($300,000/$5,500,000) × 100% = 5.45%.

> ## Working capital efficiency ratios
>
> - Purpose of working capital efficiency ratios
> - Average time to collect (debtor days or days sales outstanding)
> - Average time for holding inventory (inventory turnover)
> - Average time to pay suppliers
> - Cash operating cycle/working capital cycle

4 Working capital efficiency ratios

4.1 Purpose of working capital efficiency ratios

Working capital efficiency ratios measure the efficiency with which the entity has managed its receivables, inventory and trade payables. The ratios are usually measured in terms of an average number of days.

The working capital ratios are a useful measure of whether the entity has too much or too little invested in working capital.

Excessive investment in working capital is indicated by a long cash cycle (a long working capital cycle) that appears to be getting even longer. When too much is invested in working capital, the return on capital employed will be lower than it should be.

Under-investment in working capital is an indication of possible liquidity difficulties. When working capital is low in comparison with the industry average, this might indicate that current assets are being financed to an excessive extent by current liabilities, particularly trade payables and a bank overdraft.

4.2 Average time to collect (receivables days or days sales outstanding)

This ratio estimates the time that it takes on average to collect the payment from customers after the sale has been made. It could be described as the average credit period allowed to customers.

$$\text{Average days to collect} = \frac{\text{Trade receivables}}{\text{Sales}} \times 365 \text{ days}$$

Trade receivables should be the average value of receivables during the year. This is the average of the receivables at the beginning of the year and the receivables at the end of the year.

However, the value for receivables at the end of the year is also commonly used.

Sales are usually taken as total sales for the year. However, if sales are analysed into credit sales and cash sales, it is probably more appropriate to use the figure for credit sales only.

The average time to collect money from credit customers should not be too long. A long average time to collect suggests inefficient collection of debts

4.3 Average time for holding inventory (inventory turnover)

This ratio is an estimate of the average time that inventory is held before it is used or sold.

$$\text{Inventory turnover} \quad = \quad \frac{\text{Inventory}}{\text{Cost of sales}} \times 365 \text{ days}$$

Inventory should be the average value of inventory during the year. This is the average of the inventory at the beginning of the year and the inventory at the end of the year.

However, the value for inventory at the end of the year is also commonly used.

4.4 Average time to pay suppliers

The average time to pay suppliers may be calculated as follows:

$$\text{Average time to pay} \quad = \quad \frac{\text{Trade payables}}{\text{Cost of purchases}} \times 365 \text{ days}$$

Trade payables should be the average value of trade payables during the year. This is the average of the trade payables at the beginning of the year and the trade payables at the end of the year.

However, the value for trade payables at the end of the year is also commonly used When the cost of purchases is not available, the **cost of sales** should be used instead.

 Example

The following information is available for The Brush Company for Year 1:

	1st January Year 1	31st December Year 1
	$	$
Inventory	300,000	360,000
Trade receivables	400,000	470,000
Trade payables	150,000	180,000

Sales in Year 1 totalled $3,000,000 and the cost of sales was $1,800,000.

Required

Calculate the working capital turnover ratios.

Answer

Average inventory = [$300,000 + $360,000]/2 = $330,000

Average trade receivables = [$400,000 + $470,000]/2 = $435,000

Average trade payables = [$150,000 + $180,000]/2 = $165,000.

Turnover ratios

Average days to collect = [330,000/3,000,000] × 365 days = 40.2 days

Inventory turnover period = [435,000/1,800,000] × 365 days = 88.2 days

Average time to pay = [165,000/1,800,000] × 365 days = 33.5 days.

4.5   Cash operating cycle/working capital cycle

The cash operating cycle or working capital cycle is the average time of one cycle of business operations:

- from the time that suppliers are paid for the resources they supply
- to the time that cash is received from customers for the goods (or services) that the entity makes (or provides) with those resources and then sells.

A cash cycle or operating cycle is measured as follows. Figures are included for the purpose of illustration:

	Days	Days
Inventory turnover	A	40.2
Average days to collect	B	88.2
		128.4
Average time to pay	(C)	(33.5)
Cash cycle/operating cycle	A + B − C	94.9

The working capital ratios and the length of the cash cycle should be monitored over time. The cycle should not be allowed to become unreasonable in length, with a risk of over-investment or under-investment in working capital.

Liquidity ratios
■ The meaning of liquidity
■ Current ratio
■ Quick ratio or acid test ratio

5 Liquidity ratios

5.1 The meaning of liquidity

Liquidity means having cash or access to cash readily available to meet obligations to make payments

There are two ratios for measuring liquidity:

■ current ratio

■ quick ratio, also called the acid test ratio.

The more suitable ratio for use depends on whether inventory is considered a liquid asset that will soon be used or sold, and converted into cash from sales.

5.2 Current ratio

The current ratio is the ratio of current assets to current liabilities.

$$\text{Current ratio} = \frac{\text{Current assets}}{\text{Current liabilities}}$$

The amounts of current assets and current liabilities in the balance sheet at the end of the year may be used. It is not necessary to use average values for the year

It is sometimes suggested that there is an 'ideal' current ratio of 2.0 times (2:1).

However, this is not necessarily true and in some industries, much lower current ratios are normal. It is important to assess the liquidity ratios by considering:

■ changes in the ratio over time

■ the liquidity ratios of other companies in the same period

■ the industry average ratios.

Liquidity should be monitored by looking at changes in the ratio over time.

5.3 Quick ratio or acid test ratio

The quick ratio or acid test ratio is the ratio of current assets excluding inventory to current liabilities. Inventory is excluded from current assets on the assumption that it is not a very liquid item.

$$\text{Quick ratio} = \frac{\text{Current assets excluding inventory}}{\text{Current liabilities}}$$

The amounts of current assets and current liabilities in the balance sheet at the end of the year may be used. It is not necessary to use average values for the year.

This ratio is a better measurement of liquidity than the current ratio when inventory turnover times are very slow, and inventory is not a liquid asset.

It is sometimes suggested that there is an 'ideal' quick ratio of 1.0 times (1:1).

However, this is not necessarily true and in some industries, much lower quick ratios are normal. As indicated earlier, it is important to assess liquidity by looking at changes in the ratio over time, and comparisons with other companies and the industry norm.

Debt ratios

- Gearing ratio (leverage)
- Interest cover ratio

6 Debt ratios

Debt ratios are used to assess whether the total debts of the entity are within control and are not excessive.

6.1 Gearing ratio (leverage)

Gearing, also called leverage, measures the total long-term debt of a company as a percentage of either:

- the equity capital in the company, or
- the total capital of the company.

$$\text{Gearing} = \frac{\text{Long - term debt}}{\text{Share capital and reserves}} \times 100\%$$

Alternatively:

$$\text{Gearing} = \frac{\text{Long - term debt}}{\text{Share capital and reserves} + \text{Long - term debt}} \times 100\%$$

When there are preference shares, it is usual to include the preference shares within long-term debt, not share capital.

A company is said to be **high-geared** or **highly-leveraged** when its debt capital exceeds its share capital and reserves. This means that a company is high-geared when the gearing ratio is above either 50% or 100%, depending on which method is used to calculate the ratio.

A company is said to be **low-geared** when the amount of its debt capital is less than its share capital and reserves. This means that a company is low-geared when the gearing ratio is less than either 50% or 100%, depending on which method is used to calculate the ratio.

The gearing ratio can be used to monitor changes in the amount of debt of a company over time. It can also be used to make comparisons with the gearing levels of other, similar companies, to judge whether the company has too much debt, or perhaps too little, in its capital structure.

6.2   Interest cover ratio

Interest cover measures the ability of the company to meet its obligations to pay interest.

$$\text{Interest cover} = \frac{\text{Profit before interest and tax}}{\text{Interest charges in the year}}$$

An interest cover ratio of less than 3.0 times is considered very low, suggesting that the company could be at risk from too much debt in relation to the amount of profits it is earning.

> ### The limitations of financial ratios
>
> - Differences in accounting policy
> - Other limitations in the use of financial ratios

7 The limitations of financial ratios

There are several limitations or weaknesses in the use of financial ratios for analysing the financial position and financial performance of companies.

7.1 Differences in accounting policy

One of the uses of financial ratios is to compare the financial position and performance of one company with similar companies for the same period.

Comparisons between companies might not be reliable, however, when companies use different accounting policies, or have different judgements in applying accounting policies.

A few possible differences in accounting policy that might make inter-company comparisons unreliable are listed below.

- Entities might have different policies about the revaluation of non-current assets.
- Entities might have different policies about depreciation of non-current assets.
- Entities might use different judgements in estimating the expected profitability on incomplete construction contracts.
- Entities might use different policies in assessing whether a liability should be treated as a provision or a contingent liability.

7.2 Other limitations in the use of financial ratios

There are other problems with the use of financial ratios.

- Financial statements are published infrequently. If ratios are used to study trends and developments over time, they are only useful for trends or changes over one year or longer, and not changes in the short-term.
- Ratios can only indicate **possible** strengths or weaknesses in financial position and financial performance. They might raise questions about performance, but do not provide answers. They are not easy to interpret, and changes in financial ratios over time might not be easy to explain.
- Using ratios to measure performance can lead managers to focus on the short-term rather than the long-term success of the business.

> ## The balanced scorecard approach
>
> - The balanced scorecard: four perspectives of performance
> - Using the balanced scorecard
> - Conflicting targets for the four perspectives

8 The balanced scorecard approach

8.1 The balanced scorecard: four perspectives of performance

The balanced scorecard approach is an approach to measuring performance in relation to long-term objectives. This approach to target setting and performance measurement was developed by Kaplan and Norton in the 1990s. The most important objective for business entities is a financial objective, but to achieve long-term financial objectives, it is important to achieve goals or targets that are non-financial in nature as well as financial.

The reason for having a balanced scorecard is that by setting targets for several key factors, managers will take a more balanced and long-term view about what they should be trying to achieve. A balanced scorecard approach should remove the emphasis on financial targets and short-term results.

In a balanced scorecard, critical success factors are identified for four aspects of performance, or four 'perspectives':

- customer perspective
- internal perspective
- innovation and learning perspective
- financial perspective.

Perspective	The key question
Customer perspective	**What do customers value?** By recognising what customers value most from the organisation, the organisation can focus performance on satisfying the customer more effectively. Targets might be developed for performance such as cost (value for money), quality or place of delivery.
Internal perspective	**To achieve its financial and customer objectives, what processes must the organisation perform with excellence?** Management should identify the key aspects of operational performance and seek to achieve or maintain excellence in this area.
Innovation and learning perspective	**How can the organisation continue to improve and create value?** The focus here is on the ability of the organisation to maintain its competitive position, through the skills and knowledge of its work force and through developing new products and services.
Financial perspective	**How does the organisation create value for its owners?** Financial measures of performance in a balanced scorecard system might include share price growth, profitability and return on investment.

8.2   Using the balanced scorecard

The focus is on strategic objectives and the critical success factors necessary for achieving them. In a balanced scorecard approach, targets are set for a range of critical financial and non-financial areas covering these four perspectives. The main performance report for management each month is a balanced scorecard report, not budgetary control reports and variance reports.

Examples of measures of performance for each of the four perspectives are as follows:

Perspective	Outcome measures
Critical financial measures	Return on investment Profitability Economic value added (EVA) Revenue growth Productivity and cost control Cash flow
Critical customer measures	Market share Customer profitability Attracting new customers Retaining existing customers Customer satisfaction On-time delivery
Critical internal measures	Success rate in winning contract orders Production cycle time/throughput time Amount of re-working of defective units
Critical innovation and learning measures	Revenue per employee Employee productivity Employee satisfaction Employee retention Percentage of total revenue earned from sales of new products Time to develop new products

Example: balanced scorecard

Kaplan and Norton described the example of Mobil in the early 1990s, in their book *The Strategy-focussed Organisation*. Mobil, a major supplier of petrol, was competing with other suppliers on the basis of price and the location of petrol stations. Its strategic focus was on cost reduction and productivity, but its return on capital was low.

The company's management re-assessed their strategy, with the aim of increasing market share and obtaining stronger brand recognition of the Mobil brand name. They decided that the company needed to attract high-spending customers who would buy other goods from the petrol station stores, in addition to petrol.

As its high-level financial objective, the company set a target of increasing return on capital employed from its current level of about 6% to 12% within three years.

- From a **financial perspective**, it identified such key success factors as productivity and sales growth. Targets were set for productivity (reducing operating costs per gallon of petrol sold) and 'asset intensity' (ratio of operational cash flow to assets employed).

- From a **customer perspective**, Mobil carried out market research into who its customers were and what factors influenced their buying decisions. Targets were set for providing petrol to customers in a way that would satisfy the customer and differentiate Mobil's products from rival petrol suppliers. Key issues were found to be having petrol stations that were clean and safe, and offering a good quality branded product and a trusted brand. Targets were set for cleanliness and safety, speedy service at petrol stations, helpful customer service and rewarding customer loyalty.

- From an **internal perspective**, Mobil set targets for improving the delivery of its products and services to customers, and making sure that customers could always buy the petrol and other products that they wanted, whenever they visited a Mobil station.

8.3 Conflicting targets for the four perspectives

A criticism that has been made against the balanced scorecard approach is that the targets for each of the four perspectives might often conflict with each other. When this happens, there might be disagreement about what the priorities should be.

This problem should not be serious, however, if it is remembered that the financial is the most important of the four perspectives for a commercial business entity.

A useful sporting analogy was provided in an article in *Financial Management* magazine (Gering and Mntambo, November 2001). They compared the balanced scorecard to the judgements of a football team manager during a football match. The objective is to win the match and the key performance measure is the score.

However, as the match progresses, the manager will look at other important aspects of performance, such as the number of shots at the goal by each side, the number of corner kicks, the number of tackles and the percentage of possession of the ball enjoyed by the team.

Shots on goal corner kicks, tackles and possession of the ball are all necessary factors in scoring goals, not conceding goals, and winning the match. The manager will therefore use them as indicators of how well or badly the match is progressing. However, the score is ultimately the only thing that matters.

In the same way, targets for four perspectives are useful in helping management to judge progress towards the company's objectives, but ultimately, success in achieving those objectives is measured in financial terms. The financial objective is the most important.

The performance pyramid

- The pyramid structure: linking performance targets throughout an organisation
- Interpreting the pyramid

---

9 The performance pyramid

Another approach to structuring the performance evaluation system is the performance pyramid. The concept of a performance pyramid is based on the idea that an organisation operates at different levels. Each level has different concerns, but these should support each other in achieving the overall business objectives.

Performance can therefore be seen as a pyramid structure, with a large number of operational performance targets supporting higher-level targets, leading to targets for the achievement of overall corporate objectives at the top.

9.1 The pyramid structure: linking performance targets throughout an organisation

The performance pyramid was developed by Lynch and Cross (1991). They argued that traditional performance measurement systems were not as effective as they should be, because they had a narrow financial focus – concentrating on measures such as return on capital employed, profitability, cash flow and so on. They argued that in a dynamic business environment, achieving strategic business objectives depends on good performance with regard to:

- **Customer satisfaction** (a 'marketing' objective: here, the focus is on external/market effectiveness)
- **Flexibility** (the flexibility objective relates to both external effectiveness and internal efficiency with in the organisation)
- **Productivity** (resource utilisation: here, the focus is on internal efficiency, much of which can be measured by financial performance)

These key 'driving forces' can be monitored at the operational level with performance measures relating to quality, delivery, cycle time and waste.

Lynch and Cross argued that within an organisation, there are different levels of management and each has its own focus. However, there must be consistency between performance measurement at each management level, so that performance measures at the operational level support the corporate strategy.

They presented these ideas in the form of a pyramid of targets and performance that links operations to corporate strategy.

A performance pyramid can be presented as follows:

Performance pyramid

9.2 Interpreting the pyramid

The performance pyramid links strategic objectives with operational targets, and internally-focused with externally-focused objectives.

- Objectives and targets are set from the top level (corporate vision) down to the operational level. Performance is measured from an operational level upwards. If performance targets are achieved at the operational level, targets should be achieved at the operating systems level. Achieving targets for operating systems should help to ensure the achievement of marketing and financial strategy objectives, which in turn should enable the organisation to achieve its corporate objectives.

- A key level of performance measurement is at the operating systems level – achieving targets for customer satisfaction, flexibility and productivity. To achieve performance targets at this level, operational targets must be achieved - for quality, delivery, cycle time and waste.

- With the exception of flexibility, which has both an internal and an external aspect, performance measures within the pyramid (and below the corporate vision level) can be divided between:

    - market measures, or measures of external effectiveness, and

    - financial measures, or measures of internal efficiency.

- The measures of performance are inter-related, both at the same level within the pyramid and vertically, between different levels in the pyramid. For example:

    - New product development is a business operating system. When a new product is introduced to the market, success depends on meeting customer needs (customer satisfaction), adapting customer attitudes and production systems in order to make the changes (flexibility) and delivering the product to the customer at the lowest cost for the required quality (productivity).

- Achieving improvements in productivity depends on reducing the cycle time (from order to delivery) or reducing waste.

Lynch and Cross argued that the performance measures that are chosen should link operations to strategic goals.

■ All operational departments need to be aware of how they are contributing to the achievement of strategic goals.

■ Performance measures should be a combination of financial and non-financial measures that are of practical value to managers. Reliable information about performance should be readily available to managers whenever it is needed.

> ### Performance measurement in service industries
>
> - The characteristics of services and service industries
> - Controllable performance in service industries: Fitzgerald and Moon
> - Applying the Fitzgerald and Moon framework

10 Performance measurement in service industries

10.1 The characteristics of services and service industries

Many organisations provide services rather than products. There are many examples of service industries: hotels, entertainment, the holiday and travel industries, professional services, banking, cleaning services, and so on.

Performance measurement for services may differ from performance measurement in manufacturing in several ways:

- **Simultaneity**. With a service, providing the service ('production') and receiving consumption the service ('consumption' by the customer) happen at the same time.

- **Perishability**. It is impossible to store a service for future consumption: unlike manufacturing and retailing, there is no inventory of unused services. The service must be provided when the customer wants it.

- **Heterogeneity**. A product can be made to a standard specification. With a service provided by humans, there is variability in the standard of performance. Each provision of the service is different. For example, even if they perform the same songs at several concerts, the performance of a rock band at a series of concerts will be different each time.

- **Intangibility**. With a service, there are many intangible elements of service that the customer is given, and that individual customer might value. For example, a high quality of service in a restaurant is often intangible, but noticed and valued by the customer.

Since services differ to some extent from products, should performance setting and performance measurement be different in service companies, compared with manufacturing companies?

10.2 Controllable performance in service industries: Fitzgerald and Moon

Research by Fitzgerald and others (1993) and by Fitzgerald and Moon (1996) into performance in service industries concluded that **controllable** performance in service industries can be measured in six different dimensions.

Two of these are:

- financial performance and
- competitiveness.

However, these aspects of performance are the results of actions and decisions taken in the past. They measure the success of these past decisions and actions. The other four dimensions of performance are:

- quality
- flexibility
- resource utilisation
- innovation.

These are dimensions of competitive success now and in the future, and so are appropriate for measuring the performance of current management.

Fitzgerald and Moon developed building blocks for measurement of performance in service industries, based on these six dimensions of performance. The building blocks supporting performance in each of the six dimensions are standards for setting performance and reward systems.

Building blocks for performance measurement systems
(Fitzgerald and Moon 1996)

Dimensions

Profit
Competitiveness
Quality
Resource utilisation
Flexibility
Innovation

Standards	**Rewards**
Ownership	Clarity
Achievability	Motivation
Equity	Controllability

10.3 Applying the Fitzgerald and Moon framework

You may be required to suggest suitable measures of performance in a service industry, and the framework above might provide a useful framework for doing this.

Dimension of performance	Possible measure of performance
Financial performance	Profitability
	Growth in profits
	Profit/sales margins
	Note: return on capital is possibly not so relevant in a service industry, where the company employs fairly small amounts of capital.
Competitiveness	Growth in sales
	Retention rate for customers
	Success rate in converting enquiries into sales
	Possibly market share, although this may be difficult to measure

Table continued

Service quality	Rate/number of complaints
	Whether the rate of complaints is increasing or decreasing
	Customer satisfaction, as revealed by customer opinion surveys
	Number of errors discovered
Flexibility	Possibly the mix of different types of work done by employees
	Possibly the speed of response to customer requests
Resource utilisation	Efficiency/productivity measures
	Utilisation rates: percentage of available time utilised in 'productive' activities
Innovation	Number of new services offered
	Percentage of sales income that comes from services introduced in the last one/two years

Other measures of performance might be appropriate for each dimension, depending on the nature of the service industry. However, this framework of six dimensions provides a structure for considering what measures of performance might be suitable.

> ## Behavioural aspects of performance reporting: reward systems
>
> - Unintended consequences of performance measurement systems
> - Performance rewards
> - Designing reward schemes: factors to consider
> - Behavioural problems with reward systems

11 Behavioural aspects of performance reporting: reward systems

11.1 Unintended consequences of performance measurement systems

An aim of performance reporting systems should be to improve performance. In order to achieve this objective, it is often necessary to consider the behavioural implications of performance reports.

Performance reports should be used in the way intended. In practice, however, there may be unintended consequences, particularly when managers receive rewards for good performance.

Performance measurement systems can suffer from several problems that reduce their effectiveness.

- **Tunnel vision**. Tunnel vision means focusing on performance measurement to the exclusion of other aspects of management.

- **Sub-optimisation**. Sub-optimisation occurs when managers focus on achieving good performance in one area, but in doing so overlook other aspects of performance. As a result, overall performance is not as good as it should be. For example, management may be given performance targets for the sales of new products: they may focus on sales growth for new products, and in doing so overlook the need to maintain sales of established products. As a result total sales and profits might fall.

- **Myopia**. Myopia is short-sightedness. In the context of performance measurement, it means concentrating on short-term performance measures to the exclusion of longer-term considerations.

- **Measure fixation**. Measure fixation means taking action to ensure that specific performance targets are reached without considering the possible consequences. For example, a department might have a target for labour costs as a maximum proportion of its total operating costs. In order to meet this target, management might recruit and employ inexperienced and untrained staff who are paid less money than experienced employees. The labour cost target might be met, but the quality of work might deteriorate.

- **Misrepresentation**. Misrepresentation describes the tendency to give a false but flattering picture of performance, by disguising actual results. For example, a sales manager might represent the sales performance for a period in a flattering light – with some growth in sales volume. However, this could be misleading:

sales volume growth might have been achieved only as a result of heavy price discounting and a big reduction in gross profit margins.

- **Misinterpretation**. Misinterpretation occurs when performance measures are interpreted in an incorrect or over-simplified way. Management might read something good or something bad in a set of performance figures, when the actual situation is more complex and the results are not so easy to interpret.

- **Gaming**. Gaming occurs when there is a deliberate distortion of a performance measure or a performance target, in order to make actual results subsequently appear much better than they really are. For example, a departmental manager might argue that productivity in the department has been poor, so that a low performance target is set for productivity in the department. If the target is set at a low level, it is relatively easy to achieve, and the department's performance will therefore appear better than it really is.

- **Ossification**. Performance measurement systems should be flexible, and new performance measures should be introduced as appropriate to replace measures that are no longer appropriate. Ossification refers to an unwillingness that may exist to change any parts of the measurement system, after it has been introduced.

- **Lack of consistency**. Within an organisation, the performance targets set for individuals or groups may be inconsistent with each other. For example, a production manager may be given performance targets relating to keeping costs under control, and a quality control manager may have performance targets for ensuring the quality of completed output. The targets of the production manager and the quality control manager may be inconsistent, if lower costs are achievable by reducing quality.

These problems need to be recognised and understood. Management should continually review the performance measurement system and the appropriateness of the performance targets and performance measurements that are used.

11.2 Performance rewards

Many organisations have systems for linking the achievement of performance targets with rewards for the successful individual. Rewards may take the form of higher pay (for example, a cash bonus or a higher salary) or promotion. Individuals may also feel rewarded by a sense of personal achievement (and possibly also by a formal recognition of their achievement by senior management). In some cases, there may be systems of 'punishment' for poor performance, such as withholding a bonus or even dismissal.

Advantages of reward systems

There are several advantages in having a system of rewards linked to performance:

- A well-designed reward scheme should link rewards to performance that supports strategic objectives. This should help the organisation to implement its strategies and achieve its strategic objectives.

- Rewards can motivate individuals to achieve their performance targets. They can also help to attract and retain talented individuals.

- The payment of rewards for achieving key targets helps to inform managers and employees about what the critical aspects of performance are.

- An effective reward system will encourage employees to focus on continuous improvement.

- Where rewards involve granting shares or share options in the company, employees who benefit from the rewards may be encouraged to think more about the long-term prospects of their company and its market value.

11.3 Designing reward schemes: factors to consider

There are several factors to consider and questions to answer when designing a reward scheme.

- Should the rewards for performance be based on results (outputs) or on the effort that has been put in? A reward scheme for salesmen, for example, can be based fairly simply on results achieved (volume of sales). It is often much more difficult however to reward administrative staff for results achieved, because the results of their efforts might not be easily quantifiable, or measured against clear targets.

- Should rewards be given in a money form (a bonus or higher salary) or in non-monetary form (such as share options)?

- Should rewards be explicit or implicit? Explicit rewards are rewards that will definitely be given for meeting performance targets, such as a cash bonus. Implicit rewards are not specific promises, but there is a general understanding that the rewards will be available for good performance. For example, there is often an expectation of promotion or a higher salary for good performance, but these are not explicit promises, only an implicit understanding.

- How large should rewards be?

- Over what time period should performance be measured before rewards are given?

- Should rewards be given for individual performance, or should there be group rewards for team performance?

- Should the rewards involve equity participation – giving shares or share options to individuals?

- What are the tax implications of different reward schemes? Can a reward scheme be devised that limit the tax liabilities of the employees receiving the rewards, without breaching the tax laws?

11.4 Behavioural problems with reward systems

When individuals are rewarded for performance, some potential behavioural problems might occur.

It is often difficult to measure the performance of individuals, and the performance of groups or teams must be measured instead. When group performance is measured, there may be a problem in the following situations:

- Some members of the group or team believe that they have been responsible for the successful performance of the group, whereas other team members have not contributed as much as they should have. These individuals may be angered if rewards are paid to all members of the team, including the undeserving members.

- The reward system provides rewards to some members of a group, but not to others: for example, a departmental manager may be rewarded, but none of the departmental staff.

When performance is rewarded, the individuals affected will be inclined to focus on the measures of performance that set the level of their reward – to the exclusion of all other aspects of performance. This can have unintended consequences.

For example, a sales manager may be rewarded with a bonus for exceeding a sales target. The manager might therefore take measures to ensure that the sales target is achieved, and to do this, the manager might offer attractive terms to customers, such as large price discounts. As a result, the key performance target – sales revenue – might be achieved, but with the consequence that profit margins are much lower than planned.

CHAPTER

14

Performance analysis in not-for-profit organisations and the public sector

Contents
1   Performance measurement in not-for-profit organisations
2   Value for money

> ## Performance measurement in not-for-profit organisations
>
> - The special characteristics of not-for-profit organisations
> - Identifying performance targets for not-for-profit organisations
> - Difficulties in measuring performance
> - The public sector

1 Performance measurement in not-for-profit organisations

1.1 The special characteristics of not-for-profit organisations

Not-for-profit organisations, such as government departments and charitable organisations, differ from commercial businesses because their main objective is not financial. The main objective of any such organisation depends on the purpose for which it exists: to administer the country (government departments), to provide education (schools and universities), provide medical care (hospitals), do charitable work, and so on.

A not-for-profit organisation will nevertheless have some financial objectives:

- State-owned organisations must operate within their spending budget.

- Charitable organisations may have an objective of keeping running costs within a certain limit, and of raising as much funding as possible for their charity work.

1.2 Identifying performance targets for not-for-profit organisations

You may be required in your examination to suggest quantitative targets for a not-for-profit organisation. The selection of appropriate targets will vary according to the nature and purpose of the organisation. The broad principle, however, is that any not-for-profit organisation should have:

- strategic targets, mainly non-financial in nature

- operational targets, which may be either financial (often related to costs and keeping costs under control) or non-financial (related to the nature of operations)

A school, for example, might set targets and assess its performance on the basis of measures such as:

- examination results

- numbers of students going to university

- average class sizes

- ratio of teacher numbers to student numbers

- annual intake of new students.

These could be both long-term and shorter-term targets.

1.3   Difficulties in measuring performance

A good performance measurement system seeks to monitor the success of an organisation in achieving its objectives. To do this it must

- have clear objectives

- set targets which are linked to objectives

- measure performance against these targets.

There are great difficulties for a non-profit seeking organisations when trying to establish a good performance measurement system

- There are multiple objectives and it may be difficult to decide which are most important. Different objectives may be more important to different stakeholders.

- It may be difficult to define targets which are clearly linked to objectives and which are measurable

- Public sector organisations may be subject to political interference in the setting of performance targets

 Example

A school may have a variety of objectives. Employers and the government may all require high levels of examination results and school management may require a high intake of pupils. Pupils may aspire to develop their skills. Parents expect schools to teach life and community skills. This leads to difficulties in identifying targets.

- The main target may be the level of examination results. However, the success in achieving this target will depend on the ability of the pupils in the school as well as the skill of the teachers.

- Targets such as class sizes and ratio of teachers to pupils may impact on the ability to achieve a good level of examination results but these are measures of inputs into the school rather than outputs from the school.

- An attempt may be made to measure the value added to each pupil. This could be done by measuring a pupil's achievements on entering and leaving the school. However there are many difficulties inherent in such a system. Only certain skills could be measured and it would be possible to coach a pupil in these particular skills to ensure good results. There would be great pressure to do this if performance of each school was measured on this basis and this affected the number and ability of pupils sent to the school.

- A performance measurement system focusing on a narrow range of measures can lead to other important objectives being overlooked. If targets are centered on literacy and numeracy then other skills, such as musical and sporting ability, may not be developed. This may demotivate pupils and lead to a lowering of overall performance.

1.4   The public sector

Public sector organisations may face particular constraints when trying to improve performance.

■ There may be legal constraints concerning how budgets are spent. The public sector is funded mainly by taxation and the government is accountable to the general electorate for performance. Governments may prefer to be seen to increase investment in new services than fund increased pay awards for staff which could be criticised for fuelling wage inflation in the private sector.

■ Public sector organisations may not legally be able to borrow funds from commercial sources.

■ Budget levels may be only authorised on a short-term basis and may be subject to change if there is a change of government. It is therefore difficult for organisations to make long-term plans to achieve objectives.

> **Value for money**
>
> ■ How can performance be measured?
> ■ Benchmarking
> ■ Quantitative measures of efficiency

2 Value for money

2.1 How can performance be measured ?

The performance of not-for-profit organisations may be assessed on the basis of value for money or VFM. Value for money is often referred to as the '3Es':

■ economy

■ efficiency

■ effectiveness.

Economy

Economy means keeping spending within limits, and avoiding wasteful spending. It also means achieving the same purpose at a lower expense. A simple example of economy is found in the purchase of supplies. Suppose that an administrative department buys items of stationery from a supplier, and pays $2 each for pens. It might be possible to buy pens of the same quality to fulfil exactly the same purpose for $1.50 each. Economy would be achieved by switching to buying the $1.50 pens, saving $0.50 per pen with no loss of operating efficiency or effectiveness.

Efficiency

Efficiency means getting more output from available resources. Applied to employees, efficiency is often called 'productivity'. Suppose that a sales order clerk processes 50 customer orders each day. Efficiency would be improved if a sales order clerk increases the rate of output, and processes 60 orders each day, without any loss of effectiveness.

Effectiveness

Effectiveness refers to success in achieving end results or success in achieving objectives. Whereas efficiency is concerned with getting more outputs from available resources, effectiveness is concerned with achieving outputs that meet the required aims and objectives. For example, the efficiency of sales representatives will be improved if they increase their calls to customers from 8 to 10 each day, but their effectiveness will not be increased if they do not achieve any more sales from the extra calls.

Management accounting systems and reporting systems may provide information to management about value for money. Has VFM been achieved, and if so, how much and in what ways?

Value for money audits may be carried out to establish how much value is being achieved within a particular department and whether there have been improvements to value for money. Internal audit departments may carry out occasional VFM audits, and report to senior management and the manager of the department they have audited.

VFM budgeting can be particularly useful in not-for-profit organisations, whose purpose is to achieve a stated objective as closely as possible, with the resources available.

 Example

State-owned schools may be given a target that their pupils (of a specified age) must achieve a certain level of examination grades or 'passes' in a particular examination.

A VFM audit could be used to establish spending efficiency within a school.

- **Economy**. Was there any unnecessary spending? Could the same value have been obtained for lower spending?
- **Efficiency**. Have the school's resources been used efficiently? Could more output have been obtained from the available resources? Could the same results have been achieved with fewer resources? A study of efficiency might focus on matters such as teaching time per teacher per week, and the utilisation of resources such as science equipment and computer-based training materials.
- **Effectiveness**. The most obvious measurements of effectiveness are the number or percentage of pupils achieving the required examination 'passes', or the grades of pass mark that they have achieved. Effectiveness is improved by increasing the pass rate.

2.2   Benchmarking

Benchmarking is the comparison of performance against the best practitioners, identifying gaps and seeking ways to improve.
Benchmarking may be a very effective method for organisations in the not-for-profit sector to achieve improvements in performance as often they are not in direct competition with other similar organisations.

 Example

Local authorities provide many services to households in their geographical area. These may include rubbish collection, road maintenance and social services. By comparing performance statistics it may be possible to identify more cost effective ways of providing services which can lead to an improvement in services for everybody.

2.3 Quantitative measures of efficiency

Efficiency relates the quantity of resources to the quantity of output. This can be measured in a variety of ways

- Actual Output/Maximum output for a given resource × 100%

- Minimum input to achieve required level of output/actual input × 100%

- Actual output/actual input x 100% compared to a standard or target

Example

A hospital has an operating theatre which can be utilised for 20 hours per day. The maximum number of operations that can be performed in any day is 40. If on a particular day 35 operations were performed, this represents

35/40 × 100% = 87.5% efficiency

A local authority must ensure that all residents' rubbish is collected each week. This normally requires 1,000 man hours. If in a particular week 900 man hours were used this represents

1,000/900 × 100% = 111.1% efficiency

Schools may have a standard pupil to teacher ratio of 27. If a particular school has 550 pupils and 21 teachers then the actual ratio is 26.2 which represents

27/26.2 × 1005 = 103.05% efficiency

CHAPTER

15

Decentralisation and divisional performance

Contents
1   Divisional performance evaluation
2   Return on Investment (ROI)
3   Residual income (RI)
4   Divisional performance and depreciation

> ## Divisional performance evaluation
>
> - Decentralisation of authority
> - Benefits of decentralisation
> - Disadvantages of decentralisation
> - Controllable profit and traceable profit

1 Divisional performance evaluation

1.1 Decentralisation of authority

Decentralisation involves the delegation of authority within an organisation. Within a large organisation, authority is delegated to the managers of cost centres, revenue centres, profit centres and investment centres.

A divisionalised structure refers to the organisation of an entity in which each operating unit has its own management team which reports to a head office. Divisions are commonly set up to be responsible for specific geographical areas or product lines within a large organisation.

The term 'decentralised divisionalised structure' means an organisation structure in which authority has been delegated to the centre's manager to decide selling prices, choose suppliers, make output decisions, and so on.

1.2 Benefits of decentralisation

Decentralisation should provide several benefits for an organisation.

- Decision-making should improve, because the divisional managers make the tactical and operational decisions, and top management is free to concentrate on strategy and strategic planning.
- Decision-making at a tactical and operational level should improve, because the divisional managers have better 'local' knowledge.
- Decision-making should improve, because decisions will be made faster. Divisional managers can make decisions 'on the spot' without referring them to senior management.
- Managers may be more motivated to perform well if they are empowered to make decisions and rewarded for performing well against fair targets
- Divisions provide useful experience for managers who will one day become top managers in the organisation.
- Within a large multinational group, there can be tax advantages in creating a divisional structure, by locating some divisions in countries where tax advantages or subsidies can be obtained.

1.3 Disadvantages of decentralisation

Decentralisation can lead to problems.

- The divisional managers might put the interests of their division before the interests of the organisation as a whole. Taking decisions that benefit a division might have adverse consequences for the organisation as a whole. When this happens, there is a lack of 'goal congruence'.

- Top management may lose control over the organisation if they allow decentralisation without accountability. It may be necessary to monitor divisional performance closely. The cost of such a monitoring system might be high.

- It is difficult to find a satisfactory measure of historical performance for an investment centre that will motivate divisional managers to take the best decisions. For example, measuring divisional performance by Return on Investment (ROI) might encourage managers to make inappropriate long-term investment decisions.

- Economies of scale might be lost. For example, a company might operate with one finance director. If it divides itself into three investment centres, there might be a need for four finance directors – one at head office and one in each of the investment centres. Similarly there might be a duplication of other systems, such as accounting system and other IT systems.

1.4 Controllable profit and traceable profit

Profit is a key measure of the financial performance of a division. However, in measuring performance, it is desirable to identify:

- Costs that are controllable by the manager of the division

- Costs that are traceable to the division. These are controllable costs plus other costs directly attributable to the division over which the manager does not have control.

There may also be an allocation of general overheads, such as a share of head office costs.

In a divisionalised system, profit centres and investment centres often trade with each other, buying and selling goods and services. These are internal sales, priced at an internal selling price (a 'transfer price'). Reporting systems should identify external sales of the division and internal sales as two elements of the total revenue of the division.

	$
External sales	600,000
Internal sales	150,000
Total sales	750,000
Costs controllable by the divisional manager:	
Variable costs	230,000
Contribution	420,000
Controllable fixed costs	140,000
Profit attributable to the manager (controllable profit)	280,000
Costs traceable to the division but outside the manager's control	160,000
Profit traceable to the division	120,000
Share of general overheads	30,000
Net profit	90,000

Notes

- **Controllable profit** is used to assess the manager and is therefore sometimes called the **managerial evaluation**.

- **Traceable profit** is used to assess the performance of the division and is sometimes called the **economic evaluation**.

- The apportionment of general head office costs should be excluded from the analysis of the manager's performance and the division's performance.

These profit measures can be used with variance analysis, ratio analysis, return on investment, residual income and non-financial performance measurements to evaluate performance.

Return on Investment (ROI)

- Measuring ROI
- ROI and investment decisions
- Advantages and disadvantages of ROI for measuring performance

2 Return on Investment (ROI)

Return on investment (ROI) is a measure of the return on capital employed for an investment centre. It is also called the accounting rate of return (ARR).

It is often used as a measure of divisional performance for investment centres because:

- the manager of an investment centre is responsible for the profits of the centre and also the assets invested in the centre, and
- ROI is a performance measure that relates profit to the size of the investment.

Profit is not a suitable measure of performance for an investment centre. It does not make the manager accountable for his or her use of the net assets employed (the investment in the investment centre).

2.1 Measuring ROI

ROI is the profit of the division as a percentage of capital employed.
Performance measurement systems could use ROI to evaluate the performance of both the manager and the division.

Although ROI can be measured in different ways, the recommended measures are as follows:

- Managerial evaluation

  ROI = Controllable profit/divisions' capital employed × 100%

- Divisional/economic evaluation

  ROI = Traceable profit/divisions' capital employed × 100%

Where possible, the capital employed by the division should be analysed into:

- capital (assets less liabilities) controllable by the manager, and
- capital (assets and liabilities) traceable to the division.

Profit is usually measured as an accounting profit, after deduction of any depreciation charges on non-current assets.

2.2 ROI and investment decisions

When an investment centre manager's performance is evaluated by ROI, the manager will probably be motivated to make investment decisions that increase the division's ROI, and reject investments that would reduce ROI.

Example

A divisional manager is considering an investment in a new item of equipment that would cost $80,000.

The estimated life of the equipment is four years with no residual value.

The estimated profit before depreciation is as follows:

Year	$
1	20,000
2	25,000
3	35,000
4	25,000

The asset will be depreciated on a straight-line basis.

What would be the ROI on this investment? Would the investment centre manager decide to undertake this investment or not?

Answer

	$
Total 4-year profits before depreciation	105,000
Depreciation over four years	80,000
Total profit over 4 years	25,000
Average annual profit	6,250

Average asset carrying value over 4 years: $\dfrac{80,000+0}{2} = \$40,000$

$$\text{ROI (or investment ARR)} = \frac{6,250}{40,000} \times 100\% = 15.63\%$$

The manager might decide to undertake this investment if the average ROI of the division is less than 15.63%. By undertaking the investment, the average ROI over the next four years should increase, and the measured performance of the division would improve.

However, the manager is unlikely to undertake the investment if the average ROI of the investment centre is already higher than 15.63%. This is because over the life of the investment, the average ROI of the investment centre would fall.

The disadvantage of ROI for investment decisions

In practice, ROI (ARR) is an inappropriate basis for making investment decisions. Investment decisions should be based on DCF analysis.

 Example

The managers of investment centres A and B are considering new investments for their division. The following estimates have been prepared:

	Division A	Division B
Average investment (controllable investment)	$100,000	$100,000
Average annual profit after depreciation	$16,000	$11,000
Current controllable ROI of the division	18%	9%
Cost of capital of the company	13%	13%

Division A decision

Using ROI as a basis for the investment decision, Division A would reject their project.

- The project ROI is 16%

- The current ROI of the division is 18%. Investing in the project would reduce the division's ROI.

- However, the ROI of the project is higher than the company's cost of capital.

Division B decision

Using ROI as a basis for the investment decision, Division B would invest in their project.

- The project ROI is 11%.

- The current ROI of the division is 9%. Investing in the project would increase the division's ROI.

- However, the ROI of the project is lower than the company's cost of capital, and investing would almost certainly be undesirable because it would have a negative NPV.

The decision by Division A of whether or not to invest should be based on a DCF evaluation. There is insufficient information to calculate the project NPV.

Decisions using ROI are inappropriate because they do not make reference to the company's cost of capital.

2.3 Advantages and disadvantages of ROI for measuring performance

Advantages of using ROI

There are several advantages in using ROI as a measure of the performance of an investment centre.

- It relates the profit of the division to the capital employed, and the division manager is responsible for both profit and capital employed.

- ROI is a percentage measure and can be used to compare the performance of divisions of different sizes.

- It is an easily understood measure of financial performance.

- It focuses attention on capital as well as profit, and encourages managers to sell off unused assets and avoid excessive working capital (inventory and receivables).

Disadvantages of using ROI

There are also disadvantages in using ROI as a measure of the performance of an investment centre.

- As explained above, investment decisions might be affected by the effect they would have on ROI, and this is inappropriate for making investment decisions.

- There are different ways of measuring capital employed. ROI might be based on the net book value (carrying value) of the division at the beginning of the year, or at the end of the year, or the average for the year. Comparison of performance between different organisations is therefore difficult.

- Similarly, profit measurement may be influenced by the accounting policies of the division which may make comparisons difficult.

- When assets are depreciated, ROI will increase each year provided that annual profits are constant. The division's manager might not want to get rid of ageing assets, because ROI will fall if new (replacement) assets are purchased.

- ROI is an accounting measure of performance. An alternative system of performance measurement, such as a balanced scorecard approach, might be more appropriate.

> ### Residual income (RI)
>
> - Measuring residual income
> - Imputed interest (notional interest)
> - Residual income and investment decisions
> - Advantages and disadvantages of residual income

3 Residual income (RI)

Residual income (RI) is another way of measuring the performance of an investment centre.

Residual income = Divisional profit minus Imputed interest charge.

Notes

Divisional profit is an accounting measurement of profit, after depreciation charges are subtracted.

The interest charge is calculated by applying a cost of capital to the division's net investment (net assets). The appropriate measure of net investment is the average investment during the period.

3.1 Measuring residual income

Residual income is measured in either of the following ways:

Managerial evaluation

	$
Controllable profit	A
Less notional interest on average controllable investment	B
Controllable residual income	A – B

Divisional/economic evaluation

	$
Traceable profit	A
Less notional interest on average traceable investment	B
Divisional residual income	A – B

3.2 Imputed interest (notional interest)

Residual income is calculated by deducting an amount for imputed interest (also called notional interest) from the accounting profit for the division.

Imputed interest (notional interest) is the division's capital employed, multiplied by:

- the organisation's cost of borrowing, or
- the weighted average cost of capital of the organisation, or
- a special risk-weighted cost of capital to allow for the special business risk characteristics of the division. A higher interest rate would be applied to divisions with higher business risk.

3.3 Residual income and investment decisions

If investment centres are evaluated on the basis of residual income, their managers will be motivated to undertake new investments that increase residual income and to avoid new investments that would reduce residual income.

Residual income increases if the annual profit exceeds the notional interest charge.

- Investments with an average annual profit higher than the cost of capital are undertaken.
- Investments with an average annual profit lower than the cost of capital are rejected.

Example

The difference between the ROI and residual income can be illustrated by returning to the previous example.

	Division A	Division B
Average investment (controllable investment)	$100,000	$100,000
Average annual profit after depreciation	$16,000	$11,000
Current controllable ROI of the division	18%	9%
Cost of capital of the company	13%	13%

Division A decision

Using RI as a basis for the investment decision, Division A would invest in their project, because RI would increase.

	Division A
	$
Average annual profit after depreciation	16,000
Notional interest (13% × $100,000)	13,000
Increase in average annual RI	3,000

Average annual return on capital from the project (16%) is higher than the company's cost of capital. This is why the average annual residual income increases.

Division B decision

Using RI as a basis for the investment decision, Division B would not invest in their project, because RI would fall.

	Division B
	$
Average annual profit after depreciation	11,000
Notional interest (13% × $100,000)	13,000
Fall in average annual RI	(2,000)

Average annual return on capital from the project (11%) is less than the company's cost of capital. This is why the average annual residual income falls.

The decisions by Division A and Division B whether or not to invest should be based on a DCF evaluation. There is insufficient information to calculate the project NPV. However, using residual income for investment decisions is more likely than using ROI to result in a decision that agrees with the decision based on DCF analysis.

In the above example, it is almost certain that a DCF analysis would show that the Division B investment has a negative NPV. The decision using DCF would be to reject the investment, and the decision based on RI is consistent with this.

3.4 Advantages and disadvantages of residual income

Advantages of RI

There are several advantages in using RI as a measure of the performance of an investment centre.

- It relates the profit of the division to the capital employed, by charging an amount of notional interest on capital employed, and the division manager is responsible for both profit and capital employed.

- RI is a flexible measure of performance, because a different cost of capital can be applied to investments with different risk characteristics.

- As explained above, measuring performance with RI is more likely to encourage managers to make investment decisions that are consistent with DCF-based investment decisions.

Disadvantages of RI

There are also disadvantages in using RI as a measure of the performance of an investment centre.

- RI is an accounting-based measure, and suffers from the same problem as ROI in defining capital employed and profit.

- Its main weakness is that it is difficult to compare the performance of different divisions using RI. Larger divisions should earn a bigger RI. A small division making RI of $50,000 might actually perform much better than a much larger division whose RI is $100,000.

- RI is not easily understood by management, especially managers with little accounting knowledge.

Example

The performance of a divisional manager is evaluated by RI. The company's cost of capital is 10%.

The manager is considering whether to invest in a project to buy an asset costing $600,000. The asset would have a three-year life and no residual value. Cash flows from the investment would be $500,000 in each year.

Required

(a) Calculate the RI for each of the three years of the project, using net book value (NBV) at the start of the year as capital employed.

(b) Calculate the NPV of the project. Assume that cash flows occur at the end of each year.

Answer

(a) Residual income

	Year 1	Year 2	Year 3
	$	$	$
Opening net book value	600,000	400,000	200,000
Annual depreciation	200,000	200,000	200,000
	$	$	$
Profit	300,000	300,000	300,000
Notional interest (10%)	60,000	40,000	20,000
Residual income	240,000	260,000	280,000

(b) NPV

Year	Cash flow	Discount factor at 10%	Present value
	$		$
0	(600,000)	1.000	(600,000)
1 – 3	500,000	2.487	1,243,500
			+ 643,500

Divisional performance and depreciation
■ ROI or RI: the problem with depreciation

4 Divisional performance and depreciation

4.1 ROI or RI: the problem with depreciation

If straight-line depreciation is used and capital employed is based on carrying values (net book values) ROI and RI will rise over time if:

■ annual profits are constant and

■ assets are not replaced, and existing assets remain in use as they get older.

In the early years of an investment project, the ROI or RI might be very low. If a divisional manager is concerned about the effect that this would have on the division's ROI or RI for the next year or two, the manager might refuse to invest in the project. This is because performance in the next year or so might be much worse, even though the project might be expected to earn a high return over its full economic life.

 Example

Palace Division is a part of the Crystal Group. Its manager has the authority to invest in new capital expenditure, within limits set by head office. The senior management team of the division is considering an investment of $4.2 million. This would have a residual value of zero after four years. Net cash inflows from the investment would be $1.4million for each of the next four years.

The cost of capital for the Palace Division is 10%. It is the group's policy to use straight-line depreciation when measuring divisional profit.

For measurement purposes and reporting purposes, 'capital' is defined as the opening net book value at the start of each year.

Required

For this particular investment:

(a) Calculate residual income each year

(b) Calculate the Return on Investment each year

(c) Calculate the NPV of the investment

(d) State whether the decision would be in the best interests of the company if the manager makes the decision on the basis of the effect of the investment on:

   (i) RI or

   (ii) ROI.

Ignore taxation.

Answer

(a) Residual income

	Year 1	Year 2	Year 3	Year 4
	$000	$000	$000	$000
Opening net book value	4,200	3,150	2,100	1,050
Annual depreciation	1,050	1,050	1,050	1,050
	$	$	$	
Profit before depreciation	1,400	1,400	1,400	1,400
	1,050	1,050	1,050	1,050
	350	350	350	350
Notional interest (10%)	420	315	210	105
Residual income	(70)	35	140	245

The total residual income over the four years is $350,000 (profit of $1,400,000 minus notional interest charges of $1,050,000).

(b) Return on Investment

Capital is defined here as the value of the net assets at the beginning of the year.

	Year 1	Year 2	Year 3	Year 4
	$000	$000	$000	$000
Opening net book value	4,200	3,150	2,100	1,050
Annual depreciation	1,050	1,050	1,050	1,050
	$	$	$	
Profit before depreciation	1,400	1,400	1,400	1,400
	1,050	1,050	1,050	1,050
Profit	350	350	350	350
Return on investment (ROI)	8.3%	11.1%	16.7%	33.3%

The average return on investment = average annual profit/average investment = $350,000/$2,100,000 = 16.7%.

(c) NPV

Year		Cash flow	Discount factor at 10%	Present value
		$		$
0	Capital expenditure	4,200,000	1.000	4,200,000
1 - 4	Net cash flow	1,400,000	3.170	4,438,000
	Net present value			+ 238,000

(d) Ignoring risk and uncertainty in the forecast cash flows, the decision should be to undertake the capital investment, because the NPV is positive. In theory, undertaking the project will add to shareholders' wealth by this amount.

If the management of Palace Division are concerned about the short-term performance of the division, they might decide not to undertake the investment. This is because the ROI will be less than 10% in Year 1 and the residual income would be negative.

However, if the management team takes a longer-term view, and considers performance over the full four years, they would undertake the investment, because the average annual ROI on the new investment would be 16.7% and the average annual increase in residual income for the division would be $87,500.

Unfortunately, decision-making often focuses on the short term, and there is a possibility that the investment will not be undertaken in order to prevent a fall in ROI or residual income.

Conflicts with NPV

This previous example should demonstrate that on occasions there may be a conflict between NPV and ROI/RI.

NPV gives the correct decision under the assumption that we want to maximise shareholder wealth.

NPV cannot be used to assess historical performance, but ROI and residual income do not always indicate the most appropriate investment decision.

CHAPTER

16

Transfer pricing

Contents

Transfer pricing: purpose and objectives
■ Purpose of transfer pricing
■ Definition of a transfer price
■ The objectives of transfer pricing
■ The motivation of divisional managers
■ Goal congruence
■ Divisional autonomy

1 Transfer pricing: purpose and objectives

1.1 Purpose of transfer pricing

When an entity has a divisionalised structure, some of the divisions might supply goods or services to other divisions in the same entity.

■ One division sells the goods or services. This will be referred to as the 'selling division'.

■ Another division buys the goods or services. This will be referred to as the 'buying division'.

For accounting purposes, these internal transfers of goods or services are given a value. Transfers could be recorded at cost. However, when the selling division is a profit centre or investment centre, it will expect to make some profit on the sale.

1.2 Definition of a transfer price

A transfer price is the price at which goods or services are sold by one division within an entity to another division in the same entity. Internal sales are referred to as transfers, so the internal selling and buying price is the transfer price.

1.3 The objectives of transfer pricing

A decision has to be made about what the transfer price should be.

For the purpose of performance measurement and performance evaluation in a divisionalised organisation, it is appropriate that:

■ the selling division should earn some profit or return on sales to other divisions and

■ the buying division should pay a fair price for the goods or services that it buys from other divisions.

Transfer prices are decided by management. The objectives of transfer pricing should be to:

■ achieve goal congruence for the entity as a whole, and

- give autonomy (freedom to make decisions) to the managers of the profit centres or investment centres.

- enable the entity to measure the performance of the division in a fair way.

These objectives are often in conflict with each other.

1.4 The motivation of divisional managers

An assumption is that the managers of every profit centre will take decisions that maximise the profits of the division.

If every division maximises its profits, the profits of the entity as a whole will also be maximised.

However, a division might take action that maximises its own profit, but reduces the profits of another division. As a result, the profits of the entity as a whole might also be reduced.

1.5 Goal congruence

Every divisional manager should work towards the maximisation of the profits and returns of the entity as a whole. When every divisional manager has the same aim or goal, there is goal congruence.

- Transfer prices should therefore encourage divisional managers to take decisions that are in the best interests of the entity as a whole.

- Transfer prices should not encourage a divisional manager to take decisions that are against the interests of the entity as a whole and would reduce the profits of the entity.

1.6 Divisional autonomy

Autonomy is freedom of action and freedom to make decisions. Divisional managers should be free to make their own decisions. Autonomy should improve motivation of divisional managers.

For example, when transfer prices have been decided, the managers of all divisions within the entity should be free to decide:

- whether to sell their output to other divisions (internal transfers) or whether to sell them to external customers, if an external market exists for the output

- whether to buy their goods from another division (internal transfers) or whether to buy them from external suppliers, if an external market exists.

Divisional managers should be allowed to make their own choices. They should not have to be told what to do by senior management at head office.

If there is a conflict between the objectives of goal congruence and divisional autonomy, goal congruence should have priority. If divisional managers cannot agree to do what is best for the entity as a whole, they should be instructed what to do by senior management. However, this situation would be undesirable.

Ideally, transfer prices should be set so that divisional managers can agree on selling and buying between each other in a way that is in the best interests of all the divisions and the entity as a whole.

> ## The ideal transfer price
>
> - Assumptions
> - Market-based and cost-based transfer prices
> - The opportunity cost of transfers
> - Identifying the ideal transfer price

2 The ideal transfer price

The ideal transfer price is a price that will result in goal congruence and also allow the divisional managers autonomy to make their own decisions, without having to be told by head office what they must do.

The main problems arise when there is no external market for the goods (or services) that one division transfers to another. When an external market exists for goods or services that are also transferred internally, the market might be called an **external intermediate market**.

- The selling division can sell its goods into this market, instead of transferring them internally.
- Similarly the buying division can buy its goods from other suppliers in this market, instead of buying them internally from another division.

2.1 Assumptions

The following assumptions will be made:

- When there is an external intermediate market, divisional managers will decide between internal transfers and using the external market in a way that maximises the profits of their division.
- When there is no difference in profitability between internal transfers and selling or buying externally, the divisional managers should agree to transfer the goods internally.
- If the performance of the divisions and the divisional managers is based on divisional profitability, it is reasonable to expect that:
  - the selling division will earn some profit on internal transfers, and
  - the buying division will pay a fair price for internal transfers.

2.2 Market-based and cost-based transfer prices

As a general rule:

- when an external intermediate market does not exist for transferred goods, the transfer price will be based on cost
- when an external intermediate market does exist for transferred goods, the transfer price will be based on the external market price.

However, the situation is more complicated when:

■ there is a limit to production capacity in the selling division, or

■ there is a limit to sales demand in the external intermediate market.

In these circumstances, we need to consider the **opportunity costs** for the selling division of transferring goods internally instead of selling them externally.

2.3 The opportunity cost of transfers

The selling division and the buying division have opportunity costs of transferring goods internally when there is a shortage of capacity.

■ For the selling division, the opportunity cost of transferring goods internally to another division might include a loss of contribution and profit from not being able to sell goods externally in the intermediate market.

■ For the buying division, the opportunity cost of buying internally from another division is the price that it would have to pay for purchasing the items from external suppliers in the intermediate market.

Goal congruence is achieved when the transfer price is at a level where both the selling division and the buying division will want to do what is in the best interests of the entity as a whole, because it is also in the best interests of their divisions.

Ideal transfer prices must therefore take opportunity costs into consideration.

2.4 Identifying the ideal transfer price

The following rules should help you to identify the ideal transfer price in any situation:

■ **Step 1**. Begin by identifying the plan that maximises the profits of the entity as a whole. In other words, what is the goal congruence that we are trying to achieve?

■ **Step 2**. Having identified the plan that is in the best interests of the entity as a whole, identify the transfer price, or range of transfer prices, that will make the manager of the buying division want to work towards this plan. The transfer price must ensure that, given this transfer price, the profits of the division will be maximised by doing what is in the best interests of the entity as a whole.

■ **Step 3**. In the same way, having identified the plan that is in the best interests of the entity as a whole, identify the transfer price, or range of transfer prices, that will make the manager of the selling division want to work towards the same plan. Again, the transfer price must ensure that, given the transfer price, the profits of the division will be maximised by doing what is in the best interests of the entity as a whole.

These rules will be illustrated with a number of different examples and different situations.

Finding the ideal transfer price

- No external intermediate market
- An external intermediate market and no production limitations
- An external intermediate market and production limitations
- Transfer pricing and more than one limiting factors

3 Finding the ideal transfer price

The ideal transfer price depends on circumstances.

3.1 No external intermediate market

When there is no external intermediate market, the ideal transfer price is at cost or cost plus a contribution margin or profit margin for the selling division.

Example

An entity has two divisions, Division A and Division B. Division A makes a component X which is transferred to Division B. Division B uses component X to make end-product Y. Details of costs and selling price are as follows:

Division A	$
Cost of component X	
Variable cost	10
Fixed cost	8
Total cost	18

Division B	
Further processing costs	
Variable cost	4
Fixed cost	7
	11
Selling price per unit of product Y	40

The further processing costs of Division B do not include the cost of buying component X from Division A. One unit of component X goes into the production of one unit of Product Y.

Fixed costs in both divisions will be the same, regardless of the volume of production and sales.

Required

What is the ideal transfer price, or what is a range of prices that would be ideal for the transfer price?

Answer

Step 1

What is in the best interests of the entity as a whole?

The total variable cost of one unit of the end product, product Y, is $14 ($10 + $4). The sales price of product Y is $40. The entity therefore makes additional contribution of $26 for every unit of product Y that it sells.

It is in the best interests of the entity to maximise production and sales of product Y.

Step 2

What will motivate the buying division to buy as many units of component X as possible?

Division B will want to buy more units of component X provided that the division earns additional contribution from every unit of the component that it buys.

Division B	$
Selling price of Product Y	40
Variable further processing costs	4
	36

The opportunity cost of not buying units of component X, ignoring the transfer price, is $36 per unit. Division B should therefore be willing to pay up to $36 per unit for component X.

Step 3

What will motivate the selling division to make and transfer as many units of component X as possible?

Division A will want to make and sell more units of component X provided that the division earns additional contribution from every unit of the component that it sells.

The marginal cost of making and transferring a unit of component X is $10. Division A should therefore be willing to transfer as many units of component X as it can make (or Division B has the capacity to buy) if the transfer price is at least $10.

Ideal transfer price

The ideal transfer price is anywhere in the range $10 to $36.

In a similar way to pricing for the external market, Division A may be able to sell at marginal cost if there is excess capacity in the short-term. In the long-term, Division A will wish to cover fixed costs and make a profit. Depending on the profit target set by head office the required transfer price will be in somewhere in excess of $18. Division B will also wish to maximise profit. Whilst paying up to $36 per unit of component X will earn contribution. Division B will also have fixed costs to cover and will wish to make a profit. The realistic transfer price that would be agreed by both divisions may therefore be in a much narrower band and it may not be possible for both divisions to cover fixed costs. An element of negotiation will be required which may be difficult to resolve.

3.2 An external intermediate market and no production limitations

When there is an external intermediate market for the transferred item, a different situation applies, and if there are no production limitations in the selling division, the ideal transfer price is usually the external market price.

Example

An entity has two divisions P and Q. Division P makes a component X which it either transfers to division Q or sells in an external market. The costs of making one unit of component X are:

Component X	$
Variable cost	60
Fixed cost	30
Total cost	90

Division Q uses one unit of component X to make one unit of product Y, which it sells for $200 after incurring variable further processing costs of $25 per unit.

Required

What is the ideal transfer price or range of transfer prices, if the price of component X in the external intermediate market is:

(a) $140

(b) $58?

Answer

Step 1

What is in the best interests of the entity as a whole?

The entity will benefit by maximising the total contribution from external sales of component X and product Y.

If component X is not transferred by division P to Division Q, Division Q will have to buy units of component X in the external market. Every unit of component X transferred therefore reduces the need to purchase a unit externally.

Since the additional contribution from making and selling a unit of product Y is $175 ($200 – $25), a profit-maximising plan is to maximise the sales of division Q, and transfer component X from Division P to Division Q rather than sell component X externally.

Step 2

What will motivate the buying division to buy as many units of component X as possible from Division P?

Division Q will be prepared to buy component X from Division P as long as it is not more expensive than buying in the external market from another supplier. Division Q will be willing to buy internally if the transfer price is:

(a)   not more than $140 when the external market price is $140

(b)   not more than $58 when the external market price is $58.

Step 3

What will motivate the selling division to make and transfer as many units of component X as possible?

Division P should be prepared to transfer as many units of component X as possible to Division Q provided that its profit is no less than it would be if it sold component X externally.

Units transferred to division Q are lost sales to the external market; therefore there is an opportunity cost of transfer that division P will wish to include in the transfer price.

Component X: market price $140	$
Variable cost	60
Opportunity cost of lost external sale (140 – 60)	80
Total cost = minimum transfer price	140

Component X: market price $58	$
Variable cost	60
Opportunity cost of lost external sale (58 – 60)	(2)
Total cost = minimum transfer price	58

Ideal transfer price

The ideal transfer price is the maximum that the buying division is prepared to pay and the minimum that the selling division will want to receive. In both situations, the ideal transfer price is therefore the price in the external intermediate market.

When the external market price is $58, Division P is losing contribution by selling component X externally. It would also be cheaper for the entity as a whole to buy the component externally for $58 rather than make internally for a marginal cost of $60. Division P should consider ending its operations to produce component X.

3.3   An external intermediate market and production limitations

When there is an external intermediate market for the transferred item, and the selling division has a limitation on the number of units it can produce, the ideal transfer price should allow for the opportunity cost of the selling division. Every unit transferred means one less external sale.

Example

An entity consists of two divisions, Division A and Division B. Division A is working at full capacity on its machines, and can make either Product Y or Product Z, up to its capacity limitation. Both of these products have an external market.

The costs and selling prices of Product Y and Product Z are:

	Product Y	Product Z
	$	$
Selling price	15	17
Variable cost of production	10	7
Variable cost of sale	1	2
Contribution per unit	4	8

The variable cost of sale is incurred on external sales of the division's products. This cost is not incurred for internal sales/transfers from Division A to Division B.

To make one unit of Product Y takes exactly the same machine time as one unit of Product Z.

Division B buys Product Y, which it uses to make an end product.

The profit of the entity will be maximised by making and selling as many units as possible of Division B's end product.

Required

What is the ideal transfer price or range of transfer prices?

 Answer

Step 1

What is in the best interests of the entity as a whole?

This is stated in the example. The entity wants to make and sell as many units of the end product of Division B as follows. It is not clear, however, whether it is better for Division B to buy Product Y externally or to buy internally from Division A.

If division A does not make Product Y, it can make and sell Product Z instead. Product Z earns a higher contribution per unit of machine time, the limiting factor in Division A.

Step 2

What would motivate the buying division to buy as many units of Product Y as possible from Division A?

Division B will be prepared to buy Product Y from Division A as long as it is not more expensive than buying in the external market from another supplier.

Division B will be willing to buy Product Y internally if the transfer price is $15 or less.

Step 3

What would motivate the selling division to make and transfer as many units of Product Y as possible?

The selling division will only be willing to make Product Y instead of Product Z if it earns at least as much contribution as it would from making Z and selling it externally. (In this situation, the division can make as many units of Z as it can make of Y, and Product Z earns a higher contribution).

Product Y	$
Variable cost	10
Opportunity cost of lost external sale (17 − 7 − 2)	8
Total cost = minimum transfer price	18

Ideal transfer price/ideal production and selling plan

Division B will not want to pay more than $15 for transfers of Product Y; otherwise it will buy Product Y externally.

Division A will want to receive at least $18 for transfers of Product Y; otherwise it will prefer to make and sell Product Z, not Product Y.

The ideal solution is for Division B to buy Product Y externally at $15 and for Division A to make and sell Product Z.

Example

An entity consists of two divisions, Division A and Division B. Division A is operating at full capacity making Product X, for which there is an external market. The variable cost of making one unit of Product X is $70, and the sale price of Product X in the external market is $100 per unit.

Division B needs one unit of Product X to manufacture another product, Product Y. The variable conversion costs and further processing costs in Division B are $29 per unit of Product Y, and one unit of Product Y requires one unit of Product X as a component. The external selling price of Product Y is $140 per unit.

An external supplier has offered to sell units of Product Y to Division B for $103 per unit.

Required

(a) Identify the ideal transfer price.

(b) Calculate the contribution per unit for each Division and for the entity as a whole if this transfer price is used.

(c) Suggest with reasons whether this transfer price provides a fair measure of divisional performance.

Answer

Step 1

What is in the best interests of the entity as a whole?

For each additional unit of Product Y that division B makes and sells, the additional contribution for the entity is $41 ($140 – $29 – 70). The entity makes more contribution from making and selling Product Y than from selling Product X externally.

The production plan that will optimise the profit for the entity as a whole is for Division A to make units of Product X and transfer them to Division B.

Step 2

What would motivate the buying division to buy as many units of Product X as possible from Division A?

Division B will not want to pay more to Division A for Product X than the price it has been offered by an external supplier, $103. However, Division B can presumably find another supplier who is willing to offer the current market price of $100, and the maximum price that Division B should pay ought to be $100.

Step 3

What would motivate the selling division to make and transfer as many units of Product X as possible?

Product Y	$
Variable cost	70
Opportunity cost of lost external sale (100 – 70)	30
Total cost = minimum transfer price	100

Ideal transfer price

The ideal transfer price is $100 per unit of Product X.

Contribution per unit

	Division A	Division B	Entity as a whole
	$/unit	$/unit	$/unit
External sale	-	140	140
Internal sale	100	-	-
Sales revenue	100	140	140
Transfer: purchase cost	-	100	-
Other variable costs	70	29	99
Total variable costs	70	129	99
Contribution per unit	30	11	41

Comment

The contribution per unit for each division is a fair representation of the economic contribution of each division to the profitability of the entity as a whole.

The transfer price will achieve goal congruence and provides an appropriate measurement of divisional performance.

3.4 Transfer pricing and more than one limiting factors

The selling division might have more than one limiting factor that restricts its output capacity. When this happens, it might be necessary to use a linear programming model to identify the shadow price (also called the dual price) of each of the limiting factors.

A shadow price is the amount of contribution that will be lost for each reduction of one unit in the available scarce resource. (It is also the extra contribution that could be earned for each extra unit of the scarce resource that is available).

For example, suppose that direct labour is a scarce resource. There are only 2,000 hours available each week, and the shadow price of direct labour is $5 per hour. This means that the maximum possible contribution will be reduced by $5 if there are only 1,999 hours available, and will be reduced by $500 if there are only 1,900 hours available each week, and so on.

The ideal transfer price should include the shadow prices of any scarce resources used in the transferred product.

Example

An entity consists of two divisions, Division A and Division B. Division A can make three products, Product P, Product Q and Product R.

Product P and Product Q are sold in an external market. Their variable cost and selling price are:

	Product P	Product Q
	$/unit	$/unit
Selling price	20	28
Variable cost	10	16
Contribution	10	12

There is a limited supply of labour and machine time each week in Division A. Labour hours are restricted to 3,000 each week and machine hours are restricted to 1,000 hours each week.

Product R does not have an external market. Units of Product R are needed by Division B to go into the manufacture of one of its products.

One unit of Product R requires:

- 1 labour hour
- 2 machine hours.

The variable costs of one unit of Product R, including the direct labour cost, is $16 per unit.

A linear programming model has been used to calculate that if Division A makes only Product P and Product Q, and does not make any units of Product R, it would make 500 units of P and 500 units of Q each week. Total contribution would be $13,000. The shadow price of labour would be $3 per hour and the shadow price of machine time would be $4 per hour.

Required

What should be the transfer price for each unit of Product R?

 Answer

From the point of view of the entity as a whole, it is only worth making and transferring units of Product R if it is more profitable for Division B to use Product R than for Division A to make and sell Products P and Q.

The ideal transfer price should therefore include the shadow price of the labour and machine hours that units of Product R would require.

Transfer price of Product R	$/unit
Variable cost of making R in Division A	16
Shadow price of labour (1 hour × $3)	3
Shadow price of machine time (2 hours × $4)	8
Transfer price	27

Transfer pricing in practice
■ Transfer price at market price
■ Transfer price at full cost plus
■ Transfer price at variable cost plus or incremental cost plus
■ Two-part transfer prices
■ Dual pricing
■ Negotiated transfer prices
■ Transfer pricing in multinational groups

4   Transfer pricing in practice

Transfer prices might be decided by head office and imposed on each division. Alternatively, the managers of each division might have the autonomy to negotiate transfer prices with each other.

Ideally, the decided transfer prices meet the two objectives of goal congruence and divisional autonomy.

In practice, transfer prices might be agreed and expressed in one of the following ways.

4.1   Transfer price at market price

A transfer price might be the external selling/buying price for the item in an external intermediate market. This price is only possible when an external market exists.

If the selling division would incur some extra costs if it sold its output externally rather than transferred it internally to another division, the transfer price might be reduced below market price, to allow for the variable costs that would be saved by the selling division. This is very common as the selling division may save costs of packaging and warranties. Distribution costs may also be cheaper and there will be no need for advertising.

Advantages of market price as the transfer price

Market price is the ideal transfer price when there is an external market. A transfer price below this amount will make the manager of the selling division want to sell externally, and a price above this amount will make the manager of the buying division want to buy externally.

Transferring at market price also encourages efficiency in the supplying division, which must compete with the external competition.

Disadvantages of market price as the transfer price

The current market price is not appropriate as a transfer price when:

■ the current market price is only temporary, and caused by short-term conditions in the market, or

■ there is imperfect competition in the external market, and the selling division faces a downward-sloping demand curve when it sells its output into the market. The opportunity cost of transferring output internally is not the market price, because the selling price would have to be reduced in order to sell the extra units.

It may also be difficult to identify exactly what the external market price is. Products from rival companies may be different in quality, availability may not be so certain and there may be different levels of service backup.

4.2 Transfer price at full cost plus

A transfer price might be expressed as the full cost of production plus a margin for profit for the selling division.

Standard full costs should be used, **not actual full costs**. This will prevent the selling division from increasing its profit by incurring higher costs per unit.

Full cost plus might be suitable when there is no external intermediate market.

However, there are disadvantages in using full cost rather than variable cost to decide a transfer price.

■ The fixed costs of the selling division become variable costs in the transfer price of the buying division. This might lead to decisions by the buying division manager that are against the best interests of the entity as a whole. This is because a higher variable cost may lead to the buying division choosing to set price at a higher level which would lose sales volume.

■ The size of the profit margin or mark-up is likely to be arbitrary.

4.3 Transfer price at variable cost plus or incremental cost plus

A transfer price might be expressed as the variable cost of production plus a margin for profit for the selling division.

Standard variable costs should be used, **not actual variable costs**. This will prevent the selling division from increasing its profit by incurring higher variable costs per unit.

Variable cost plus might be suitable when there is no external intermediate market. It is probably more suitable in these circumstances than full cost plus, because variable cost is a better measure of opportunity cost.

Another type of cost plus transfer price is **incremental cost plus**. This might be used when making and transferring units results in an increase in total fixed costs (the fixed costs are stepped costs).

Incremental cost =

Variable cost + Share of incremental fixed costs + Profit margin

A major disadvantage with this approach is that the selling division will make a loss unless the mark up is sufficient to cover fixed costs and provide an acceptable profit.

The main problem with cost based transfer prices is therefore:

- Variable cost based transfer prices will lead to goal congruence but are unlikely to be chosen by a selling division because it will make a loss

- Full cost based transfer prices will not lead to goal congruence but are more likely to be chosen by the selling division.

How can head office encourage goal congruence without imposing a transfer pricing system which would be seen as unfair by the selling division?

There are two main methods

- Two-part transfer prices

- Dual pricing

Alternatively transfer prices could be negotiated.

4.4 Two-part transfer prices

With two-part transfer prices, the selling division charges the buying division for units transferred in two ways:

- a standard variable cost per unit transferred, plus

- a fixed charge in each period.

The fixed charge is a lump sum charge at the end of each period. The fixed charge would represent a share of the contribution from selling the end product, which the supplying division has helped to earn. Alternatively, the charge could be seen as a charge to the buying division for a share of the fixed costs of the selling division in the period.

Using this method, divisions would be encouraged to trade at variable cost thus ensuring goal congruent decisions. The fixed charge would also ensure that a fair profit is made by each division.

4.5 Dual pricing

In some situations, two divisions might be unable to agree a transfer price, because there is no transfer price at which the selling division will want to transfer internally or the buying division will want to buy internally. However, the profits of the entity as a whole would be increased if transfers did occur.

These situations are rare.

However, when they occur, head office might find a solution to the problem by agreeing to dual transfer prices.

- the selling division sells at one transfer price, and
- the buying division buys at a lower transfer price.

There are two different transfer prices. The transfer price for the selling division should be high enough to motivate the divisional manager to transfer more units to the buying division. Similarly, the transfer price for the buying division should be low enough to motivate the divisional manager to buy more units from the selling division.

In the accounts of the entity, the transferred goods are:

- sold by the selling division to head office and
- bought by the buying division from head office.

The loss from the dual pricing is a cost for head office, and treated as a head office overhead expense.

However, dual pricing can be complicated and confusing. It also requires the intervention of head office and therefore detracts from divisional autonomy.

4.6 Negotiated transfer prices

A negotiated transfer price is a price that is negotiated between the managers of the profit centres.

The divisional managers are given the autonomy to agree on transfer prices. Negotiation might be a method of identifying the ideal transfer price in situations where an external intermediate market does not exist.

An **advantage** of negotiation is that if the negotiations are honest and fair, the divisions should be willing to trade with each other on the basis of the transfer price they have agreed.

Disadvantages of negotiation are as follows:

- The divisional managers might be unable to reach agreement. When this happens, management from head office will have to act as judge or arbitrator in the case.
- The transfer prices that are negotiated might not be fair, but a reflection of the bargaining strength or bargaining skills of each divisional manager.

4.7 Transfer pricing in multinational groups

Multinational companies have subsidiaries in different countries for many reasons. Each subsidiary will be treated as a profit centre or an investment centre within the group. These subsidiaries may trade with each other, exchanging goods and services. When they do, a transfer price must be agreed.

The same broad principles already described in this chapter should apply to transfer pricing within multinationals. When deciding a transfer price for transfers between subsidiaries in different countries, the following additional factors may be relevant:

- taxation
- import duties
- currency fluctuations
- repatriation of funds

Taxation

The taxation rules in each country, and tax rules relating to the pricing of transfers between group companies, may affect the choice of transfer prices. There may be a transfer price that will minimise the tax cost for the group as a whole, when there are differing rates of tax in the different countries.

- A multinational might choose to locate a selling division in a country with a low marginal rate of tax and a buying division in a country with a high marginal rate of tax.
- If the transfer price is high, the selling division will make high profits and the buying division will make low profits.
- The total tax charge for the group as a whole can be reduced, because the high profits are taxed at a low rate and the high tax rate is applied only to low profits.

However, anti-avoidance legislation exists to prevent companies from using transfer pricing to move profits from subsidiaries in high-tax countries to subsidiaries in low-tax countries.

Import duties

A transfer price may be kept low in order to minimise the import duty or tariff payable on transfers to another country. However, there may be anti-avoidance legislation to prevent international companies from using transfer prices to minimise their payments of import duties.

Currency fluctuations

Transfers will be priced in one currency, and this will expose the investment centres to the risk of losses from adverse currency movements. A group should give careful consideration to the currency or currencies for pricing transfers. The problem of currency exposures is particularly severe when the exchange rate between the domestic currencies of the two investment centres is volatile and subject to large movements. Adverse movements in an exchange rate could wipe out an investment centre's trading profit on transfers.

Repatriation of funds

Decisions about transfer prices may also need to take account of foreign exchange restrictions in the country of one of its investment centres. The aim should be to avoid having surplus funds tied up in a country from which they cannot be repatriated.

 Example

The marginal rate of tax in country A is 30% and the marginal rate of tax in country B is 50%. A multinational company locates a supplying division in country A and the buying division in country B.

If the transfer price is made higher, the total tax charge for the group will be reduced by 20% for each $1 of goods transferred.

However the taxation authorities in many countries are aware of the possibilities for tax avoidance. The Organisation for Economic and Social Development in 1995 produced guidelines stating that transfers should be at 'arm's length' and the transfer prices used should be prices that would be negotiated between two unrelated parties.

Practice questions

Contents		
		Page

1   HEN

HEN has a single production process, for which the following costs have been estimated for the period ending 31st December Year 7:

	$
Material receipt and inspection costs	31,200
Power costs	39,000
Material handling costs	27,300

HEN makes three products - X, Y and Z. These products are made by the same group of employees, using power drills. The employees are paid $8 per hour.

The following budgeted information has been obtained for the period ending 31st December Year 7:

	Product X	Product Y	Product Z
Production quantity (units)	2,000	1,500	800
Batches of material	10	5	15
For each unit of product:			
Direct material (metres)	5	6	2.5
Direct material cost ($)	4	3	6
Direct labour (minutes)	24	40	60
Number of power drill operations (per unit)	8	4	5

Overhead costs are currently absorbed into the cost of production units using an absorption rate per direct labour hour. A factory-wide absorption rate is used for work in all the production departments.

An activity based costing investigation has revealed that the cost drivers for the overhead costs are as follows:

- Material receipt and inspection: number of batches of material

- Power: number of power drill operations

- Material handling: quantity of material (metres) handled.

Required

Prepare a summary of the budgeted production cost per unit for each of the products X, Y and Z for the period ending 31 December Year 7:

(a)   using the existing method for the absorption of overhead costs, and

(b)   using an approach based on activity based costing, and the information available about cost drivers.

2   Lard Company

Lard Company is a warehousing and distribution company. It receives and stores products from customers, and then re-packs them for distribution as required. There are three customers for whom the service is provided – Customer A, Customer B and Customer C. The products stored and re-packaged for all three customers are similar in nature and size, but some are more fragile than others and break more easily. These have to be packaged more carefully.

Basic budget information has been gathered for the year to 31st December 20X6 and is shown in the following table:

	Products handled
	units
Customer A	30,000
Customer B	45,000
Customer C	25,000
	Costs
	$000
Packaging materials (See note)	1,950
Labour:	
basic pay	350
overtime pay	30
Occupancy costs	500
Administration and management costs	60

Note

Packaging materials are used in re-packing each unit of product for Customer A, Customer B and Customer C in the ratio 1:2:3 respectively. This ratio is linked to the relative fragility of the goods for each customer. It applies to the cost of packaging materials but not to the costs of labour and overhead.

Additional information has been obtained so that unit costs can be prepared for each of the three customers using an activity based costing approach. The additional information for the year to 31st December 20X6 has been estimated as follows:

(1) Labour and overhead costs have been identified as attributable to each of three work centres: receipt and inspection, storage, and packing as follows:

(2)

	Cost allocation proportions		
	Receipt and inspection	**Storage**	**Packing**
	%	%	%
Labour:			
Basic pay	20	10	70
Occupancy cost	20	60	20
Administration cost	40	10	50
Labour: overtime pay	$15,000	$6,250	$8,750

(3) A study has shown that the fragility of different goods affects the receipt and inspection time needed for the products for each customer. Storage required is related to the average size of the basic incoming product units from each customer. The re-packing of goods for distribution is related to the complexity of packaging required by each customer. The relevant requirements per unit of product for each customer have been evaluated as follows:

	Customer A	**Customer B**	**Customer C**
Receipt and inspection (minutes)	6	9	15
Storage (square metres)	0.3	0.3	0.3
Packing (minutes)	36	45	60

Required

(a) Calculate the average cost per unit of packaged products for each customer using each of the following methods:

(i) Ignoring the ABC study, calculate a cost per unit using traditional absorption costing.

(ii) Taking an activity based costing approach, using the information provided.

(b) Suggest ways in which activity based costing might improve product costing and cost control for Lard Company.

3 LC Company

LC Company has total budgeted production overheads for next year of $816,000 and has traditionally absorbed overheads on a machine hour basis. It makes two products, Product V and Product W.

	Product V	Product W
Direct material cost per unit	$20	$60
Direct labour cost per unit	$50	$40
Machine time per unit	3 hours	4 hours
Annual production	6,000 units	4,000 units

Required

(a) Calculate the product cost for each of the two products on the assumption the firm continues to absorb overhead costs on a machine hour basis.

(b) The firm is considering changing to an activity based costing (ABC) system and has identified the following information:

	Product V	Product W
Number of setups	18	32
Number of purchase orders	48	112
Overhead cost analysis	$	
Machine-related overhead costs	204,000	
Setup related overhead costs	280,000	
Purchasing-related overhead costs	332,000	
Total production overheads	816,000	

You are required to calculate the unit cost for each of the two products on the assumption that the firm changes to an ABC system, using whatever assumptions you consider appropriate.

(c) Suggest how ABC analysis could be useful for measuring performance and improving profitability.

4 Customer profitability

PQR Company sells a range of five products. Budgeted annual data for sales and costs are as follows:

Product	Selling price	Variable cost
	$	$
A	3.60	2.40
B	2.50	2.00
C	4.00	2.80
D	2.40	1.50
E	6.00	4.00

Budgeted total annual sales are:

Product	Annual sales
	units
A	100,000
B	150,000
C	120,000
D	180,000
E	80,000

The products are sold to four different types or category of customer, as follows:

% of annual sales

	Category of customer			
Product	C1	C2	C3	C4
A	10%	20%	20%	50%
B	40%	-	30%	30%
C	10%	20%	10%	60%
D	30%	10%	20%	40%
E	20%	-	20%	60%

Rebates on sales

At the end of each year, the company will pay rebates to Category 3 and Category 4 customers, as follows:

- Category 3 customers: rebate = 5% of annual sales
- Category 4 customers: rebate = 10% of annual sales.

Fixed costs

Budgeted total fixed costs for the year are $465,000, analysed as follows:

	$
Delivery costs	250,000
Order processing costs	105,000
Cost of promotion events	30,000
	385,000
Other fixed costs	80,000
	465,000

The company operates an activity based costing system. Relevant budgeted data relating to activities is as follows:

	Category of customer			
	C1	C2	C3	C4
Number of deliveries	40	80	50	100
Number of orders	30	70	50	60
Number of promotion events	0	0	2	10
Average km per delivery	100	200	300	150

The cost drivers for each activity are:

■ Delivery: kilometres (km)

■ Order processing: number of orders

■ Promotion events: number of promotion events

■ The other fixed costs are general fixed costs, and are not allocated to activities, products or customers.

Required

Using activity based costing, prepare a statement of budgeted customer profitability, for each category of customer.

5 Backflush

Transactions for the year for AYZ are as follows:

Purchases of raw materials	$5,000,000
Conversion costs	$3,000,000
Finished goods manufactured	100,000 units
Sales	98,000 units at $100 per unit

There was no inventory at the beginning of the year. The cost per unit is $80, consisting of $50 per unit for materials and $30 per unit for conversion costs.

Required

Show the book-keeping entries in the cost accounting system using backflush accounting, with two trigger points.

6 Throughput

A company manufactures two products, product X and product Y, on the same machines. Sales demand for the products exceeds the machine capacity of the company's production department. The potential sales demand in each period is for 8,000 units of Product X and 12,000 units of Product Y. Sales prices cannot be increased due to competition from other firms in the market. The maximum machine capacity in the production department is 32,000 hours in each period.

The following cost and profitability estimates have been prepared:

	Product X	Product Y
	$	$
Sales price	22	27
Direct materials	10	9
Direct labour and variable overhead	6	11
Contribution per unit	6	7
Machine hours per unit	1.5 hours	2 hours

Fixed costs in each period are $90,000.

Required

(a)   Using marginal costing principles, calculate the profit-maximising output in each period, and calculate the amount of profit.

(b)   Explain how throughput accounting differs from marginal costing in its approach to maximising profit.

(c)   Use throughput accounting to calculate the throughput accounting ratio for Product X and for Product Y. You should assume that the direct labour cost and variable overhead cost in your answer to part (a) is fixed in the short term.

(d)   Using throughput accounting principles, calculate the profit-maximising output in each period, and calculate the amount of profit.

7   Throughput ratio

Dust Company exports cases to Spain. Each pallet of cases costs $2,000 in material costs and are sold for $3,000. Production and sales are limited by a shortage of highly trained quality control inspectors. Only 200 inspection hours are available per week. Every pallet is inspected and an inspection takes 30 minutes.
Other factory costs are $300,000 per week.

Required

Calculate the throughput accounting ratio.

8   Four products

A company makes four products, W, X, Y and Z, using the same single item of direct material in the manufacture of all the products. Budgeted data for the company is as follows:

Product	W	X	Y	Z
Annual sales demand (units)	4,000	4,000	6,000	3,000
	£	£	£	£
Direct materials cost	5.0	4.0	8.00	6.00
Direct labour cost	4.0	6.0	3.00	5.00
Variable overhead	1.0	1.5	0.75	1.25
Fixed overhead	8.0	12.0	6.00	10.00
Full cost	18.0	23.5	17.75	22.25
Sales price	50.0	31.5	59.75	54.25
Profit per unit	32.0	8.0	42.00	32.00

Due to restricted supply, only £78,000 of direct materials will be available during the year.

Required

Identify the quantities of production and sales of each product that would maximise annual profit.

8 Limiting factors

(a) Company X manufactures four liquids: A, B, C and D. The selling price and unit cost details for these products are as follows:

	Liquid A	Liquid B	Liquid C	Liquid D
	£ per litre	£ per litre	£ per litre	£ per litre
Selling price	100	110	120	120
Costs:				
Direct materials	24	30	16	21
Direct labour (£6/hour)	18	15	24	27
Direct expenses	0	0	3	0
Variable overhead	12	10	16	18
Fixed overhead (note 1)	24	20	32	36
Total cost per litre	78	75	91	102
Profit per litre	22	35	29	18

Note 1

Fixed overhead is absorbed on the basis of labour hours, based on a budget of 1,600 hours per quarter (three months).

During the next three months the number of direct labour hours is expected to be limited to 1,345 hours. The same labour is used for all products.

The marketing director has identified the maximum demand for each of the four products during the next three months as follows:

Liquid A   200 litres
Liquid B   150 litres
Liquid C   100 litres
Liquid D   120 litres

No stock is held at the beginning of the period that could be used to satisfy demand in the period.

Required

(i) Determine the number of litres of liquids A, B, C and D to be produced and sold in the next three months in order to maximise profits.

(ii) Calculate the profit that this would yield.

(b) Suppose that a contract has been made before the beginning of the period by Company X and one of its customers, Company Y. Company X has agreed to supply Company Y with supply 20 litres of each A, B, C and D during the three month period.

This sales demand from Company Y is included in the demand levels shown above in part (a) of the question.

Required

(i)   Given the contract with Company Y, determine the number of litres of liquids A, B, C and D to be produced and sold in the next three months in order to maximise profits, if the maximum number of labour hours remain 1,345 hours for the period.

(ii)   Calculate the profit that this would yield.

9   Shortages

An engineering company has been experiencing problems with restricted availability of resources. The company manufactures a variety of casings. It makes four types of casing. Each casing requires the same bought-in component and some high-grade steel. The standard costs for the four types of casing are as follows:

Casing	A	B	C	D
	$	$	$	$
Steel	250	500	190	390
Bought-in component	50	50	50	50
Direct labour	60	60	50	100
Variable production costs	40	50	40	50
Fixed production costs	180	240	150	270
Selling and administration costs	145	225	120	215
Profit	35	55	30	55
Selling price	760	1,180	630	1,130

All the selling and administration costs are fixed and the same single component is used for each of the four products. Direct labour is paid $8 per standard hour and each member of the workforce is capable of producing any of the casings.

The company's main customer has ordered 30 units of Casing A, 20 units of B, 30 units of C and 20 units of D for production and delivery in the next month. Senior management have agreed that this order should be treated as a priority order and that these casings must be manufactured and delivered to the customer next month. This is necessary to maintain the goodwill of the customer. It is estimated that this order represents 10% of the total demand next month for each type of casing.

The company operates a just in time system, and has no inventories of steel, components or finished goods.

Required

If the aim is to maximise profit for the month, establish the production and selling plan for the company next month in each of the following situations:

(a)   **Situation 1**. Supplies of steel are limited to $250,000.

(b)   **Situation 2**. Only 400 bought-in components are available from suppliers.

(c)   **Situation 3**. A labour dispute restricts available productive labour hours in the month to 2,125.

(d) **Situation 4**. A labour dispute restricts available productive labour hours in the month to 2,125; but the manufacture of any quantities of the four casings could be sub-contracted to and outside supplier. The cost of buying the casings externally would $475, $705, $380 and $640 for Casing A, Casing B, Casing C and Casing D respectively. In addition, it should be assumed that the major customer insists that its order is completed by the company itself and the manufacture should not be sub-contracted.

Each of the restrictions on production should be treated independently, as four different situations.

10 Proglin

(a) Proglin is a manufacturing company. It makes and sells two versions of a product, Mark 1 and Mark 2. The two products are made from the same direct materials and by the same direct labour employees.

The following budgeted data has been prepared for next year:

	Mark 1	Mark 2
Direct materials per unit	£2	£4
Direct labour hours per unit	3 hours	2 hours
Maximum sales demand	5,000 units	unlimited
Contribution per unit	£10 per unit	£15 per unit

Direct materials and direct labour will be in restricted supply next year, as follows:

	Maximum available
Direct materials	£24,000
Direct labour hours	18,000 hours

There is no stock of finished goods at the beginning of the year.

Required

Use the graphical method of linear programming to identify the quantities of Mark 1 and Mark 2 that should be made and sold during the year in order to maximise profit and contribution.

Calculate the amount of contribution that will be earned.

(b) Suppose that the maximum available amount of direct materials next year is £24,001, not £24,000.

Required

(i) Identify the quantities of Mark 1 and Mark 2 that should be made and sold during the year in order to maximise profit and contribution.

(ii) Calculate the amount of contribution that will be earned.

(iii) Compare the total contribution you have calculated in (b) with the total contribution that you calculated in (a), to calculate the shadow price per £1 of direct materials.

11   Price

A company has developed a new product that it wishes to introduce to the market. The cost per unit is expected to be as follows, assuming annual sales of 40,000 units.

	£
Direct materials:	
Material M1 (2 litres at £15)	30
Material M2 (0.5 litres at £8)	4
Direct labour (3 hours at £10)	30
Fixed overheads (3 hours at £12)	36
Full cost	100

It has been company policy to price products to achieve a profit of 16.67% (one-sixth) on the sales price.

Required

(a)   Calculate the selling price that would be charged if the company applies its normal pricing policy.

(b)   If the company decided to price products at marginal cost plus, what mark-up on the marginal cost would be required to obtain the same selling price as in (a)?

(c)   Suggest two other pricing strategies that might be applied to decide a selling price for the product.

12   Marginal

The marketing director of a company selling home entertainment products has estimated that at a sales price of $250, a new product (the Blaze) will sell 400,000 units in the next year. He also estimates that for every $10 increase or reduction in price, annual sales will fall or increase by 20,000 units below or above this 400,000 units level.

The production engineer has estimated that the costs of making the Blaze will be a variable cost of $210 per unit sold and annual fixed costs of $20 million.

You are given the following formulae:

Price function: $P_q = P_0 - bq$

Total revenue function (TR): $P_0 q - bq^2$

Marginal revenue function (MR): $P_0 - 2bq$

where

P_0 = Price at zero units of demand

P_q = Price at q units of demand

b = relationship between price and demand

q = units of annual demand

Required

(i) Calculate the price at which the Blaze should be sold in order to maximise profit for the year.

(ii) Calculate the quantity of units that will be sold in the year, if the marketing director's forecast is correct.

(iii) Calculate the annual profit that will be made from selling the Blaze.

13 MC = MR

A business entity has estimated that it faces the following price/quantity relationship:

Sales price	Quantity demanded
$	Units
50	1,000
30	2,000
10	3,000

Required

(a) Calculate a formula for the demand curve, assuming that the demand curve can be drawn as a straight line on a graph.

(b) Find the formula for total revenue.

(c) If the marginal cost per unit is $8, calculate the price at which contribution is maximised.

14 Snap Company

Snap Company makes product SP8 in department C. For the year commencing 1st January 20X7 the following budget has been formulated for department C:

	$000
Direct costs	
Materials	60
Labour	40
	100
Production overheads	100
Full production cost	200
Administrative and marketing overheads	50
Full cost of sale	250
Profit	50
Revenue (see note)	300

Note: From budgeted sales of 20,000 units.

Production overheads are absorbed on the basis of 100% of direct costs. However, half of these costs are fixed, and the other half are variable. It is assumed that they vary with the cost of materials.

The administrative and marketing overheads are based on 25% of factory costs and do not vary within wide ranges of activity. A profit margin of 20% is applied to the full cost of sale. This also results in a price that appears to be fair to customers.

Halfway through the year to 31st December 20X7, it became clear that actual sales of SP8 would be 25% below budget. At about the same time that this shortfall in sales became evident, a customer asked about buying 5,000 units of a simplified version of product SP8. If Snap Company were to produce this simplified model for the customer, the direct material and labour costs would be lower. It is estimated that materials costing $12,000 and direct labour of $8,000 would be required to produce the 5,000 units. As the production could take place within the firm's existing capacity, fixed costs would not be affected.

Required

(a)   Calculate the prices that Snap Company should quote to the customer for each unit of the simplified product, assuming that the following pricing policies are applied:

(i)   Full cost plus pricing, on the current basis.

(ii)   A price that would enable the company to achieve its original budgeted profit.

(b)   Give your advice on the price that should be quoted to the customer.

15   Bridge Company

The following costs per unit relate to the production and sale of 20,000 of a product by Bridge Company, for the financial year that has just ended:

	$ per unit
Direct material	30
Direct labour	10
Overheads:	
Variable	10
Fixed	10
	60

It has been estimated that major cost increases will apply to the following year, assuming that production and sales volumes are still 20,000 units.

	Increase
Direct material	20%
Direct labour	5%
Variable overhead	5%
Fixed overhead	10%

It would be possible to substitute a cheaper grade of direct material, allowing the cost of direct materials to be $31.25 per unit. However, a rejection rate of 5% will arise. (There are currently no rejected units.) This would require an additional annual inspection cost of $30,000.

In the past, the selling price has been set using a mark-up of 50% on full cost and a price of $90 per unit was charged in the current year. However, the sales manager has estimated the price/demand relationships as follows:

Price	$80	$84	$88	$90	$92	$96	$100
Demand (000s units)	25	23	21	20	19	17	15

Required

(a) Decide whether the product should use the regular or the cheaper grade of material.

(b) Calculate the price that should be charged for the product to maximise the annual profit, and the profit that should be expected.

16 Materials and relevant costs

A company is considering whether to agree to do a job for a customer. It has sufficient spare capacity to take on this job.

To do the job, three different direct materials will be required, Material X, Material Y and Material Z. Data relating to these materials is as follows:

Material	Quantity needed for the job	Quantity currently in stock	Original cost of units currently in stock	Current purchase price	Current disposal value
	units	units	£ per unit	£ per unit	£ per unit
X	800	200	20	23	22
Y	600	400	15	19	12
Z	500	300	30	40	20

Material X is regularly used by the company for other work. Material Y is no longer in regular use, and the units currently held in stock have no alternative use. Material Z is also no longer in regular use, but if the existing stocks of the material are not used for this job, they can be used as a substitute material on a different job, where the contribution would be £25 per unit of Material Z used.

Required

Calculate the total relevant costs of the materials for this job for the customer.

17 Printing leaflets

(a) The manager of a small printing business has received enquires about printing three different types of advertising leaflet, type A, type B and type C. Selling price and cost information for these leaflets is shown below:

Leaflet type:	Type A	Type B	Type C
	£	£	£
Selling price, per 1,000 leaflets	300	660	1,350
Estimate printing costs:			
Variable costs, per 1,000 leaflets	120	210	390
Specific fixed costs per month	7,200	12,000	28,500

In addition to the specific fixed costs, £12,000 per month will be incurred in general fixed costs.

Required

Assuming that fixed orders have been received to print 50,000 of Leaflet A and 50,000 of Leaflet B each month, calculate the quantity of Leaflet C that must be sold to produce an overall profit, for all three leaflets combined, of £5,400 per month.

(b) The printing business now receives an enquiry from a customer about printing 30,000 of a different type of leaflet. The customer is willing to pay £25,000. The variable labour and overhead costs of producing these leaflets would be £80 per 1,000 leaflets.

The leaflets would be printed on a special type of paper. This costs £500 per 1,000 leaflets. However, there are already sufficient quantities of the paper in store for 20,000 of the leaflets. This special paper was purchased three months ago for a customer who then cancelled his order. The material has a disposal value of £1,500, but it could also be used to produce 20,000 units of leaflet C. The cost of normal paper for leaflet C is £300 per 1,000 leaflets.

Required

Calculate the relevant costs of making the leaflets for this special order, and indicate by how much profit would increase as a result of undertaking the order.

18   Company JB

Company JB is a small specialist manufacturer of electronic components and much of its output is used by the makers of aircraft. One of the small number of aircraft manufacturers has offered a contract to Company JB for the supply of 400 identical components over the next twelve months.

The data relating to the production of **each component** is as follows:

(a) **Material requirements:**

3 kilograms material M1:	see note 1 below
2 kilograms material P2:	see note 2 below
1 Part No. 678:	see note 3 below

Note 1

Material M1 is in continuous use by the company. 1,000 kilograms are currently held in stock at a carrying amount of £4.70 per kilogram but it is known that future purchases will cost £5.50 per kilogram.

Note 2

1,200 kilograms of material P2 are held in stock. The original cost of the material was £4.30 per kilogram but as the material has not been required for the last two years it has been written down to £1.50 per kilogram (scrap value). The only foreseeable alternative use is as a substitute for material P4 (in current use) but this would involve further processing costs of £1.60 per kilogram. The current cost of material P4 is £3.60 per kilogram.

Note 3

It is estimated that the Part No. 678 could be bought for £50 each.

(b) Labour requirements

Each component would require five hours of skilled labour and five hours of semi-skilled. An employee possessing the necessary skills is available and is currently paid £5 per hour. A replacement would, however, have to be obtained at a rate of £4 per hour for the work that would otherwise be done by the skilled employee. The current rate for semi-skilled work is £3 per hour and an additional employee could be appointed for this work.

(c) Overhead

Company JB absorbs overhead by a machine hour rate, currently £20 per hour of which £7 is for variable overhead and £13 for fixed overhead. If this contract is undertaken it is estimated that fixed costs will increase for the duration of the contract by £3,200. Spare machine capacity is available and each component would require four machine hours.

A price of £145 per component has been suggested by the large aircraft manufacturer.

Required

State whether or not the contract should be accepted and support your conclusion with appropriate figures for presentation to management.

19 Product B22

BB Company has received an enquiry from a customer for the supply of 500 units of a new product, product B22. Negotiations on the final price to charge the customer are in progress and the sales manager has asked you to supply relevant cost information.

The following information is available:

(1) Each unit of product B22 requires the following raw materials:

Raw material type

X   4 kg

Y   6 kg

(2) The company has 5,000 kg of material X currently in stock. This was purchased last year at a cost of $7 per kg. If not used to make product B22, this stock of X could either be sold for $7.50 per kg or converted at a cost of $1.50 per kg, so that it could be used as a substitute for another raw material, material Z, which the company requires for other production. The current purchase price per kilogram for materials is $9.50 for material Z and $8.25 per kg for material X.

(3) There are 10,000 kilograms of raw material Y in stock, valued on a FIFO basis at a total cost of $142,750. Of this current stock, 3,000 kilograms were purchased six months ago at a cost of $13.75 per kg. The rest of the stock was purchased last month. Material Y is used regularly in normal production work. Since the last purchase of material Y a month ago, the company has been advised by the supplier that the price per kilogram has been increased by 4%.

(4) Each unit of product B22 requires the following number of labour hours in its manufacture:

Type of labour:

Skilled: 5 hours

Unskilled: 3 hours

Skilled labour is paid $8 per hour and unskilled labour $6 per hour.

(5) There is a shortage of skilled labour, so that if production of B22 goes ahead it will be necessary to transfer skilled workers from other work to undertake it. The other work on which skilled workers are engaged at present is the manufacture of product B16. The selling price and variable cost information for B16 are as follows:

	$/unit	$/unit
Selling price		100
Less: variable costs of production		
Skilled labour (3 hours)	24	
Other variable costs	31	
		55
		45

(6) The company has a surplus of unskilled workers who are paid a fixed wage for a 37-hour week. It is estimated that there are 900 hours of unused unskilled labour time available during the period of the contract. The balance of the unskilled labour requirements could be met by working overtime, which is paid at time and a half.

(7) The company absorbs production overheads by a machine hour rate. This absorption rate is $22.50 per hour, of which $8.75 is for variable overheads and the balance is for fixed overheads. If production of product B22 is undertaken, it is estimated that an extra $4,000 will be spent on fixed costs. Spare machining capacity is available and each unit of B22 will require two hours of machining time in its manufacture using the existing equipment. In addition, special finishing machines will be required for two weeks to complete the B22. These machines will be hired at a cost of $2,650 per week, and there will be no overhead costs associated with their use.

(8) Cash spending of $3,250 has been incurred already on development work for the production of B22. It is estimated that before production of the B22 begins, another $1,750 will have to be spent on development, making a total development cost of $5,000.

Required

Calculate the minimum price that the company should be prepared to accept for the 500 units of product B22. Explain briefly but clearly how each figure in the minimum price calculation has been obtained.

(Note: the minimum price is the price that equals that the total relevant costs of producing the items. Any price in excess of the minimum price will add to total profit).

20 Make or buy

Company S makes two components, A and B, for which costs in the next year are expected to be as follows:

	A	B
Production (units)	30,000	20,000
Variable costs per unit:	£	£
Direct materials	6	5
Direct labour	3	9
Variable production overheads	1	3
Variable production cost	10	17

Direct labour is paid £12 per hour. There will be only 19,500 hours of direct labour time available next year, and any additional components must be purchased from an external supplier.

Total fixed costs per annum are expected to be as follows:

	£
Incurred as a direct consequence of making A	40,000
Incurred as a direct consequence of making B	50,000
Other fixed costs	30,000
	120,000

An external supplier has offered to supply units of A for £12.50 and units of B for £23.

Required

(a) Recommend whether Company S should shut down internal production of Component A or Component B and switch to external purchasing.

(b) Recommend the quantities that Company S should make of the components, and the quantities that it should buy externally, in order to obtain the required quantities of both components at the minimum cost. Calculate what the total annual cost will be.

Tutorial note. To answer part (b), you will need to consider that labour is a limiting factor.

21 Villaco

Villaco produces two products with the following costs and revenue per unit:

	Product A	Product B
	$	$
Sales price	20	10
Variable cost	8	6
Fixed cost	4	3
	units	units
Sales demand	2,000	3,000

There are only 7,000 machine hours available, and Product A requires 4 machine hours per unit and Product B requires 1 machine hour per unit

Required

(a) Calculate the profit-maximising production and sales mix.

(b) Assume that all the data is the same, except that we are able to sub-contract the products for an additional variable cost of $1 per unit for A and $0.50 per unit for B.

What is the profit-maximising decision?

22 Payoff table

A baker pays $0.10 for buns and sells them for $0.30. At the end of a day, any pastries that have not been sold must be thrown away. On any particular day, the probability distribution of sales demand is as follows:

Number of pastries demanded by customers	20	40	60
Probability	0.3	0.5	0.2

Required

a) Construct a payoff matrix to show all the possible outcomes

b) How many buns should the baker make if he bases his decision on expected value?

23 Probabilities

A company is considering whether or not to invest in a project where the initial cash investment would be $6,250,000. The project would have a five-year life, and the estimated annual cash flows are as follows:

Year	Cash inflows	Cash outflows
	$	$
1	3,000,000	1,500,000
2	4,000,000	1,800,000
3	5,000,000	2,400,000
4	4,000,000	1,700,000
5	3,000,000	1,000,000

The cost of capital is 10%.

The estimates of cash outflows are considered fairly reliable. However, the estimates of cash inflows are much more uncertain. Several factors could make the annual cash flows higher or lower than expected.

■ Factor 1: There is a 20% probability that government measures to control the industry will reduce annual cash inflows by 20%.

■ Factor 2: There is a 30% probability that another competitor will also enter the market: this would reduce the estimated cash inflows by 10%.

■ Factor 3: There is a 40% probability that demand will be stronger than expected. The company would not be able to supply more products to the market, but it would be able to sell at higher prices and cash inflows would be 5% higher than estimated.

Required

Calculated the expected net present value of the project.

24 Grab Company

Grab Company engages in site clearance and site preparation work. Information about its operations is as follows:

(1) It is Grab Company's policy to hire all the plant and machinery it needs, rather than to purchase its own plant and machinery.

(2) Grab Company will enter into an advance hire agreement contract for the coming year at one of three levels – high, medium or low – which correspond to the requirements of a high, medium or low level of orders obtained.

(3) The level of orders obtained will not be known when the advance hire agreement contract is entered into. Probabilities have been estimated by management as to the likelihood of the orders being at a high, medium or low level.

(4) Where the advance hire agreement entered into is lower than that required for the level of orders actually obtained, a premium rate must be paid to obtain the additional plant and machinery required.

(5) No refund is obtainable where the advance hire agreement for plant and machinery is at a level in excess of that required to satisfy the site clearance and preparation orders actually obtained.

A summary of the information relating to the above points is as follows:

| Level of orders | Sales revenue | Probability | Plant and machinery hire costs | |
			Advance hire	Conversion premium
	$000		$000	$000
High	15,000	0.25	2,300	
Medium	8,500	0.45	1,500	
Low	4,000	0.30	1,000	
Low to medium				850
Medium to high				1,300
Low to high				2,150
Variable cost (as a percentage of turnover) 70%				

Required

(a) Prepare a summary which shows the forecast net margin earned by Grab Company for the coming year for each possible outcome.

(b) On the basis of maximising expected value, advise Grab Company whether the advance contract for the hire of plant and machinery should be at the low, medium or high level.

(c) Explain how the risk preferences of the management members responsible for the choice of advance plant and machinery hire contract may alter the decision reached in (b) above.

25   Zero based budgeting

State briefly where zero-based budgeting is likely to be of the greatest value and suggest how often ZBB should be used.

26   Learning

A company has developed a design for a new product, the Widgette. It intends to sell the product at full production cost plus a profit margin of 40%. The estimated production cost and selling price for the first unit of the Widgette are as follows:

	$
Direct materials	2,000
Direct labour (200 hours at $15 per hour)	3,000
Fixed production overhead ($20 per direct labour hour)	4,000
Full production cost	9,000
Profit margin (40%)	3,600
Selling price	12,600

The company's management expects reductions in the time to produce subsequent units of the Widgette, and an 80% learning curve is expected.

A customer has expressed an interest in buying units of the Widgette, and has asked the following questions:

(1)   If we bought the first Widgette for $12,600 and immediately ordered another one, what would be the selling price for the second Widgette?

(2)   If we waited until you have sold the first two Widgettes to another customer, and then ordered the third and the fourth units that you produce, what will be the average price for the third and fourth units?

(3)   If we decided to buy eight Widgettes immediately, and asked you to quote a single price for all eight units, what price would you charge?

Required

(a)   Answer each of these questions, assuming that the policy of the company remains to make a profit margin of 40% on every unit that it makes and sells.

(b)   List three limitations of learning curve theory.

27   Greenears

Greenears is a new business producing woollen hats, which it makes in small batches of a standard size. It estimates that the first batch of a new design of hand-made hats will have a labour cost of $2,000. There will be an 85% learning curve effect for subsequent batches.

In month 1 production is 5 batches, and in month 2 production is 7 batches.

Required

Estimate the total labour cost in month 2 for making the hats.

28   Regression

A company has achieved the following total sales in each year for the past five years:

Year	Total sales
	$ million
20X2 = Year 1	12
20X3 = Year 2	15
20X4 = Year 3	15
20X5 = Year 4	18
20X6 = Year 5	19

Required

(a)   Use linear regression analysis to establish a formula for the trend line in sales, and use this formula to estimate what total sales should be in 20X7 and 20X8.

(b)   Calculate the correlation coefficient to decide how much reliance you can place in your forecasts.

To produce your answer, you can make use of the following calculations:

Year	Total sales			
x	y	xy	x²	y²
1	12	12	1	144
2	15	30	4	225
3	15	45	9	225
4	18	72	16	324
5	19	95	25	361
15	79	254	55	1,279

29   Flexed budget

LAW operates a system of flexible budgets and the flexed budgets for expenditure for the first two quarters of Year 3 were as follows:

Flexed budgets - quarters 1 and 2

Activity	Quarter 1	Quarter 2
Sales units	9,000	14,000
Production units	10,000	13,000
Budget cost allowances	$	$
Direct materials	130,000	169,000
Production labour	74,000	81,500
Production overhead	88,000	109,000
Administration overhead	26,000	26,000
Selling and distribution overhead	29,700	36,200
Total budgeted cost	347,700	421,700

The cost structures in quarters 1 and 2 are expected to continue during quarter 3 as follows:

(a)   The variable cost elements behave in a linear fashion in direct proportion to volume. However, for production output in excess of 14,000 units, the variable cost per unit for production labour increases by 50%. This is due to a requirement for overtime working. The extra amount is payable only on the production above 14,000 units.

(b)   Fixed costs are not affected by changes in activity levels.

(c)   The variable elements of production costs are directly related to production volume.

(d)   The variable element of selling and distribution overhead is directly related to sales volume.

Required

Prepare a statement of the budgeted cost allowance for quarter 3. The activity levels during quarter 3 were:

	Units
Sales	14,500
Production	15,000

30   Budget preparation

BRO makes and sells a single product, product A. The following information is available for use in the budgeting process for the year to 31st December Year 8:

(i)   **Sales**: Selling price per product unit $20.

	Year 8				Year 9
	Quarter 1	Quarter 2	Quarter 3	Quarter 4	Quarter 1
Sales (units)	6,000	4,000	3,600	5,600	4,800

(ii)

Inventory levels	
At 31st December Year 7:	Finished product A: 1,500 units
	Raw material X: 3,500 kilos

Closing inventory of finished product A at the end of each quarter is budgeted as a percentage of the sales units of the following quarter, as follows:

■ At the end of quarters 1 and 2: inventory of A = 25% of sales in the next quarter

■ At the end of quarters 3 and 4: inventory of A = 35% of sales in the next quarter.

Closing inventory of raw material X is budgeted to fall by 300 kilos at the end of each quarter in order to reduce holdings by 1,200 kilos during Year 8.

(iii)   **Product A unit data:**

Material X: 4 kilos per unit at $1.60 per kilo

Direct labour: 0.3 hours per unit at $7.00 per hour.

(iv)   **Other quarterly expenditure**

	Quarter 1	Quarter 2	Quarter 3	Quarter 4
	$	$	$	$
Fixed overheads	45,000	48,000	47,000	50,000
Capital expenditure		50,000		

(v)   **Forecast balances at 31st December Year 7**

Trade receivables $40,000
Bad debts provision: $2,000
Cash in the bank $22,000

Non-current assets (at cost) $500,000
Trade payables (all for materials) $9,600

(vi)   **Cash flow timing information**

(1)   Sales revenue: 60% of trade receivables are paid during the first quarter of sale, and 38% during the next quarter. Expected bad debts are 2% of sales.

(2)   Material purchases: 70% of purchases will be paid for during the quarter of purchase, and the remaining 30% will be paid during the next quarter.

(3)   Direct wages, fixed overheads and capital expenditure: 100% is payable during the quarter in which the expenditures occur.

(vii)   Non-current assets are depreciated on a straight-line basis at a rate of 5% of cost per year, with a residual value of $0. This depreciation is based on the total cost of non-current assets held at any point during the year.

(viii)   All forecast receivables and payables balances at 31st December Year 7 will be received or paid as relevant during the first quarter of Year 8.

(ix)   Inventories of product A are valued on a marginal cost basis for internal budgeting purposes.

Required

(a)   Prepare a cash budget for BRO for each quarter of the year to 31st December Year 8.

(b)   Prepare a budgeted income statement for the year to 31st December Year 8.

31   Cash calculations

(a)   A company has actual and budgeted monthly sales as follows:

Month		$
November	(actual)	60,000
December	(actual)	120,000
January	(budget)	80,000
February	(budget)	40,000
March	(budget)	92,000

Receipts from customers are as follows:

In the month of sale	10%
One month later	40%
Two months later	49%
Bad debts	1%

Bad debts are written off at the end of the second month following the month of sale. There are no provisions for doubtful debts, and trade receivables at 1st January were $138,000.

Required

Calculate the budgeted cash receipts in each of the months January, February and March.

(b)   The same company pays for its material purchases as follows:

In the month of sale	30%
One month later	70%

Materials costs amount to 25% of the value of sales.

The material inventory is $18,000 at 1st January, and is expected to increase to $20,000 by the end of January and to $25,000 by the end of February and March.

Trade payables for materials at 1st January are $21,000.

Actual and budgeted sales are as shown in part (a) above.

Required

Calculate the budgeted cash payments for materials in each of the months January, February and March.

32   Cash budget

The following information relates to Entity XY:

Month	Wages incurred	Materials purchases	Overheads	Sales
	$000	$000	$000	$000
February	6	20	10	30
March	8	30	12	40
April	10	25	16	60
May	9	35	14	50
June	12	30	18	70
July	10	25	16	60
August	9	25	14	50
September	9	30	14	50

(a)   It is expected that the cash balance on 31st May will be $22,000.

(b)   All wages are paid in the month they are incurred.

(c) It is company policy to pay suppliers for materials three months after receipt of the materials.

(d) Trade receivables: customers are expected to pay two months after sale.

(e) Included in the overhead figure is $2,000 per month for depreciation of non-current assets.

(f) There is a one-month delay in paying the other overhead expenses.

(g) 10% of the monthly sales are cash sales and 90% are credit sales.

(h) A sales commission of 5% is paid to agents on all the credit sales, but this is not paid until the month after the sales to which the commission relates. This expense is not included in the overhead figures shown above.

(i) It is intended to repay a bank loan of $25,000 on 30th June.

(j) Delivery is expected in July of a new machine costing $45,000 of which $15,000 will be paid on delivery and $15,000 in each of the following two months.

(k) Assume that a bank overdraft facility is available if required.

Required

Prepare a cash budget for each of the months June, July and August.

33 Cost estimation

The following recorded monthly costs of production will be used to estimate fixed costs per month and the variable cost per unit:

Output	Total cost
000 units	$000
17	63
15	61
12	52
22	74
18	68

Required

(a) Using the high low method, estimate the fixed costs per month and the variable cost per unit. Use your estimate to budget the total costs in a month when output is 15,000 units.

(b) Using linear regression analysis, estimate the fixed costs per month and the variable cost per unit. Use your estimate to budget the total costs in a month when output is 15,000 units.

(c) Calculate the correlation coefficient and comment on what it shows.

34   Reconcile

A company makes a single product and uses standard absorption costing. The standard cost per unit is as follows:

	£ per unit
Direct materials	8
Direct labour	6
Fixed production overheads	12
	26

Budgeted production is 14,000 units per month. Last month, actual production was 14,800 units, and actual costs were as follows:

Total costs	£
Direct materials	125,000
Direct labour	92,000
Fixed production overheads	170,000
	387,000

Required

Prepare a statement for the month that reconciles budgeted costs, standard costs and actual costs

35   Simple variances

(a)   Z plc uses a standard costing system and has the following labour cost standard in relation to one of its products:

4 hours of skilled labour at £6.00 per hour: £24.00

During October, 3,350 units of this products were made, which was 150 units less than budgeted. The labour cost incurred was £79,893 and the number of direct labour hours worked was 13,450.

Required

Calculate the direct labour rate and efficiency variances for the month.

(b)   Company J uses a standard costing system and has the following data relating to one of its products:

	£ per unit	£ per unit
Selling price		9.00
Variable cost	4.00	
Fixed cost	3.00	
		7.00
Profit		2.00

The budgeted sales for October Year 5 were 800 units, but the actual sales were 850 units. The revenue earned from these sales was £7,480.

Required

Calculate the sales price and sales volume variances for October using:

■ standard absorption costing

■ standard marginal costing.

(c) The budget was to produce 15,000 units. The standard fixed production cost of a product is £20, which is 4 hours at a rate of £5 per direct labour hour. Actual production was 14,600 units and actual fixed production overhead expenditure was £325,000. The production output was manufactured in 58,000 hours of work.

Required

Calculate:

■ the fixed production overhead total cost variance

■ the fixed production overhead expenditure variance and volume variance

■ the fixed production overhead efficiency variance and capacity variance

36   Manufacturing cost variance

A manufacturing company uses a standard absorption costing system in accounting for its production costs.

The standard cost of a unit of product is as follows:

	Standard quantity	Standard price/rate	Standard cost
		£	£
Direct materials	5 kilos	6.00	30.00
Direct labour	20 hours	4.00	80.00
Variable production overhead	20 hours	0.20	4.00
Fixed production overhead	20 hours	5.00	100.00

The following data relates to Period 1:

Budgeted output	25,000 units
Actual output - produced	20,000 units
Units sold	15,000 units
Materials put into production	120,000 kilos
Materials purchased	200,000 kilos
Direct labour hours paid	500,000 hrs

Due to a power failure 10,000 hours were lost.

Cost of materials purchased and used	£825,000
Rate per direct labour hour	£5
Variable production overhead	£70,000
Fixed production overhead	£2,100,000

Required

Calculate, for Period 1:

1   the material price variance

2   the material usage variance

3   the direct labour rate variance

4   the direct labour idle time variance

5   the direct labour efficiency variance

6   the variable overhead total cost variance

7   the fixed overhead expenditure variance

8   the fixed overhead volume variance

9   the manufacturing cost variance.

37   Variances and operating statements

Standard data per unit of Product Q is as follows:

	£ per unit	£ per unit
Standard sales price		6.00
Direct labour cost	0.64	
Direct material cost	3.00	
Variable production overheads	0.16	
		3.80
Contribution		2.20
Fixed overheads		0.20
Profit		2.00

The budgeted production and sales volume for Product Q was 12,000 units. Budget for 2,400 direct labour hours (12,000 units):

- 5 units to be made per hour

- Standard labour cost is £3.20 per hour

- Standard material cost is £1.50 per kilogram and each unit requires 2 kilos

- Budgeted fixed overheads £2,400

- Budgeted variable overhead cost per direct labour hour = £0.80.

Actual results for the same period:

- 11,500 units were manufactured

- 2,320 direct labour hours were worked, and cost £7,540

- 25,000 kilos of direct material were purchased (and used) at a cost of £1.48 per kilogram.

- Stock is valued at standard cost.

- Actual variable overheads were £1,750

- Actual fixed overheads were £2,462

- 10,000 units were sold for £62,600.

Required

Prepare operating statements for the period using:

(a)   standard absorption costing and

(b)   standard marginal costing.

To prepare the absorption costing operating statement, you should show the variable overhead expenditure and efficiency variances, and the fixed overhead expenditure and volume variances.

38   Standard cost sheet

The following data relates to actual output, actual costs and variances for the four-weekly accounting period number 4 of a company which makes only one product.

The value of work-in-progress at the end of period 4 was the same as the value of work-in-progress at the beginning of the month.

Actual production of Product XY	18,000 units
Actual costs incurred:	£000
Direct materials purchased and used (150,000 kg)	210
Direct labour costs (32,000 hours)	136
Variable production overhead	38

Variances:	£000	
Direct materials price	15	Favourable
Direct materials usage	9	Adverse
Direct labour rate	8	Adverse
Direct labour efficiency	16	Favourable
Variable production overhead expenditure	6	Adverse
Variable production overhead efficiency	4	Favourable

Variable production overhead varies with labour hours worked.
A standard marginal costing system is operated.

Required

Present a standard product cost sheet for one unit of Product XY, showing how the standard marginal production cost of the product is made up.

39   Variances

MKL makes and sells a single product, product Q. The sales budget for a period and the standard cost and selling price of product Q is as follows:

Budgeted sales		6,000 units
Budgeted selling price		$50
Standard cost per unit:		$
Direct materials	4 metres at $3 per metre	12
Direct labour	0.5 hours at $16 per hour	8
Variable production overhead	0.5 hours at $4 per hour	2
Fixed production overhead	0.5 hours at $20 per hour	10
		32

All other overhead costs are ignored.

Actual sales and costs in the period were as follows:

Actual sales		5,700 units
sales revenue		$288,300
Costs		$
Direct materials	23,200 metres	70,500
Direct labour	2,740 hours	47,900
Variable production overhead		10,600
Fixed production overhead		65,000
		194,000

Required

Prepare an operating statement that reconciles the budgeted profit for the period to the actual profit, and showing variances in as much detail as possible.

40 Standard costing

A manufacturing company produces a single product, the Sigma. The standard cost card for Sigma is as follows:

Direct materials:	$
2 kilos of A at $2 per kilo	4.00
1 kilo of B at $6 per kilo	6.00
Direct labour:	
3 hours at $6 per hour	18.00
Overheads:	
Variable - 3 hours at $4 per direct labour hour	12.00
Fixed - 3 hours at $8 per direct labour hour	24.00
Total standard cost	64.00
Standard profit mark-up (25%)	16.00
Standard selling price	80.00

The company planned to produce 10,000 units of Sigma in the month of April (budgeted fixed overheads for the month being $240,000).

The actual results for April are as follows:

	$
Sales: 9,000 units	756,000
Direct materials:	
A: 19,000 kilos	41,800
B: 10,100 kilos	56,560
Direct labour: 28,500 hours	182,400
Variable overheads	104,000
Fixed overheads	232,000
	616,760
Profit	139,240

Manufacturing overheads are charged to production on the basis of direct labour hours. Actual production for the period was 9,000 units.

Required

(a)   Prepare a reconciliation of budget and actual profit for the month.

(b)   Explain how this would differ using standard marginal costing.

41   Sales variances

A company makes and sells three products Q, R and S. During a period, budgeted and actual results were as follows:

Budget

Product	Total sales revenue	Sales volume	Price	Margin	Total margin
	$	units	$	$	$
Q	18,000	600	30	10	6,000
R	16,500	300	45	15	4,500
S	6,500	100	65	25	2,500

Actual

Product	Total sales revenue	Sales volume	Price	Margin	Total margin
	$	units	$	$	$
Q	14,560	520	28	8	4,160
R	14,210	290	49	19	5,510
S	5,670	90	63	23	2,070

Required

Calculate all relevant sales margin variances.

42   Mix and yield variances

A chemical company has the following standard cost for producing 9 litres of a lubricant:

■   5 litres of material P at $0.70 per litre

■   5 litres of material Q at $0.92 per litre.

There are no inventories of materials, and all material price variances relate to materials used. Actual results showed that 100,000 litres of materials were used during a particular period as follows:

■   45,000 litres of material P: cost $36,000

■   55,000 litres of material Q: cost $53,350

During the period 92,070 litres of the lubricant were produced.

Required

Calculate the total materials cost variance and analyse it into its price, usage, yield and mix components.

43   More mix and yield

The standard cost for a product, product Z, includes the following direct materials costs:

		$ per unit
Material X	5 kilos at $8 per kilo	40
Material Y	3 kilos at $12 per kilo	36
		76

The materials can be mixed in differing proportions.

Actual production during April was 1,250 units of Product Z, with the following direct materials costs:

		$
Material X	6,700 kilos	51,400
Material Y	2,900 kilos	39,500
		90,900

Required

(a)   Calculate the direct materials price, mix and yield variances for the month.

(b)   Reconcile the actual and standard direct materials costs for the month.

44   Planning and operational variances

CAD manufactures product X. In the annual budget for the current year, the standard direct labour cost for Product X is:

3 hours per unit × $15 per hour = $45 per unit.

This cost was based on the expectation that new working procedures and new equipment would be used to reduce the labour time per unit. The changes have not yet been introduced, however, in retrospect, it is decided that a more appropriate direct labour cost for product X should be:

4 hours per unit × $15 per hour = $60 per unit.

In the current period, 2,000 units of Product X were produced. These took 8,200 hours to make, and the direct labour cost was $120,800.

Required

(a)   Reconcile the actual direct labour costs to the original standard costs, using planning and operational variances.

(b)   Show the planning and operational variances if 2,000 units were made in the period in 8,200 hours at a direct labour cost of $101,600, and it was decided in retrospect that the appropriate direct labour cost for product X should be:

4 hours per unit × $12 per hour = $48 per unit.

45 Sam

Sam imports and retails wine. Extracts from the financial statements for this year and last are set out below.

Income statements for the years ended 30th September

	Year 7	Year 6
	$000	$000
Revenue	2,160	1,806
Cost of sales	(1,755)	(1,444)
Gross profit	405	362
Administrative expenses	(260)	(198)
Distribution costs	(130)	(108)
Profit before tax	15	56
Tax expense	(6)	(3)
Profit for the period	9	53

Balance sheets as at 30th September

	Year 7		Year 6	
	$000	$000	$000	$000
Assets				
Non-current assets				
Property, plant and equipment		78		72
Current assets				
Inventories	106		61	
Trade receivables	316		198	
Cash	-		6	
		422		265
Total assets		500		337
Equity and liabilities				
Capital and reserves				
Equity shares	110		85	
Preference shares	23		11	
Share premium	15		-	
Revaluation reserve	20		20	
Accumulated profits	78		74	
		246		190
Current liabilities				
Bank overdraft	49		-	
Trade payables	198		142	
Current tax payable	7		5	
		254		147
Total equity and liabilities		500		337

Required

Comment critically on Sam's results, using appropriate ratios.

46 Chris and Caroline

The income statements and balance sheets of two manufacturing companies in the same sector are set out below.

	Chris	Caroline
	$	$
Revenue	150,000	700,000
Cost of sales	(60,000)	(210,000)
Gross profit	90,000	490,000
Interest payable	(500)	(12,000)
Administrative expenses	(15,000)	(35,000)
Distribution costs	(13,000)	(72,000)
Profit before tax	61,500	371,000
Tax expense	(16,605)	(100,170)
Profit for the period	44,895	270,830

	Chris		Caroline	
	$	$	$	$
Assets				
Non-current assets				
Property	-		500,000	
Plant and equipment	190,000		280,000	
		190,000		780,000
Current assets				
Inventories	12,000		26,250	
Trade receivables	37,500		105,000	
Cash at bank	500		22,000	
		50,000		153,250
Total assets		240,000		933,250
Equity and liabilities				
Capital and reserves				
Issued capital	156,000		174,750	
Accumulated profits	51,395		390,830	
		207,395		565,580
Non-current liabilities				
Long-term debt		10,000		250,000
Current liabilities				
Trade payables		22,605		117,670
Total equity and liabilities		240,000		933,250

Required

Using ratio analysis, briefly compare the profitability, efficiency/liquidity and solvency of the two entities. State, giving reasons, which is the stronger company in each case.

47 Balanced

A balanced scorecard approach may be used to set performance targets and monitor performance.

(a) List the four aspects of performance in a balanced scorecard approach.

(b) Suggest how a professional football club might use a balanced scorecard approach. Indicate what key aspects of performance might be identified and suggest performance targets that a football club might use in a balanced scorecard approach.

48 Pyramid

(a) Describe briefly the performance pyramid.

(b) List the dimensions of performance for a service industry, as suggested by Fitzgerald and others.

49 Three services

A company provides three types of delivery service to customers: service A, service B and service C. Customers are a mix of firms with a contract for service with the company, and non-contract customers.

The following information relates to performance in the year to 31st December Year 1:

	Service A	Service B	Service C
Number of deliveries made	350,000	250,000	20,000
% of deliveries to contract customers	60%	60%	80%
Price charged per delivery:			
Contract customers	$9	$15	$300
Premium for non-contract customers	+ 30%	+ 50%	+ 20%

The premium for non-contract customers is in addition to the rate charged to contract customers.

All employees in the company were paid $45,000 per year and sundry operating costs, excluding salaries and fuel costs, were $4,000,000 for the year.

The following operational data for the year relates to deliveries:

	Services A and B	Service C
Average kilometres per vehicle/day	400	600
Number of vehicles	50	18
Operating days in the year	300	300

For Year 2, the company has agreed a fixed price contract for fuel. As a result of this contract, fuel prices will be:

(a) $0.40 per kilometre for Services A and B

(b) $0.80 per kilometre for Service C.

Sales prices will be 3% higher in Year 2 than in Year 1, and salaries and operational expenses will be 5% higher. Sales volume will be exactly the same as in Year 1.

The number of employees will also be the same as in Year 1: 60 employees working full-time on Services A and B and 25 employees working full-time on Service C.

Required

(a) Prepare a budgeted income statement for the year to 31st December Year 2.

(b) Comment on vehicle utilisation.

50   Private medical practice

A private medical practice has five full-time doctors, five full-time assistants and two administrators.

Each doctor treats 18 patients each day on average. The medical centre is open for five days each week, 46 weeks each year.

Charges for patients vary according to the age of the patient and the nature of the treatment provided.

Charges	Adults below 65 year of age	Children and individuals aged 65 years old and over
	$	$
No treatment: consultation only	50	30
Minor treatment	200	120
Major treatment	600	280

The patient mix and the treatment mix are as follows:

Patients:		Treatment	
Adults	45%	No treatment	20%
Children	25%	Minor treatment	70%
Over 65 years old	30%	Major treatment	10%

The salary of each doctor is $240,000, assistants earn $100,000 and administrators earn $80,000. In addition, everyone receives a 5% bonus at the end of the year.

The medical practice expects to pay $414,300 for materials next year and other (fixed) costs will be $733,600.

Required

Using the information provided, present an income statement for the medical practice for next year. (Ignore the effects of inflation.)

51   Train times

A railway company has two operating divisions, Northern Region and Southern Region. Each division runs inter-city train services and suburban ('commuter') train services. Performance figures for the most recent reporting period are as follows:

| | Northern Region | | Southern Region | |
	Inter-city services	Suburban services	Inter-city services	Suburban services
Journeys	1,500	34,000	1,800	42,000
Completed on schedule	1,240	25,100	1,590	38,600
Completed within 5 minutes of schedule	1,350	29,500	1,690	40,300
Completed within 10 minutes of schedule	1,440	33,100	1,730	41,500
Cancelled journeys	16	405	2	220
Target for on-time completion of journeys	90%	95%	90%	95%

The chief executive officer of the railway company is trying to improve standards of service, and targets have been set for the number of train journeys that should end with the train arriving at its destination on schedule. It is his intention to raise the standards still further in the future.

Required

Assess the service performance of the two regions

52   Growth objective

A company has an objective in its long-term business plan of achieving significant growth in its business in the period Year 1 to Year 5. It is now the end of Year 2.

Its results for the years to 31st December Year 1 and Year 2 are summarised below.

Income statement for the year ended 31st December

	Year 2	Year 1
	$	$
Sales	31,200,000	26,000,000
Cost of sales	18,720,000	15,600,000
	12,480,000	10,400,000
Operating expenses	6,780,000	5,200,000
Interest charges	500,000	0
Depreciation	3,000,000	3,000,000
Net profit	2,200,000	2,200,000

Balance sheet as at 31st December

	Year 2	Year 1
	$	$
Non-current assets	27,300,000	26,000,000
Net current assets	15,600,000	7,800,000
	42,900,000	33,800,000
Loan	9,000,000	0
	33,900,000	33,800,000
Share capital	19,500,000	19,500,000
Accumulated profit	14,400,000	14,300,000
	33,900,000	33,800,000

Sales are seasonal, and are much higher in the first six months of the year than in the second six months. The half-yearly sales figures in the past two years have been as follows:

Sales

	Year 2	Year 1
	$	$
1st January – 30th June	21,645,000	16,900,000
1st July – 31st December	9,555,000	9,100,000
	31,200,000	26,000,000

The company employs part-time workers during the first six-months of each year. Part-time workers operate for a full working week during the weeks that they are employed. Employee numbers have been as follows:

Employee numbers

	Year 2	Year 1
Full time employees	318	260
Part time (seasonal) employees	494	310

The company introduced four new products to the market in Year 1 and another five new products in Year 2.

Required

Explain with reasons whether the company appears to be on course for achieving its objective of growing the business.

In particular, you should consider growth in sales, profits, investment and product range.

53   Responsibility

A multinational company established a new operating division in Fenland four years ago. The operating division has been established as a profit centre. Decisions relating to the purchase of capital equipment for the division, and borrowing to finance the capital, have been taken at head office.

The results for the first four years of operation have been as follows:

	Year 1	Year 2	Year 3	Year 4
	$000	$000	$000	$000
Sales revenue	172	646	810	1,792
Operating costs	167	620	718	1,490
Depreciation	25	104	187	530
Interest charges	0	132	240	462
Profit/(loss)	(20)	(210)	(335)	(690)

The managing director of the division has been asked to explain its poor performance and the escalating losses. In response, the managing director has argued that the performance of the division has improved, and is not getting worse.

Required

(a)   Identify a measure of performance that would suggest that the performance of the division has been improving over the four-year period.

(b)   Suggest how the performance of the division should be assessed, and state whether you agree or disagree with the view of the managing director that performance has improved.

54   Cross Streets Hotel

Cross Streets Hotel owns five hotels in the same country, providing accommodation mainly to business people and tourists. Each hotel has a bar and restaurant open to residents and non-residents.

The directors of the company work in two offices in the oldest hotel in the southern region of the country, where the small finance office is also located. Until now the company has only produced statutory financial accounts, and has not produced management accounts.

The directors disagree with each other about the profitability of each of the individual hotels owned and operated by the company. The head of the finance office has proposed that performance reports should be produced, based on a system of responsibility accounting for each of the hotels. The performance of all five hotels should also be amalgamated to prepare performance reports at company level.

Required

Suggest:

■ what reports this management information system should produce

■ what information the reports should contain

55 Non-financial performance measurements

Suggest **three** non-financial measures of performance that might be helpful to management in assessing the following aspects of operations in a commercial bank:

(1)   service quality

(2)   marketing effectiveness

(3)   personnel

56 Decentralisation

(a)   Define the following concepts:

    (i)   Responsibility accounting

    (ii)   An investment centre

    (iii)   Return on investment (for a division)

    (iv)   Residual income (for a division).

(b)   The following information available about Divisions M and W, which are investment centres in LK Group:

	Division M	Division W
Divisional investment	$200,000	$5,000,000
Division profit	$20,000	$410,000

The weighted average cost of capital for LK Group is 8%.

Ignore taxation.

Required

(a)   Evaluate the performance of division M and division W.

(b)   Re-evaluate the situation given that the weighted cost of capital is

    (1)   6%

    (2)   10%.

57 West Division

Large Group has several separate divisions, each operating as an investment centre within the group. West Division makes and sells three products, A, B and C. All three products are sold under the Titan brand label, but Product A and Product B are also sold through a supermarket group as unbranded products.

Budgeted data for the year to 31st December Year 7 is as follows:

Product sales

	Product A	Product B	Product C
	units	units	units
Titan brand	160,000	120,000	50,000
Unbranded	450,000	600,000	-

Selling prices

	Product A	Product B	Product C
	$ per unit	$ per unit	$ per unit
Titan brand	2.50	3.20	5.00
Unbranded	1.50	2.00	-

Variable costs

	Production	Packaging
	$ per unit	$ per unit
Product A:		
Titan brand	1.20	0.30
Unbranded	1.20	0.10
Product B:		
Titan brand	1.60	0.40
Unbranded	1.60	0.20
Product C:		
Titan brand	2.50	0.50

Budgeted marketing expenditure is $180,000 for the year, and other budgeted expenditure for other fixed costs is $375,000. The average capital employed in West Division in Year 7 is expected to be $400,000 and the division's cost of capital is 10%.

Required

(a) Calculate the budgeted ROI for West Division for the year to 31st December Year 7.

(b) Calculate the budgeted residual income for West Division for the year to 31st December Year 7.

58 Residual

A company is organised into several investment centres. In the past, investment centres have been required to achieve a DCF return of at least 12% on all new investment projects. The annual performance of each investment centre is measured on the basis of ROI. ROI is measured each year as the profit before interest as a percentage of the average investment/average capital employed in the investment centre.

One of the investment centres has achieved a ROI in excess of 35% in each of the past four years. Its managers are considering a new investment project that will have the following cash flows:

Year	Cash flow
	$
0	(42,000)
1 – 3	19,000 each year

The Year 0 investment will be in an item of machinery that will have no residual value at the end of Year 3. Assume that depreciation is charged on a straight-line basis.

The NPV of the investment is $3,638 at a cost of capital of 12%.

Required

(a) Calculate the ROI for the project, each year and on average for the three-year period.

(b) Suggest whether the managers of the investment centre are likely to invest in the project.

(c) Calculate the residual income for the project, assuming that a cost of capital of 12% is applied. Suggest how the decision by the centre's managers about investing in the project might be changed if residual income rather than ROI were used to measure divisional performance.

59   Two divisions

A company has two operating divisions, X and Y, that are treated as profit centres for the purpose of performance reporting.

Division X makes two products, Product A and Product B. Product A is sold to external customers for $62 per unit. Product B is a part-finished item that is sold only to Division Y.

Division Y can obtain the part-finished item from either Division X or from an external supplier. The external supplier charges a price of $55 per unit.

The production capacity of Division X is measured in total units of output, Products A and B. Each unit requires the same direct labour time. The costs of production in Division X are as follows:

	Product A	Product B
	$	$
Variable cost	46	48
Fixed cost	19	19
Full cost	65	67

Required

You have been asked to recommend the optimal transfer price, or range of transfer prices, for Product B.

(a) What is an optimal transfer price?

(b)   What would be the optimal transfer price for Product B if there is spare production capacity in Division X?

(c)   What would be the optimal transfer price for Product B if Division X is operating at full capacity due to a limited availability of direct labour, and there is unsatisfied external demand for Product A?

60   Training company

A training company has two training centres, each treated as a profit centre for the purpose of transfer pricing.

Each training centre hires its training staff to client organisations, and charges a fixed rate for each 'trainer day'. Trainers are either full-time staff of the company, or are hired externally. Externally-hired trainers are all vetted for quality, and are used when client demand for training exceeds the ability of the division to meet from its full-time staff.

The London centre is very busy and charges its client £2,000 per trainer day. It pays £1,200 per day to external trainers. The variable cost of using its own full-time trainers is £200 per day.

The other training centre is in Liverpool. The manager of the Liverpool centre is meeting with the manager of the London centre to discuss the possibility of the London centre using trainers from the Liverpool centre instead of external trainers. They have agreed this arrangement in principle, but need to agree a daily fee that the London centre should pay the Liverpool centre for these of its trainers.

It has been estimated that if trainers from the Liverpool centre are used in London, the variable costs incurred will be £200 per day, plus £250 per day for travel and accommodation costs. These costs will be paid by the Liverpool centre.

Required
Identify the optimal charge per day for the use of Liverpool trainers by the London training centre, in each of the following circumstances:

(a)   assuming that the Liverpool centre has spare consulting capacity

(b)   assuming that the Liverpool training centre is fully occupied charging clients £750 per trainer day

(c)   assuming that the Liverpool training centre is fully occupied charging clients £1,100 per trainer day.

61   Shadow price

Division A supplies a special chemical to Division B, another profit centre in the same group. The output capacity for making the special chemical in Division A is limited.

■   The variable cost of making the chemical is $500 per kilo.

■   There is no external intermediate market for the chemical.

■   Division B uses the chemical to manufacture a tablet. Each tablet uses ten grams of the chemical.

Sales demand for the tablet exceeds the production capacity of Divisions A and B.

The selling price for each tablet is $10. Further variable processing costs in Division B to make the tablet from the special chemical are $2 per tablet.

Required

(a) Calculate the shadow price of each kilo of the special chemical.

(b) Identify the ideal transfer price.

(c) Suggest whether this transfer price will provide a suitable basis for performance evaluation of the two divisions.

62 Bricks

ABC Company is organised into two trading groups. Group X makes materials that are used to manufacture special bricks. It transfers some of these materials to Group Y and sells some of the materials externally to other brick manufacturers. Group Y makes special bricks from the materials and sells them to traders in building materials.

The production capacity of Group X is 2,000 tonnes per month. At present, sales are limited to 1,000 tonnes to external customers and 600 tonnes to Group Y.
The transfer price was agreed at $200 per tonne in line with the external sales trade price at 1st July which was the beginning of the budget year. From 1st December, however, strong competition in the market has reduced the market price for the materials to $180 per tonne.

The manager of Group Y is now saying that the transfer price for the materials from Group X should be the same as for external customers. The manager of Group X rejects this argument on the basis that the original budget established the transfer price for the entire financial year.

From each tonne of materials, Group Y produces 1,000 bricks, which it sells at $0.40 per brick. It would sell a further 400,000 bricks if the price were reduced to $0.32 per brick.

Other data relevant are given below.

	Group X	Group Y
	$	$
Variable cost per tonne	70	60
Fixed cost per month	100,000	40,000

The variable costs of Group Y exclude the transfer price of materials from Group X.

Required

(a) Prepare estimated profit statements for the month of December for each group and for ABC Company as a whole, based on transfer prices of $200 per tonne and of $180 per tonne, when producing at

(i) 80% capacity

(ii) 100% capacity, on the assumption that Group Y reduces the selling price to $0.32.

(b) Comment on the effect that might result from a change in the transfer price from $200 to $180.

(c) Suggest an alternative transfer price that would provide an incentive for Division Y to reduce the selling price and increase sales by 40,000 bricks a month.

63   International transfers

An international company has two operating subsidiaries, one in Country X and one in Country Y. The subsidiaries operate independently, and report to head office as investment centres. Each investment centre manager has the freedom to make his own decisions about what products they should sell, who to sell them to, and the prices at which they should be sold. Each investment centre is required to maximise its annual profit

The main subsidiary (X Division) is in Country X. It makes and sells two products, Product P and Product Q.

Sales and cost data for X Division is as follows:

	Product P	Product Q
Annual sales demand	150,000 units	600,000 units
	$	$
Selling price	9.00	
Variable cost of production	3.40	
Contribution per unit	5.60	0.50

Products P and Q are made on the same machines and with the same work force, at a production centre in Country X. Each product requires exactly the same amount of machine time and labour time, and production can be switched easily from one product to another. Total production capacity is 800,000 units each year, for Product P and Product Q in total.

The investment centre in Country Y (Y Division) is considering a decision to sell Product P. It would not manufacture the product itself, but would buy units of Product P either from Division X or from an external supplier. The external supplier would be willing to sell units of Product P to Division Y at a price of $5 per unit.

The manager of Division Y has asked the manager of Division X to quote a price for supplying Product P. Division X has replied by saying that they would be willing to supply units of Product P at its normal selling price less 40%.

Division Y is not yet sure whether it will want to buy 50,000 units of Product P each year, or 120,000 units.

Required

(a)   If Division X offers to sell units of Product P at the normal selling price in Country X less 40%, what will be the decision of the manager of Division Y if annual purchase requirements are:

(i)   50,000 units of Product P

(ii)   120,000 units of Product P?

(b)   Recommend a transfer price, or a range of transfer prices, at which Division X should offer to sell units of Product P to Division Y, **if the annual profits of the company as a whole are to be maximised** and annual purchase requirements are:

(i)   50,000 units of Product P

(ii)   120,000 units of Product P?

Ignore taxation.

(c)   Suppose that the rate of taxation on company profits is 50% in Country X and 30% in Country Y.

Recommend, with reasons, whether Division Y should obtain units of Product P from Division X or from the external supplier, if its annual purchase requirements are 120,000 units and if the transfer price is the market price in Country X less 40%.

64   Long and Short

Long and Short are two divisions in the Range Group of companies. Both require components S and M for their operations. Component S is available from Division A and component M is available from Division B.

Long Division converts the components S and M into a final product, RDZ. Short Division converts the components S and M into another final product, BL.

The market demand for RDZ and BL exceeds the production capacity of Range Group, because of the limited availability of components S and M. There is no external intermediate market for S or M. No other intermediate product market is available to the Long and Short Divisions.

Other data

Long Division

RDZ		
	Selling price per unit	$45
	Processing cost per unit	$12
	Components required per unit of RDZ	
	Component S	3 units
	Component M	2 units

Short Division

BL	Selling price per unit	$54
	Processing cost per unit	$14
	Components required per unit of BL	
	Component S	2 units
	Component M	4 units

Division A

| Component S | Variable cost per unit | $6 |
| | Maximum production capacity | 1,200 units |

Division B

| Component M | Variable cost per unit | $4 |
| | Maximum production capacity | 1,600 units |

The solution to a linear programming model for production planning in Range Group shows that the imputed scarcity value (shadow price) of product S is $0.50 and the imputed scarcity value of product M is $2.75 per unit. The model also indicates that the components S and M should be transferred to Long and Short Divisions such that 200 units of RDZ and 300 units of BL are produced and sold.

Required

(a) Calculate the contribution earned by the Range Group if the production and sales plan indicated by the linear programming model is implemented.

(b) If the transfer prices are set on the basis of variable cost plus shadow price, show detailed calculations for the following:

(i) the contribution per unit of intermediate product earned by divisions A and B.

(ii) the contribution per unit of products RDZ and BL.

(c) Comment on the results in (b) above and on the possible attitude of management of the various divisions to the proposed transfer pricing and the production and sales plan.

(d) In the following year the capacities of Divisions A and B have each doubled and the following changes have taken place:

(i) Component S – There is still no external market for this product, but Division A has a large demand for other products which could use its spare capacity and earn a contribution of 5% over cost. The variable cost per unit for the other products would be the same as for Component S and these products would use capacity in Division A at the same rate as Component S.

(ii) Component M – An intermediate market for this product now exists and Component M can be bought and sold in unlimited amounts at $7.50 per unit. External sales of Component M would incur additional transport costs of $0.50 per unit which are not incurred in inter-divisional transfers.

The sales demand for units of RDZ and BL will still exceed the production capacity of Divisions A and B to make component S and M for Long and Short Divisions.

Calculate the transfer prices at which Components S and M should now be offered to Long and Short Divisions, in order that the transfer policy implemented will lead to the maximisation of group profit.

Determine the production and sales pattern for Component S, Component M, product RDZ and product BL that will now maximise contribution for the Range Group, and calculate the amount of this total contribution.

You should assume that all the divisions will make decisions that are consistent with the financial data available.

Answers

Contents		
		Page

Performance measurement

Divisional performance and transfer pricing

1   HEN

(a)   **Current full costing method**

Budgeted hours	hours
Product X: (2,000 × 24/60)	800
Product Y: (1,500 × 40/60)	1,000
Product Z: (800 × 60/60)	800
	2,600

Overhead recovery rate using the current absorption costing method:

$$\frac{\text{Total overheads}}{\text{Total hours}} = \frac{\$\left(31,200+39,000+27,300\right)}{2,600}$$

= \$37.50.

Full cost per unit (current method)

	Product X		Product Y		Product Z	
		\$		\$		\$
Direct materials		4.00		3.00		6.00
Direct labour	(\$8 × 24/60)	3.20	(\$8 × 40/60)	5.33	(\$8 × 60/60)	8.00
Overheads	(\$37.50 × 4/60)	15.00	(\$37.50 × 40/60)	25.00	(\$37.50 × 60/60)	37.50
		22.20		33.33		51.50

(b)   **ABC method**

Materials receipt and inspection costs:

Cost driver = Number of batches of material

Total number of batches = (10 + 5 +15) = 30

Overhead cost per batch = \$31,200/30 batches = \$1,040 per batch

Power costs:

Cost Driver = Number of power drill operations

Total number of drill operations

= (2,000 × 8) + (1,500 ×4) + (800 × 5) = 26,000

Overhead cost per drill operation = \$39,000/26,000 = \$1.50.

Materials handling costs:

Cost driver = Quantity of materials handled

Number of metres handled = (2,000 × 5) + (1,500 × 6) + (800 × 2.5) = 21,000
Overhead costs per metre handled = \$27,300/21,000 = \$1.30.

	Overhead costs				
	Product X		**Product Y**		**Product Z**
		$		$		$
Materials receipt	($1,040 × 10)	10,400	($1,040 × 5)	5,200	($1,040 × 15)	15,600
Power	($1.50 × 2,000 × 8)	24,000	($1.50 × 1,500 × 4)	9,000	($1.50 × 800 × 5)	6,000
Materials handling	($1.30 × 2,000 × 5)	13,000	($1.30 × 1,500 × 6)	11,700	($1.30 × 800 × 2.5)	2,600
		44,700		25,900		24,200
Number of units produced		2,000		1,500		800
Overhead cost per unit		$22.35		$17.27		$30.25

Cost per unit (ABC method)

	Product X	Product Y	Product Z
	$	$	$
Direct materials	4.00	3.00	6.00
Direct labour	3.20	5.33	8.00
Overheads	22.35	17.27	30.25
	29.55	25.60	44.25

2 Lard Company

(a) (i) Budgeted cost: traditional absorption costing

It is assumed that the weighting of 1:2:3 applies to packaging materials, but not to labour and overhead costs.

Packaging material

	Output		Material usage		
Customer A	30,000	×	1 =		30,000
Customer B	45,000	×	2 =		90,000
Customer C	25,000	×	3 =		75,000
Weighted units of material					195,000

Therefore, packaging material per weighted unit = $1,950,000/195,000 = $10.

Labour and overheads

Total cost of labour and overheads (000s) = 350 + 30 + 500 + 60 = 940

Total units = (30,000 + 45,000 + 25,000) = 100,000.

Labour and overhead cost per unit = $940,000/100,000 = $9.40.

Budgeted average cost/unit

	Customer A	Customer B	Customer C
	$	$	$
Material	10.0	20.0	30.0
Labour/overhead	9.4	9.4	9.4
Product cost/metre	19.4	29.4	39.4

(ii) Activity based costing analysis of labour and overhead costs

	Receipts and inspection	Storage	Packaging
	$	$	$
Labour			
Basic pay (20:10:70)	70,000	35,000	245,000
Overtime	15,000	6,250	8,750
Occupancy cost (20: 60: 20)	100,000	300,000	100,000
Administration cost (40: 10: 50)	24,000	6,000	30,000
	209,00	347,250	383,750

Activity levels (cost drivers)

Customer	Units		Receipts and inspection (hours)		Storage (metres^2)		Packaging (hours)
A	30,000	(× 6/60)	3,000	(× 0.3)	9,000	(× 36/60)	18,000
B	45,000	(× 9/60)	6,750	(× 0.3)	13,500	(× 45/60)	33,750
C	25,000	(× 15/60)	6,250	(× 0.3)	7,500	(× 60/60)	25,000
			16,000		30,000		76,750

	Receipts and inspection	Storage	Packaging
Cost	$209,000	$347,250	383,750
Cost/unit of activity	$13.0625 per hour	$11.575 per m·	$5 per hour

ABC-based costs

	Customer A	Customer B	Customer C
	$	$	$
Material	10.00	20.00	30.00
Receipts ($13.0625/hour)	1.31	1.96	3.27
Storage ($11.575/m·)	3.47	3.47	3.47
Packing ($5/hour)	3.00	3.75	5.00
Product cost/unit	17.78	29.18	41.74

(b) Total costs per unit for Lard Company are not much different using activity based costing than they are with traditional absorption costing. However, ABC analysis allows management to look at the costs of overhead-related activities. This may help them to control these costs, through better management of these activities and the resources they use.

3   LC Company

(a)

Budgeted machine hours	hours
Product V: 6,000 × 3	18,000
Product W: 4,000 × 4	16,000
Total budgeted machine hours	34,000
Budgeted production overheads	$816,000
Absorption rate per machine hour	$24

	Product V	Product W
	$	$
Direct materials	20	60
Direct labour	50	40
Production overhead (3 hours/4 hours × $24)	72	96
Full production cost per unit	142	196

(b) **Machine-related overhead costs:**
Overhead cost per machine hour = $204,000/34,000 hours = $6 per machine hour

Setup related overhead costs:
Overhead cost per setup = $280,000/(18 + 32) = $5,600 per setup.

Purchasing-related overhead costs:
Cost per purchase order = $332,000/ (48 + 112) = $2,075 per order.

Overhead cost analysis		Product V Total cost	Cost/ unit		Product W Total cost	Cost/ unit
Overheads:		$	$		$	$
Machine-related	(18,000 × 6)	108,000	18.0	(16,000 × 6)	96,000	24.0
Setup related	(18 × 5,600)	100,800	16.8	(32 × 5,600)	179,200	44.8
Purchasing-related	(48 × 2,075)	99,600	16.6	(112 × 2,075)	232,400	58.1
		308,400	51.4		507,600	126.9

Unit costs	V	W
	$	$
Direct materials	20.0	60.0
Direct labour	50.0	40.0
Production overhead	51.4	126.9
Full production cost per unit	121.4	226.9

(c)   ABC analysis could be used by LC Company to analyse the profitability of Products V and W. Using ABC, the overhead cost per unit of W is much higher than with traditional absorption costing, and the cost per unit of V is less. This is because Product W has a relatively large amount of setup activity and purchasing-related activity.

Management could look at the reasons why Product W needs so many setups and purchase orders, and by trying to reduce the resources used up by these activities, it might be possible to reduce the costs (and increase the profitability) of Product W.

4   Customer profitability

Workings

Product	Units	Contribution per unit	Total contribution	Total sales revenue
		$	$	$
A	100,000	1.20	120,000	360,000
B	150,000	0.50	75,000	375,000
C	120,000	1.20	144,000	480,000
D	180,000	0.90	162,000	432,000
E	80,000	2.00	160,000	480,000
			661,000	2,127,000

Contribution per customer category

	Total contribution	Category of customer			
		C1	C2	C3	C4
	$	$	$	$	$
Product A	120,000	12,000	24,000	24,000	60,000
Product B	75,000	30,000	0	22,500	22,500
Product C	144,000	14,400	28,800	14,400	86,400
Product D	162,000	48,600	16,200	32,400	64,800
Product E	160,000	32,000	0	32,000	96,000
Total	661,000	137,000	69,000	125,300	329,700

Rebates

	Total sales		C3		C4
	$		$		$
Product A	360,000	20%	72,000	50%	180,000
Product B	375,000	30%	112,500	30%	112,500
Product C	480,000	10%	48,000	60%	288,000
Product D	432,000	20%	86,400	40%	172,800
Product E	480,000	20%	96,000	60%	288,000
Total			414,900		1,041,300
Rebate %			5%		10%
Rebate in $			$20,745		$104,130

ABC apportionment rates

	Number of deliveries	Km per delivery	Total kilometres
C1	40	100	4,000
C2	80	200	16,000
C3	50	300	15,000
C4	100	150	15,000
			50,000

Apportionment rates

- Delivery costs: $250,000/50,000 = $5 per kilometre

- Order processing: $105,000/(30 + 70 + 50 + 60) = $500 per order

- Promotion events: $30,000/12 = $2,500 per event.

Statement of customer profitability

	C1	C2	C3	C4	Total
	$	$	$	$	$
Contribution	137,000	69,000	125,300	329,700	661,000
Rebates	0	0	(20,745)	(104,130)	(124,875)
	137,000	69,000	104,555	225,570	536,125
Activity costs					
Delivery	(20,000)	(80,000)	(75,000)	(75,000)	(250,000)
Order processing	(15,000)	(35,000)	(25,000)	(30,000)	(105,000)
Promotion events	0	0	(5,000)	(25,000)	(30,000)
Customer profitability	102,000	(46,000)	(445)	95,570	151,125
Other fixed costs					(80,000)
Company profit					71,125

5 Backflush

Backflush accounting, with two trigger points

Raw materials inventory account

	$		$
Creditors	5,000,000	Finished goods inventory	5,000,000

Finished goods inventory account

		$		$
Raw materials	(100,000 × 50)	5,000,000	Income statement (98,000 × 80)	7,840,000
Conversion costs	(100,000 × 30)	3,000,000	Balance c/f (2,000 × 80)	160,000
		8,000,000		8,000,000

Conversion costs account

	$		$
Creditors (overheads)	3,000,000	Finished goods inventory	3,000,000
	3,000,000		3,000,000

Sales

	$		$
Income statement (98,000 × 100)	9,800,000	Receivables (98,000 × 100)	9,800,000

Income statement

	$		$
Finished goods	7,840,000	Sales	9,800,000
Profit	1,960,000		
	9,800,000		9,800,000

6 Throughput

(a) **Marginal costing approach**

Profit will be maximised by producing output to maximise the contribution per machine hour (contribution per unit of limiting factor).

	Product X	Product Y
Contribution per unit	$6	$7
Machine hours per unit	1.5 hours	2 hours
Contribution per machine hour	$4	$3.50
Priority for manufacture	1st	2nd

Profit will be maximised by making and selling 8,000 units of Product X in each period (maximum sales demand). This will require 12,000 machine hours. The remaining 20,000 machine hours should be used to make and sell 10,000 units of Product Y.

	$
Contribution from Product X: 8,000 × $6	48,000
Contribution from Product Y: 10,000 × $7	70,000
Total contribution	118,000
Fixed costs	90,000
Profit	28,000

(b) Throughput accounting is based on the view that value is not added to a product until the product is eventually sold. There is no value in inventory. When there is a limiting factor restricting production, all costs except for the cost of bought-in materials (raw materials, purchased components) are fixed costs in the short-term, including direct labour costs and associated 'variable' overheads.

The aim should be to maximise throughput in a period, where throughput is defined as sales minus the cost of bought-in materials.

The main difference between throughput accounting and marginal costing is in the treatment of direct labour and variable overhead costs as a 'fixed cost' in the short-term. In throughput accounting, fixed costs are referred to as 'factory cost'.

(c)   Throughput accounting ratio =

Return per bottleneck unit / Factory cost per bottleneck unit

Here, the bottleneck resource is machine time.

	Product X	Product Y
	$	$
Sales price	22	27
Materials cost	10	9
Throughput	12	18
Machine hours per unit	1.5 hours	2 hours
Throughput/return per machine hour	$8	$9

To calculate the cost per factory hour, we need to make an assumption about direct labour cost and variable overhead costs. It is assumed that the direct labour cost and variable overhead cost in the answer to part (a) is fixed in the short-term.

	$
Direct labour and variable overhead costs:	
Product X: 8,000 × $6	48,000
Product Y: 10,000 × $11	110,000
Total contribution	158,000
Fixed costs	90,000
Factory cost in each period	248,000

Factory cost per machine hour = $248,000/32,000 hours = $7.75.

	Product X	Product Y
Return per machine hour	$8	$9
Factory cost per machine hour	$7.75	$7.75
Machine hours per unit	1.5 hours	2 hours
Throughput accounting ratio	1.03	1.16
Priority for manufacture	2ⁿᵈ	1ˢᵗ

Tutorial note: The aim should be to maximise the throughput accounting ratio, and to ensure that the ratio is higher than 1.0. The throughput accounting ratio for both Product X and Product Y is low, close to the minimum acceptable level.

(d)   Profit will be maximised by making and selling 12,000 units of Product Y (maximum sales demand). This will use up 24,000 machine hours. The remaining 8,000 machine hours should be used to make 5,333.33 units of Product X.

	$
Return from Product Y: 12,000 × $18	216,000
Return from Product Y: 5,333.33 × $12	64,000
Total return/throughput	280,000
Fixed costs	248,000
Profit	32,000

7   Throughput ratio

Throughput per pallet = $3,000 – $2,000 = $1,000.

Throughput per inspection hour = $1,000/0.5 hours = $2,000.

Operating expenses per inspection hour = $300,000/200 = $1,500.

Throughput accounting ratio = $2,000/$1,500 = 1.33.

8   Four products

	W	X	Y	Z
	£	£	£	£
Sales price/unit	50.0	31.5	59.75	54.25
Variable cost/unit	10.0	11.5	11.75	12.25
Contribution per unit	40.0	20.0	48.00	42.00
Direct materials per unit (£)	5	4	8	6
Contribution/£1 direct material	£8.0	£5.0	£6.0	£7.0
Priority for making and selling	1·	4·	3·	2·

Profit-maximising budget

Product	Sales units	Direct materials	Contribution per unit	Total contribution
		£	£	£
W (1st)	4,000	20,000	40	160,000
Z (2nd)	3,000	18,000	42	126,000
Y (3rd) - balance	5,000	40,000	48	240,000
		78,000		526,000

8   Limiting factors

(a)

	A	B	C	D
	£	£	£	£
Sales price	100	110	120	120
Variable cost per litre	54	55	59	66
Contribution per litre	46	55	61	54
Direct labour hours/unit	3	2.5	4	4.5
Contribution /direct labour hour	£15.33	£22	£15.25	£12
Priority for manufacture/sale	2nd	1st	3rd	4th

The fixed overhead absorption rate is £8 per hour. This can be calculated from the overhead cost and direct labour hours for any of the four products.

The budgeted labour hours for calculating this absorption rate was 1,600 hours, therefore budgeted fixed costs are 1,600 hours × £8 = £12,800.

The output and sales that will maximise contribution and profit is as follows:

Product	Litres	Hours	Contribution/litre	Contribution/profit
			£	£
B	150.0	375	55	8,250.0
A	200.0	600	46	9,200.0
C (balance)	92.5	370	61	5,642.5
		1,345		23,092.5
Fixed costs (see above)				12,800.0
Profit				10,292.5

(b)   In this situation, there is a minimum sales demand from Company Y that must be met:

Product	Litres	Hours	Contribution/litre	Contribution
			£	£
A: (3 hours/litre)	20	60	46	920
B: (2.5 hours/litre)	20	50	55	1,100
C: (4 hours/litre)	20	80	61	1,220
D: (4.5 hours/litre)	20	90	54	1,080
		280		4,320
Total hours available		1,345		
Hours remaining		1,065		

The remaining 1,065 hours should be used to maximise contribution, using the same priorities as before. However, maximum sales demand should be reduced by 20 litres for each product, to allow for the sales to Company Y.

The output and sales that will maximise contribution and profit, allowing for the sales to Company Y, are as follows:

Product	Litres	Hours	Contribution/litre	Contribution/profit
			£	£
B	130	325	55	7,150
A	180	540	46	8,280
C (balance)	50	200	61	3,050
		1,065		18,480
Contribution from sales to Y				4,320
Total contribution				22,800
Fixed costs				12,800
Profit				10,000

9   Shortages

Working: contribution per unit

	A	B	C	D
	$/unit	$/unit	$/unit	$/unit
Profit	35	55	30	55
Fixed costs:				
Production	180	240	150	270
Selling	145	225	120	215
Contribution	360	520	300	540

Resources required for the priority order for the major customer

Casing	Units required	Steel		Direct labour	
		per unit	Total	per unit	Total
		$	$	hours	hours
A	30	250	7,500	7.5	225.0
B	20	500	10,000	7.5	150.0
C	30	190	5,700	6.25	187.5
D	20	390	7,800	12.5	250.0
Total			31,000		812.5

(a) **Steel in short supply and restricted to $250,000**

Casing	A	B	C	D
	$	$	$	$
Contribution/unit	360	520	300	540
Steel costs/unit	250	500	190	390
Contribution/$1 steel cost	1.44	1.04	1.58	1.38
Ranking for manufacture	2nd	4th	1st	3rd

It is assumed that the sales forecasts for the month are correct.

Profit-maximising production schedule

	Steel used	A	B	C	D
	$	units	units	units	units
Priority order	31,000	30	20	30	20
Sales of C	51,300			270	
Sales of A	67,500	270			
Sales of D	70,200				180
	220,000				
Balance: Sales of B	30,000		60		
Total steel available	250,000				
Total production/sales		300	80	300	200

(b) **Components are in short supply and restricted to 400 units**

	A	B	C	D
Contribution/unit	$360	£520	$300	$540
Components/unit	1	1	1	1
Contribution/component	£360	$520	$300	$540
Ranking for manufacture	3rd	2nd	4th	1st

Profit-maximising production schedule

	Components used	A	B	C	D
	units	units	units	units	units
Priority order	100	30	20	30	20
Sales of D	180				180
	280				
Balance: Sales of B	120		120		
Total available	400				
Total production/sales		30	140	30	200

(c) Labour is in short supply and restricted to 2,125 hours

Casing	A	B	C	D
Contribution/unit	$360	$520	$300	$540
Labour hours/unit	7.5	7.5	6.25	12.5
Contribution per hour	$48.00	$69.33	$48.00	$43.20
Ranking for manufacture	2nd	1st	2nd	4th

Profit-maximising production schedule

	Labour hours	A	B	C	D
		units	units	units	units
Special order	812.5	30	20	30	20
Remaining hours	1,312.5		175		
Total hours	2,125.0				
Total production/sales		30	195	30	20

(d) Make or buy decision

	A	B	C	D
	$	$	$	$
Contribution if made	360	520	300	540
Contribution if bought in	285	475	250	490
Extra contribution if made	75	45	50	50
Labour hours	7.5	7.5	6.25	12.5
Extra contribution per hour	$10	$6	$8	$4
Ranking/priority for making	1st	2nd	3rd	4th

Profit-maximising production schedule

Casing	Hours	A	B	C	D
Special order	1,625	30	20	30	20
Remaining hours	2,625	175			
Total hours	4,250				
Made internally		205	20	30	20
Purchased externally		95	180	270	180
Total sales		300	200	300	200

10 Proglin

Let the number of units of Mark 1 be x
Let the number of units of Mark 2 be y.

The objective function is to maximise total contribution: 10x + 15y.

Subject to the following constraints:

Direct materials	$2x + 4y$	$\leq$	24,000
Direct labour	$3x + 2y$	$\leq$	18,000
Sales demand, Mark 1	x	$\leq$	5,000
Non-negativity	x, y	$\geq$	0

These constraints are shown in the graph below. The graph also shows an iso-contribution line 10x + 15y = 60,000.

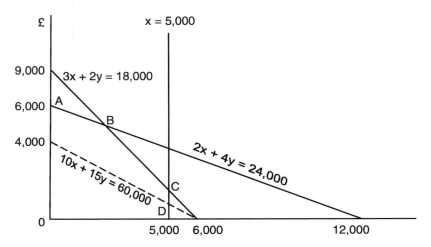

The feasible solutions are shown by the area 0ABCD in the graph.

Using the slope of the iso-contribution line, it can be seen that contribution is maximised at point B on the graph.

At point B, we have the following simultaneous equations:

(1)	2x + 4y	=	24,000
(2)	3x + 2y	=	18,000

Multiply (2) by 2

| (3) | 6x + 4y | = | 36,000 |

Subtract (1) from (3)

| | 4x | = | 12,000 |

Therefore

| | x | = | 3,000 |

Substitute in equation (1)

	2 (3,000) + 4y	=	24,000
	4y	=	18,000
	y	=	4,500

The objective in this problem is to maximise 10x + 15y.

The total contribution where x = 3,000 and y = 4,500 is as follows:

	£
3,000 units of Mark 1 (× £10)	30,000
4,500 units of Mark 2 (× £15)	67,500
Total contribution	97,500

(b)   The graph for a linear programming solution is virtually identical to the graph shown above, and the solution is still at point B. However, at point B:

(1)	2x + 4y	=	24,001
(2)	3x + 2y	=	18,000

Multiply (2) by 2

| (3) | 6x + 4y | = | 36,000 |

Subtract (1) from (3)

4x	=	11,999

Therefore x = 2,999.75

Substitute in equation (2)

3 (2,999.75) + 2y	=	18,000
2y	=	9,000.75
y	=	4,500.375

The objective in this problem is to maximise $10x + 15y$.

The total contribution where $x = 2,999.75$ and $y = 4,500.375$ is as follows:

	£
2,999.75 units of Mark 1 (× £10)	29,997.500
4,500.375 units of Mark 2 (× £15)	67,505.625
Total costs	97,503.125

The effect of having £1 more of direct materials would be an increase of £3.125 in total contribution.

The shadow price of direct materials is therefore £3.125 per £1 of direct materials.

11 Price

(a) If the profit margin is one-sixth of the selling price:

	£
Selling price	100.00
Profit as a % of sales price	16.67
Full cost as % of sales price	83.33

Profit as % of full cost = $(16.67/83.33) \times 100\% = 20\%$.

	£
Full cost	100
Profit margin (20%)	20
Selling price	120

(b)

	£
Direct materials:	
Material M1	30
Material M2	4
Direct labour	30
Variable cost	64
Selling price	120
Mark-up	56

The required mark-up on variable cost would be $56/64 = 0.875$ or 87.5%.

(c) Alternative pricing strategies are price skimming and penetration pricing.

Premium pricing would also be an acceptable solution.

Price discrimination, with different prices charged for the same product in different geographical markets, would also be acceptable.

12 Marginal

When p = 250, q = 400,000.

The quantity sold will fall by 20,000 for every $10 increase in price.

Therefore the price when q = 0 will be 250 + [(400,000/20,000) × $10] = 450

The price function can be stated as:

P_q = 450 – (10/20,000)q = 450 – 0.0005q.

Total revenue = pq = (450 – 0.0005q)q = 450q – 0.0005q²

Marginal revenue = 450 – (2 × 0.0005 × q) = 450 – 0.001q

Marginal cost = variable cost per unit = 210.

Profit is maximised where MR = MC:

450 – 0.001q = 210

0.001q = 240

q = 240,000 units.

At this volume of sales, p = 450 – 0.0005 (240,000) = 330.

Profit is maximised at a price of $330 per unit, and annual sales will be 240,000 units.

	$000
Sales (240,000 × 330)	79,200
Variable costs (240,000 × 210)	50,400
Contribution	28,800
Fixed costs	20,000
Profit	8,800

The annual profit will be $8,800,000.

13 MC = MR

(a) The demand falls by 1,000 units for every $20 increase in price.

Demand will be 0 when the sales price is $50 + $20 × (1,000/1,000) = $70. The quantity demanded rises by 20/1,000 = 0.02 for every unit of demand.

The **demand curve** can therefore be expressed as:

P = 70 – 0.02Q

(b) **Total revenue** = PQ = (70 – 0.02Q)Q
= 70Q – 0.02Q²

(c) Marginal revenue = 70 – 0.04Q
Marginal cost = 8

Profit is maximised where MC = MR

8 = 70 – 0.04Q

Q = 62/0.04 = 1,550

P = 70 – 0.02Q = 70 – 0.02 (1,550) = 39.

The profit is maximised at a price of $39, when demand will be 1,550 units.
Contribution per unit will be $31 ($39 – $8).
Total contribution will be $48,050 ($31 × 1,550).

14   Snap Company

(a)   (i)   Full cost pricing plus, on the current basis

	$000
Direct materials	12
Direct labour	8
Direct cost	20
Production overheads (100% of direct cost)	20
Full production cost	40
Administrative and marketing overheads (25%)	10
Full cost of sale	50
Profit (20% of full cost of sale)	10
Selling price for order (5,000 units)	60

Sales price per unit = $12.

(ii)   Price to maintain budgeted profit of $50,000

If sales of SP8 falls are 25% below budget, the expected profit will be as
follows.

		$000
Direct costs	75% × 100,000	75.0
Variable overheads	75% × 50,000	37.5
Total variable costs		112.5
Fixed production overhead		50.0
Other fixed overheads		50.0
Total costs		212.5
Sales	75% × 300,000	225.0
Profit		12.5

In order to make a profit of $50,000 for the year, the simplified units of
SP8 must make $37,500 contribution to profit. The price for the order
should be as follows:

	$000
Materials	12.0
Labour	8.0
Direct cost	20.0
Variable overhead (see note)	10.0
Variable cost	30.0
Contribution	37.5
Selling price	67.5

Note: Variable overheads are assumed to vary with direct materials cost. In the original budget, variable overheads are $50,000 and direct material costs are $60,000. Variable overheads are therefore 50/60 × material costs. For the simplified units, variable overheads will be $12,000 × 50/60 = $10,000.

The selling price per unit would need to be $67,500/5,000 units = $13.50.

(b)   Advice

The price of SP8 is currently $15 ($300,000/20,000 units). The price for the simplified units of SP8 must be lower than this; otherwise the customer will not buy them.

A price of $13.50 is needed to achieve the budgeted profit, but the customer may be unwilling to pay this amount. A price of $12 will give a profit of 20% on full cost, using the budgeted absorption rates for overhead, but there will be some under-absorbed overheads.

Any price in excess of the minimum price of $30,000 ($6 per unit) will make profit higher than it will be if the simplified units are not sold to the customer.

However, the company must think of the longer term. Will the customer want to buy more units of the simplified product next year? If so, the company will want to charge a price at which it will make satisfactory profits.

The recommendation should therefore be to negotiate with the customer. If the agreed price is lower than $13.50, Snap Co might want to warn the customer that more units of the simplified SP8 might not be available in the future, except at a higher price.

15   Bridge Company

(a)   Budgeted variable production costs

	Cost in current year	Inflation	Cost next year Current material	New material
	$	%		
Direct material	30	20	36.0	31.25
Direct labour	10	5	10.5	10.50
Variable o'hd	10	5	10.5	10.50
	50		57.0	52.25
Cost of rejected units (5%)				2.75
				55.00

Using the cheaper substitute material will reduce the variable unit cost by $2, but fixed costs will increase by $30,000. Since annual sales at the current price will be 20,000 units, it will be more profitable to use the cheaper material.

The unit variable cost will be $55.

Annual fixed costs will be:

	$
Costs in the current year ($10 × 20,000 units)	200,000
Add inflation (10%)	20,000
Inspection costs	30,000
Total fixed costs for the year	250,000

(b) Optimal selling price

Method 1

It is assumed that the only sales prices to be considered are those in the sales manager's estimates of sales demand.

The variable cost will be $55 per unit.

Price	Contribution/unit	Sales	Total contribution
$	$	000 units	$000
80	25	25	625
84	29	23	667
88	33	21	693
90	35	20	700
92	37	19	703
96	41	17	697
100	45	15	675

Contribution will be maximised at a price of $92, and sales will be 19,000 units.

	$
Total contribution	703,000
Fixed costs	250,000
Profit	453,000

Method 2

It is assumed that the sales manager has identified a straight-line demand curve, and any sales price on this curve may be selected.

Sales demand falls by 1,000 units for every $2 increase in the sales price.

Sales demand will be 0 when the sales price is $130 [$100 + (15 × $2)]

Demand curve:

$P = 130 - 2Q$, where Q is sales demand in 000s units

Total revenue $TR = (130 - 2Q)Q = 130Q - 2Q^2$

Marginal revenue $MR = 130 - 4Q$

Marginal cost MC = variable cost per unit = 55.

Profit is maximised when MR = MC

$130 - 4Q = 55$

$Q = 18.75$

Price $= 130 - 2(18.75) = \$92.50$.

Profit will be maximised at a price of $92.50, and the contribution per unit will be $37.50.

	$
Total contribution (18,750 × $37.50)	703,125
Fixed costs	250,000
Profit	453,125

16   Materials and relevant costs

Material X: This material is in regular use. Its relevant cost is therefore its current replacement cost, because any existing stocks will be replaced if they are used on the job.

Materials Y and Z: The relevant cost of the additional quantities that will have to be purchased is their current replacement cost.

Material Y: units already in stock. The relevant cost of these units is their opportunity cost, which is the cash that could be obtained by disposing of them.

Material Z: units already in stock. The relevant cost of these units is the higher value of their disposal value (£20 per unit) and the contribution that they would earn if they are used as a substitute material on a different job (£25 per unit)

Relevant costs

	£	£
Material X: 800 units × £23		18,400
Material Y:		
Opportunity cost of units in stock = disposal value (400 units × £12)	4,800	
Purchase cost of additional units (200 units × £19)	3,800	
		8,600
Material Z:		
Opportunity cost of units in stock = (300 units × £25)	7,500	
Purchase cost of additional units (200 units × £40)	8,000	
		15,500
Total relevant cost of materials		42,500

17   Printing leaflets

(a)   **Tutorial note**: The volume of sales required to achieve a target profit is an application of CVP analysis.

	£	£
Target profit		5,400
General fixed costs		12,000
Specific fixed costs:		
Leaflet Type A		7,200
Leaflet Type B		12,000
Leaflet Type C		28,500
Total contribution required		65,100
Contribution from:		
50,000 Leaflets Type A: (50 × (300 − 120))	9,000	
50,000 Leaflets Type B: (50 × (660 − 210))	22,500	
		31,500
Contribution required from Leaflets Type C		33,600

The contribution from Leaflets Type C is £(1,350 − 390) = £960 per 1,000 leaflets.

The sales quantity of Leaflets Type C required to achieve a target profit of £5,400 each month is therefore £33,600/£960 per 1,000 = 35,000 leaflets.

(b)

Relevant costs	£
Materials	
To be purchased: 10,000 × £500/1,000	5,000
Currently held in stock	6,000
(Relevant cost = higher of [£1,500 and (20,000 × £300/1,000)]	
Variable costs of labour/overheads	2,400
(30,000 × £80/1,000)	
Total relevant costs	13,400
Contract price	25,000
Incremental profit	11,600

18   Company JB

The contract should be accepted if the revenue from the contract will exceed the relevant costs of the contract.

Workings

Material M1. This material is in continuous/regular use. The relevant cost of the 1,000 kilograms is their replacement cost.

Relevant cost = 400 components × 3 kilos × £5.50 per kilo = £6,600.

Material P2. The material held in stock has a relevant cost that is the higher of its scrap value (£1.50) and the costs saved by putting it to an alternative use, which is £2 (£3.60 – £1.60).

There are more units held in stock than are needed for the contract. The excess quantity should be ignored.

Relevant cost of material in stock = 400 components × 2 kilos × £2 per kilo = £1,600.

Part 678. Relevant cost = 400 components × £50 = £20,000.

Skilled labour. The relevant cost of skilled labour is the extra cash that would have to be spent to hire additional labour.

Relevant cost = 400 components × 5 hours per component × £4 per hour = £8,000.

Semi-skilled labour. Relevant cost = 400 components × 5 hours per component × £3 per hour = £6,000.

Variable overheads. It is assumed that the overhead absorption rate for variable overheads is the rate at which cash expenditure is incurred on variable overheads.

Relevant cost = 400 components × 4 machine hours per component × £7 per machine hour = £11,200.

Relevant cost statement	£
Material M1	6,600
Material P2	1,600
Part 678	20,000
Skilled labour	8,000
Semi-skilled labour	6,000
Variable overheads	11,200
Incremental fixed costs	3,200
Total relevant costs	56,600
Contract sales value (400 × £145)	58,000
Incremental profit	1,400

Undertaking the contract will add £1,400 to total profit. On a purely financial basis, this means that the contract is worth undertaking. However, management might take the view that a higher profit margin is desirable, and the suggested price of £145 per component might be negotiable.

19 Product B22

Workings for relevant costs

Material X

The company has enough kilograms of material X in stock for the contract. When it is used, the stocks of material X will not be replaced. The relevant cost of the material is therefore its opportunity cost, not its replacement cost. The opportunity cost is the higher of its current sale value ($7.50 per kg) or the net saving obtained if it is used as a substitute for material Z ($9.50 – $1.50 = $8 per kg). The relevant cost of material X is therefore $8 per kg.

Material Y

Material Y is in regular use, so its relevant cost is its current replacement cost.

	kg		$
Total inventory	10,000		142,750
Purchased six months ago	3,000	(× $13.75)	41,250
Purchased last month	7,000		101,500

Purchase price last month = $101,500/7,000 kg = $14.50 per kg.

Current purchase price = 4% higher = $14.50 × 1.04 = $15.08.

Skilled labour

Skilled labour is in short supply. If it is used to make product B22, workers will have to be taken off other work. The relevant cost of skilled labour is the wages for the skilled workers for the time spent on B22, plus the lost contribution (net of skilled labour cost) from not being able to make units of product B16.

Opportunity cost of skilled labour

Skilled labour cost per unit of Product B16 = $24
Number of hours per unit = 3 hours
Contribution per unit of B16 = $45
Contribution per skilled labour hour from B16 = $15
Opportunity cost of skilled labour if it is used to make B22 = (500 × 5) × $15 = $37,500

Unskilled labour

900 unskilled labour will be available at no incremental cost to the company (as it is already being paid and is not fully employed). There is no relevant cost for these hours. The additional 600 hours required will involve extra wage payments, including overtime payments. The relevant cost of these 600 hours is $6 per hour × 150% = $9 per hour, including the overtime premium.

Overheads

Variable overheads are included as relevant costs because they will be additional costs if the units of B22 are made. The only incremental fixed costs, however, are the extra cash costs of $4,000. The fixed overhead absorption rate is ignored. The additional costs of hiring special finishing machinery are also included as a relevant cost.

Development costs

Those costs already incurred are past costs (sunk costs) and are not relevant. The future development costs involve additional expenditure and are included as relevant costs.

Minimum price for making 500 units of B22

Materials:		£
X	(500 units × 4kg) × $8	16,000
Y	(500 units × 6kg) × $15.08	45,240
Labour:		
Skilled wages	(500 units × 5 hours) × $8	20,000
Opportunity cost	(500 units × 5 hours) × $15	37,500
Unskilled	[(500 × 3) − 900] x 6 × 1.5	5,400
Overheads:		
Variable	(500 units × 2 hours) × 8.75	8,750
Fixed	Incremental spending	4,000
Machine hire	(2 weeks × $2,650)	5,300
Development costs		1,750
Minimum price		143.940

20 Make or buy

(a)

	Component A	Component B
	£	£
Cost of making internally	10.0	17.0
Cost of buying	12.5	23.0
Extra variable cost of buying	2.5	6.0
Quantities required next year	30,000	20,000
	£	£
Total extra variable cost of buying	75,000	120,000
Fixed costs saved by closure	40,000	50,000
Net extra costs of buying	35,000	70,000

It appears that it would cost the company more each year to shut down internal production of either component and switch to external purchasing.

(b)

Production hours required	hours
Component A (30,000 × 0.25 hours)	7,500
Component B (20,000 × 0.75 hours)	15,000
Total hours required	22,500
Total hours available	19,500
Shortfall	3,000

There are insufficient hours available to manufacture everything internally. Some components must be purchased externally.

	Component A	Component B
	£ per unit	£ per unit
Cost of making internally	10.0	17.0
Cost of buying	12.5	23.0
Cost saved by making	2.5	6.0
Hours required to make internally (£3/£12 per hour: £9/£12 per hour)	0.25 hours	0.75 hours
Costs saved per hour by making (£2.50/0.25 hours: £6/0.75 hours)	£10	£8

It is better to make Component A internally than Component B.

Component	Units	Hours	Cost/unit	Cost
			£	£
A	30,000	7,500	10	300,000
B (balance)	16,000	12,000	17	272,000
Variable cost of internal manufacture		19,500		572,000
Cost of external purchase – balance of units required	4,000		23	92,000
Fixed costs				120,000
Total costs				784,000

21 Villaco

(a) Total machine hours required to meet sales demand = (2,000 × 4) + (3,000 × 1) = 11,000. Since only 7,000 hours are available, machine hours are a limiting factor.

	Product A	Product B
	$	$
Sales price	20	10
Variable cost	8	6
Contribution	12	4
Machine hours per unit	4	1
Contribution per hour	$3	$4
Priority for manufacture	2nd	1st

Decision: produce and sell the following products:

Product	Units	Machine hours	Contribution per unit	Total contribution
			$	$
B	3,000	3,000	4	12,000
A (balance)	1,000	4,000	12	12,000
		7,000		24,000

(b)

	Product A	Product B
	$	$
Extra cost of external purchase	1	0.50
Machine hours saved by external purchase	4	1
Extra cost per machine hour saved	$0.25	$0.50
Priority for manufacture	2nd	1st

Item	Number of units	Machine hours	Contribution per unit	Contribution
			$	$
Make				
A	1,750	7,000	12	21,000
Buy				
A (balance)	250	(12 − 1)	11	2,750
B	3,000	(4 − 0.5)	3.5	10,500
Total contribution				34,250

22 Payoff table

a)

Cost of production Quantity	$	Revenue from selling Quantity	$
20	2	20	6
40	4	40	12
60	6	60	18

Pay-off table

	Sales demand per day		
	20	40	60
Production per day	$	$	$
20	4	4	4
	(6 − 2)	(6 − 2)	(6 − 2)
40	2	8	8
	(6 − 4)	(12 − 4)	(12 − 4)
60	0	6	12
	(6 − 6)	(12 − 6)	(18 − 6)

b)

	Sales demand			EV of daily profit
	20	**40**	**60**	**$**
Probability	0.3	0.5	0.2	
Production per day	$	$	$	
20	4	4	4	
EV	1.2	2.0	0.8	4.0
40	2	8	8	
EV	0.6	4.0	1.6	6.2
60	0	6	12	
EV	0	3.0	2.4	5.4

On the basis of EV the decision should be to produce 40 buns per day, and the EV of daily profit will be $6.20.

23 Probabilities

Cash inflows for the project can be calculated as an EV of expected annual cash inflows.

The first step is to establish a probability distribution of possible outcomes.

	Factor 1	Factor 2	Factor 3	Joint probability
Yes, No, No	0.2	0.7	0.6	0.084
Yes, Yes, Yes	0.2	0.3	0.4	0.024
Yes, No, Yes	0.2	0.7	0.4	0.056
Yes, Yes, No	0.2	0.3	0.6	0.036
No, No, No	0.8	0.7	0.6	0.336
No, Yes, Yes	0.8	0.3	0.4	0.096
No, No, Yes	0.8	0.7	0.4	0.224
No, Yes, No	0.8	0.3	0.6	0.1440

Probability of outcome		Cash inflows as a proportion of expectation	EV
0.084	(- 25%)	0.75	0.0630
0.024	(- 25% − 10% + 5%)	0.70	0.0168
0.056	(- 25% + 5%)	0.80	0.0448
0.036	(- 25% − 10%)	0.65	0.0234
0.336		1.00	0.3360
0.096	(- 10% + 5%)	0.95	0.0912
0.224	(+ 5%)	1.05	0.2352
0.144	(- 10%)	0.90	0.1296
1.000			0.9400

The EV of cash inflows, allowing for the three additional factors, will be 94% of the original estimates.

Year	Cash inflows (0.94 of original estimate)	Cash outflows	Net cash flow	Discount factor at 10%	PV
	$m	$m	$m		$m
0	(6.25)		(6.25)	1.000	(6.25)
1	2.82	1.50	1.32	0.909	1.20
2	3.76	1.80	1.96	0.826	1.62
3	4.70	2.40	2.30	0.751	1.73
4	3.76	1.70	2.06	0.683	1.41
5	1.88	1.00	1.88	0.621	0.55
				NPV	+ 0.26

24 Grab Company

(a) Outcomes

Decision	Outcome	Turnover	Variable cost	Advance hire	Conversion premium	Profit
Low	Low	4,000	2,800	1,000	0	200
	Medium	8,500	5,950	1,000	850	700
	High	15,000	10,500	1,000	2,150	1,350
Medium	Low	4,000	2,800	1,500	0	(300)
	Medium	8,500	5,950	1,500	0	1,050
	High	15,000	10,500	1,500	1,300	1,700
High	Low	4,000	2,800	2,300	0	(1,100)
	Medium	8,500	5,950	2,300	0	250
	High	15,000	10,500	2,300	0	2,200

(b) Pay-off matrix

	Low	Medium	High	Expected value
Probability (p)	0.30	0.45	0.25	Σpx
Decision	x =	x =	x =	
Low	200	700	1,350	712.5
Medium	(300)	1,050	1,700	807.5
High	(1,100)	250	2,200	332.5

The highest expected value is earned if the medium advance hire usage contract is signed.

(c) Risk preferences

The above decision assumes a neutral risk preference. It is possible the organisation may adopt a different decision criterion than expected value. Other decision criteria may be based on a risk-seeking approach or a risk-averse approach.

Risk-seeking managers would prefer a maximax approach. This is to maximise the highest possible outcome. In this example this would require a high advance hire contract.

Risk-averse managers would prefer a maximin approach. This is to maximise the lowest possible outcome of a course of action. This would require a low advance hire contract.

25 Zero based budgeting

Zero based budgeting is most useful when:

- There is a lot of budget slack, and wasteful spending. Zero based budgeting can be much more effective than incremental budgeting in identifying and eliminating unnecessary expenditure in a budget.

- There is a shortage of resources for 'overhead' spending, and decisions have to be made about priorities for spending.

Zero based budgeting is more effective for the planning and control of overhead spending on overhead activities than for controlling direct costs of production.

A zero based budgeting operation can be time-consuming and expensive. It should not be needed every year. A ZBB approach to the budget might be sufficient, say, every three or four years.

26 Learning

(a)   (1)

	hours
Average time for 1st 2 units (200 hours × 80%)	160
Total time for 1st 2 units (160 × 2)	320
Time for first unit	200
Time for second unit	120

Selling price for the second unit:	$
Direct materials	2,000
Direct labour (120 hours × $15)	1,800
Fixed production overhead (120 hours × $20)	2,400
Full production cost	6,200
Profit margin (40%)	2,480
Selling price	8,680

(2)

	hours
Average time for 1st 4 units (200 hours × 80% × 80%)	128
Total time for 1st 4 units (128 × 4)	512
Time for 1st 2 units	320
Time for 3rd and 4th units	192
Average time per unit for 3rd and 4th units	96

Average price for the 3rd and 4th units:	$
Direct materials	2,000
Direct labour (96 hours × $15)	1,440
Fixed production overhead (96 hours × $20)	1,920
Full production cost	5,360
Profit margin (40%)	2,144
Average selling price	7,504

(3)

	hours
Average time for 1st 8 units (200 hours × 80% × 80% × 80%)	102.4
Total time for 1st 8 units (102.4 × 8)	819.2

Selling price for the first 8 units	$
Direct materials ($2,000 × 8)	16,000.0
Direct labour (819.2 hours × $15)	12,288.0
Fixed production overhead (819.2 hours × $20)	16,384.0
Full production cost	44,672.0
Profit margin (40%)	17,868.8
Selling price	62,540.8

This gives an average selling price of $7,817.6 per unit.

(b) (1)   It may be difficult to establish an expected learning rate. Reliable statistical evidence of a constant learning rate (for example, as in the aircraft manufacturing industry) is required.

(2)   Learning curve theory is of little value for the development of low-cost items where direct labour input is small. The benefits from the learning curve would be small and fairly insignificant.

(3)   Learning curve theory assumes that when the first unit has been made, every other unit will be similar. It does not allow for changes in design or other factors that could disrupt the learning effect and change the learning rate.

27   Greenears

The cost of producing batches 6 – 12 is the difference between:

■ the cost of producing batches 1 – 5, and
■ the cost of producing batches 1 – 12.

(1) Learning factor

$$\frac{\text{Logarithm } 0.85}{\text{Logarithm } 2} = \frac{-0.07058}{0.30103} = -0.23446$$

(2) Average labour cost of producing the first 5 batches

$$y = \$2,000 \times \frac{1}{5^{0.23446}}$$

$$= \$2,000 \, (0.68568)$$

$$= \$1,371 \text{ per batch}$$

(3) Average labour cost of producing the first 12 batches

$$y - \$2,000 \times \frac{1}{12^{0.23446}}$$

$$= \$2,000 \, (0.55844)$$

$$= \$1,117 \text{ per batch}$$

(4) Labour cost of producing batches 6 – 12

	$
Total cost for the first 12 batches (12 × $1,117)	13,404
Total cost for the first 5 batches (5 × $1,371)	6,855
Labour cost for batches 6 – 12	6,549

28 Regression

(a)

$$b = \frac{5(254) - (15)(79)}{5(55) - (15)(15)}$$

$$= \frac{1,270 - 1,185}{275 - 225}$$

$$b = 85/50 = 1.7$$

$$a = \frac{79}{5} - \frac{1.7(15)}{5}$$

$$a = 10.7$$

Forecast: Sales in $millions = 10.7 + 1.7x

Forecast for Year 6 (20X7) = 10.7 + 1.7(6) = 20.9 ($20.9 million)

Forecast for Year 7 (20X8) = 10.7 + 1.7(7) = 22.6 ($22.6 million).

(b)

$$r = \frac{85}{\sqrt{(50)[5(1,279) - (79)(79)]}}$$

$$r = 85/87.75 = + 0.97$$

This is very close to + 1, suggesting that the forecast will be very reliable.

29 Flexed budget

Workings

The high low method will be used to estimate fixed and variable costs.

	Production labour	Production overhead
	$	$
Total cost of 13,000 units	81,500	109,000
Total cost of 10,000 units	74,000	88,000
Variable cost of 3,000 units	7,500	21,000

Variable production labour cost per unit = $7,500/3,000 units = $2.50.

Variable production overhead cost per unit = $21,000/3,000 units = $7.00.

	Production labour	Production overhead
	$	$
Total cost of 10,000 units	74,000	88,000
Variable cost of 10,000 units (× $2.50/$7)	25,000	70,000
Fixed costs	49,000	18,000

Selling and distribution overhead	$
Total cost of 14,000 units	36,200
Total cost of 9,000 units	29,700
Variable cost of 5,000 units	6,500

Variable selling and distribution overhead cost per unit = $6,500/5,000 units = $1.30.

Selling and distribution overhead	$
Total cost of 9,000 units	29,700
Variable cost of 9,000 units (× $1.30)	11,700
Fixed costs	18,000

Summary	Fixed cost	Variable cost per unit
	$	$
Direct materials ($130,000/10,000 units)	-	13.00
Direct labour (excluding overtime)	49,000	2.50
Production overhead	18,000	7.00
Administration overhead (all fixed)	26,000	-
Selling and distribution overhead	18,000	1.30

Budgeted cost allowance – quarter 3

Production units: 15,000
Sales units: 14,500

	$
Materials (15,000 × $13)	195,000
Labour ($49,000 + (15,000 × $2.50))	86,500
Overtime (1,000 × $2.50 × 50%)	1,250
Production 0verhead ($18,000 + (15,000 × $7))	123,000
Administration overhead	26,000
Selling and distribution ($18,000 + (14,500 × $1.30))	36,850
	468,600

30　Budget preparation

(a)　Note: It is assumed that the trade receivables at the beginning of quarter 1 ($40,000) represent 40% of sales in Quarter 4 of the previous year. Sales in the previous quarter were therefore $100,000 ($40,000/0.40). From these sales, 38% ($38,000) will be received in cash in quarter 1 and 2% ($2,000) will be bad debts.

	Quarter 1	Quarter 2	Quarter 3	Quarter 4
	$	$	$	$
Receipts:				
From trade receivables (W1)				
38% of previous quarter sales	38,000	45,600	30,400	27,360
60% of this quarter sales	72,000	48,000	43,200	67,200
Total receipts	110,000	93,600	73,600	94,560
Payments:				
To suppliers of materials:				
Purchases in previous quarter	9,600	10,416	7,344	8,803
Purchases this quarter	24,304	17,136	20,541	23,498
Wages	11,550	8,190	9,786	11,172
Fixed overhead	45,000	48,000	47,000	50,000
Capital expenditure	-	50,000	-	-
Total payments	90,454	133,742	84,671	93,473
Receipts minus payments	19,546	(40,142)	(11,071)	1,087
Opening cash balance	22,000	41,546	1,404	(9,667)
Closing cash balance	41,546	1,404	(9,667)	(8,580)

Workings

(W1)

Sales budget:	Quarter 1	Quarter 2	Quarter 3	Quarter 4
Units	6,000	4,000	3,600	5,600
× $20	$120,000	$80,000	$72,000	$112,000
Received in:	$	$	$	$
Quarter 1	72,000			
Quarter 2	45,600	48,000		
Quarter 3		30,400	43,200	
Quarter 4			27,360	67,200
Bad debts (2%)	2,400	1,600	1,440	

(W2)

Production budget:	Quarter 1	Quarter 2	Quarter 3	Quarter 4
	units	units	units	units
Closing inventory	1,000	900	1,960	1,680
Sales in the month	6,000	4,000	3,600	5,600
	7,000	4,900	5,560	7,280
Opening inventory	1,500	1,000	900	1,960
Production in the month	5,500	3,900	4,660	5,320
Wages budget: $2.10 per unit	$11,550	$8,190	$9,786	$11,172

(W3)

Material purchases	Quarter 1	Quarter 2	Quarter 3	Quarter 4
	kilos	kilos	kilos	kilos
Closing inventory	3,200	2,900	2,600	2,300
Required for production				
(4 kilos per unit)	22,000	15,600	18,640	21,280
	25,200	18,500	21,240	23,580
Opening inventory	(3,500)	(3,200)	(2,900)	(2,600)
Purchases	21,700	15,300	18,340	20,980
Purchases ($1.60/ kilo)	$34,720	$24,480	$29,344	$33,568
Payable in:				
Quarter 1	$24,304			
Quarter 2	$10,416	$17,136		
Quarter 3		$7,344	$20,541	
Quarter 4			$8,803	$23,498

(b)   The variable cost per unit = (4 kilos × $1.60) + (0.3 hours × $7) = $8.50.

Production volume = (5,500 + 3,900 + 4,660 + 5,320) units = 19,380 units.

Budgeted income statement for the year	$	$
Sales (19,200 units at $20)		384,000
Minus Variable cost of sales		
Opening inventory (1,500 × $8.50)	12,750	
Production (19,380 × $8.50)	164,730	
	177,480	
Minus: Closing inventory (1,680 units × $8.50)	14,280	
		163,200
Contribution		220,800
Minus:		
Fixed overhead	190,000	
Depreciation (5% × $550,000)	27,500	
Bad debts written off (2% of sales)	7,680	
		225,180
Budgeted net loss		$(4,380)

31   Cash calculations

(a)   Cash receipts

| Sales | Total sales | Receipts in | | |
		January	February	March
	$000	$000	$000	$000
November	60	29.4	-	-
December	120	48.0	58.8	-
January	80	8.0	32.0	39.2
February	40	-	4.0	16.0
March	92	-	-	9.2
Total receipts		85.4	94.8	64.4

(b)   Cash payments

	January	February	March
	$	$	$
Budgeted closing inventory	20,000	25,000	25,000
Materials in cost of sales (25% of sales)	20,000	10,000	23,000
	40,000	35,000	48,000
Opening inventory	(18,000)	(20,000)	(25,000)
Material purchases	22,000	15,000	23,000

| Payments | Total purchases | Payments in | | |
		January	February	March
	$000	$000	$000	$000
Opening payables	21	21.0	-	-
January	22	6.6	15.4	-
February	15	-	4.5	10.5
March	23	-	-	6.9
Total payments		27.6	19.9	17.4

32   Cash budget

	June	July	August
	$	$	$
Cash sales	7,000	6,000	5,000
Cash from receivables	54,000	45,000	63,000
	61,000	51,000	68,000
Payments:			
Wages	12,000	10,000	9,000
To suppliers	30,000	25,000	35,000
Overhead: cash payments	12,000	16,000	14,000
Commission	2,250	3,150	2,700
Loan repaid	25,000		
Machine purchase		15,000	15,000
	81,250	69,150	75,700
Receipts minus payments	(20,250)	(18,150)	(7,700)
Opening cash balance	22,000	1,750	(16,400)
Closing cash balance	1,750	(16,400)	(24,100)

33   Cost estimation

(a)   High low method

		$
Total cost of	22,000 units	74,000
Total cost of	12,000 units	52,000
Therefore variable cost of	10,000 units	22,000

Variable cost per unit = $22,000/10,000 units = $2.20.

			$
Total cost of	22,000 units		74,000
Variable cost of	22,000 units	($\times$ $2.20)	48,400
Therefore fixed costs	10,000 units		25,600

Fixed costs = $25,600 per month.

In a month when output is 15,000 units, the estimated total costs are:

		$
Fixed costs		25,600
Variable costs	(15,000 $\times$ $2.20)	33,000
Total costs		58,600

(b)   Linear regression analysis

Workings

Output		Total cost		
x	y	x^2	xy	y^2
17	63	289	1,071	3,969
15	61	225	915	3,721
12	52	144	624	2,704
22	74	484	1,628	5,476
18	68	324	1,224	4,624
84	318	1,466	5,462	20,494

$$b = \frac{5(5,464)-(84)(318)}{5(1,466)-(84)^2}$$

$$= \frac{27,310-26,712}{7,330-7,056}$$

$$= \frac{598}{274} = 2.18$$

$$a = \frac{318}{5} - \frac{2.18(84)}{5}$$

$$= 63.6 - 36.6 = 27.0$$

Variable costs = \$2.18 per unit and fixed costs per month are \$27,000.

		$
Fixed costs		27,000
Variable costs	(15,000 × \$2.18)	32,700
Total costs		59,700

(c) **Correlation coefficient**

$$r = \frac{598}{\sqrt{(274)\left[5(20,494)-(318)^2\right]}}$$

$$= \frac{598}{\sqrt{(274)(102,470-101,124)}}$$

$$= \frac{598}{\sqrt{(274)(1,346)}}$$

$$= \frac{598}{607.3} = 0.98$$

A correlation coefficient close to + 1 indicates very strong positive correlation. The estimate of total costs using linear regression analysis should be very reliable.

34   Reconcile

Workings

Direct materials total cost variance

	£
14,800 units should cost (× £8)	118,400
They did cost	125,000
Direct materials total cost variance	6,600(A)

Direct labour total cost variance

	£
14,800 units should cost (× £6)	88,800
They did cost	92,000
Direct labour total cost variance	3,200(A)

Fixed production overheads total cost variance

	£
14,800 units: standard fixed overhead cost (× £12)	177,600
Actual fixed overhead cost	170,000
Fixed production overheads total cost variance	7,600(F)

Note: The fixed overhead total cost variance can be divided into:

(a)   an expenditure variance

(b)   a volume variance

Fixed production overheads expenditure variance

	£
Budgeted fixed overhead expenditure (14,000 × £12)	168,000
Actual fixed overhead expenditure	170,000
Fixed production overheads expenditure variance	2,000(A)

Fixed production overheads volume variance

	units
Budgeted units of production	14,000
Actual units produced	14,800
Fixed production overheads volume variance in units	800(F)

Standard fixed overheads per unit	£12
Fixed production overheads volume variance in £	£9,600(F)

Solution

Reconciliation statement

	£
Budgeted costs for the month (14,000 units × £26)	364,000
Extra standard costs of additional production (800 units × £26)	20,800
Standard costs of actual production (14,800 units × £26)	384,800
Cost variances	
Direct materials total cost variance	6,600(A)
Direct labour total cost variance	3,200(A)
Fixed overheads expenditure variance	2,000(A)
Fixed overheads volume variance	9,600(F)
Actual total costs in the month	387,000

35 Simple variances

(a)

Direct labour rate variance

	£
13,450 hours should cost (× £6)	80,700
They did cost	79,893
Labour rate variance	807(F)

Direct labour efficiency variance

	hours
3,350 units should take (× 4 hours)	13,400
They did take	13,450
Efficiency variance in hours	50(A)

Standard rate per hour	£6
Direct labour efficiency variance in £	£300(A)

(b)

Sales price variance

	£
850 units should sell for (× £9)	7,650
They did sell for	7,480
Sales price variance	170(A)

Sales volume variance, absorption costing

	units
Actual sales volume (units)	850
Budgeted sales volume (units)	800
Sales volume variance in units	50(F)

Standard profit per unit	£2
Sales volume variance (profit variance)	£100(F)

Sales volume contribution variance, marginal costing

Sales volume variance in units	50 (F)

Standard contribution per unit (£9 - £4)	£5
Sales volume variance (contribution variance)	£250(F)

(c)
(i)

Fixed production overhead total cost variance

	£
Standard fixed overhead cost of 14,600 units (× £20)	292,000
Actual fixed overhead expenditure	325,000
Fixed overhead total cost variance (under-absorption)	3,000(A)

(ii)

Fixed production overhead expenditure variance

	£
Budgeted fixed overhead expenditure (15,000 × £20)	300,000
Actual fixed overhead expenditure	325,000
Fixed overhead expenditure variance	25,000(A)

Fixed production overhead volume variance

	units
Budgeted production volume	15,000
Actual production volume	14,600
Volume variance in units	400(A)
Standard fixed overhead rate per unit	£20
Fixed production overhead volume variance in £	£8,000(A)

(iii)

Fixed production overhead efficiency variance

	hours
14,600 units should take (× 4 hours)	58,400
They did take	58,000
Efficiency variance in hours	400(F)
Standard fixed overhead rate per hour	£5
Fixed production overhead efficiency variance in £	£2,000(F)

Fixed production overhead capacity variance

	hours
Budgeted hours of work (15,000 × 4 hours)	60,000
Actual hours of work	58,000
Capacity variance in hours	2,000(A)
Standard fixed overhead rate per hour	£5
Fixed production overhead capacity variance in £	£10,000(A)

36　Manufacturing cost variance

Material price variance

	£
120,000 kilos of materials should cost (× £6)	720,000
They did cost	825,000
Material price variance	105,000(A)

Material usage variance

	kilos
20,000 units should use (× 5 kilos)	100,000
They did use	120,000
Material usage variance in kilos	20,000(A)
Standard price per kilo of material	£6
Material usage variance in £	£120,000(A)

Direct labour rate variance

	£
500,000 hours should cost (× £4)	200,000
They did cost (× £5)	250,000
Labour rate variance	50,000(A)

Direct labour idle time variance = 10,000 hours (A) × £4 per hour = £40,000 (A)

Direct labour efficiency variance

	hours
20,000 units should take (× 20 hours)	400,000
They did take (500,000 – 10,000)	490,000
Efficiency variance in hours	90,000(A)
Standard rate per hour	£4
Direct labour efficiency variance in £	£360,000(A)

Variable overhead total cost variance

	£
20,000 units should cost (× £4)	80,000
They did cost	70,000
Variable overhead total cost variance	10,000(F)

Fixed production overhead expenditure variance

	£
Budgeted fixed overhead expenditure (25,000 units × £100)	2,500,000
Actual fixed overhead expenditure	2,100,000
Fixed overhead expenditure variance	400,000(F)

Fixed production overhead volume variance

	units
Budgeted production volume	25,000
Actual production volume	20,000
Volume variance in units	5,000(A)
Standard fixed overhead rate per unit	£100
Fixed production overhead volume variance in £	£500,000(A)

Summary

Variance	Favourable	Adverse	
	£	£	
Material price		105,000	
Material usage		120,000	
Direct labour rate		50,000	
Direct labour idle time		40,000	
Direct labour efficiency		360,000	
Variable overhead cost	10,000		
Fixed overhead expenditure	400,000		
Fixed overhead volume		500,000	
	410,000	1,175,000	
Manufacturing cost total variance			£765,000 (A)

37 Variances and operating statements

(a) Standard absorption costing

Budgeted fixed overheads = £2,400
Budgeted labour hours = 2,400 hours
Budgeted fixed overhead rate per hour = £1.

Materials price variance

	£
25,000 kilos of materials should cost (× £1.50)	37,500
They did cost (× £1.48)	37,000
Material price variance	500(A)

Materials usage variance

	kilos
11,500 units of Product Q should use (× 2 kilos)	23,000
They did use	25,000
Material usage variance in kilos	2,000(A)
Standard price per kilo of material	£1.50
Material usage variance in £	£3,000(A)

The material price variance and the material usage variance add up to the material total cost variance.

Direct labour rate variance

	£
2,320 hours should cost (× £3.20)	7,424
They did cost	7,540
Labour rate variance	116(A)

Direct labour efficiency variance

	hours
11,500 units of Product Q should take (× 0.20 hours)	2,300
They did take	2,320
Efficiency variance in hours	20(A)
Standard rate per hour	£3.20
Direct labour efficiency variance in £	£64(A)

Variable overhead expenditure variance

	£
2,320 hours should cost (× £0.80)	1,856
They did cost	1,750
Labour rate variance	106(F)

Variable overhead efficiency variance = 20 hours (A) × £0.80 per hour = £16 (A).

Fixed production overhead expenditure variance

	£
Budgeted fixed overhead expenditure	2,400
Actual fixed overhead expenditure	2,462
Fixed overhead expenditure variance	62(A)

Fixed production overhead volume variance

	units
Budgeted production volume	12,000
Actual production volume	11,500
Volume variance in units	500(A)

Standard fixed overhead rate per unit	£0.20
Fixed production overhead volume variance in £	£100(A)

Sales price variance

	£
10,000 units should sell for (× £6)	60,000
They did sell for	62,600
Sales price variance	2,600(F)

Sales volume profit variance

	units
Actual sales volume (units)	10,000
Budgeted sales volume (units)	12,000
Sales volume variance in units	2,000(A)

Standard profit per unit	£2
Sales volume variance (profit variance)	£4,000(A)

Operating statement (standard absorption costing)

			£
Budgeted profit (12,000 units × £2)			24,000
Sales price variance			2,600(F)
Sales volume variance			4,000(A)
			22,600

Cost variances	(F) £	(A) £	
Direct materials price	500		
Direct materials usage		3,000	
Direct labour rate		116	
Direct labour efficiency		64	
Variable production overhead expenditure	106		
Variable production o'head efficiency		16	
Fixed production overhead expenditure		62	
Fixed production overhead volume		100	
Total cost variances	606	3,358	2,752(A)
Actual profit			19,848

(b)   Standard marginal costing

Sales volume contribution variance

Sales volume variance in units	2,000(A)

Standard contribution per unit	£2.20
Sales volume variance (contribution variance)	£4,400(A)

Operating statement: standard marginal costing

			£
Budgeted profit			24,000
Add budgeted fixed costs			2,400
Budgeted contribution			26,400
Sales price variance			2,600(F)
Sales volume variance			4,400(A)
			24,600

	(F)	(A)	
Variable cost variances	£	£	
Direct materials price	500		
Direct materials usage		3,000	
Direct labour rate		116	
Direct labour efficiency		64	
Variable production o'head expenditure	106		
Variable production o'head efficiency		16	
Total variable cost variances	606	3,196	2,590(A)
Actual contribution			22,010
Budgeted fixed overhead expenditure		2,400	
Fixed overhead expenditure variance		62 (A)	
Actual fixed production overheads			2,462
Actual profit			19,548

Note: The difference in profit is accounted for by the difference in the increase in closing stock (1,500 units × £0.20 per unit = £300).

38 Standard cost sheet

Tutorial note: This problem tests your understanding of the formulae for calculating variances. Here, you are given the actual costs and the variances, and have to work back to calculate the standard cost. The answer can be found by filling in the balancing figures for each variance calculation.

Materials price variance

	£
150,000 kilos of materials did cost	210,000
Material price variance	15,000(F)
150,000 kilos of materials should cost	225,000

(The variance is favourable, so the materials did cost less to buy than they should have cost.)

Therefore the standard price for materials is £225,000/150,000 kilograms = £1.50 per kilo.

Materials usage variance

Materials usage variance in £ = £9,000 (A)
Standard price for materials = £1.50
Materials usage variance in kilograms = 9,000/1.50 = 6,000 kilos (A)

	kilos
18,000 units of the product did use	150,000
Material usage variance in kilos	6,000(A)
18,000 units of the product should use	144,000

Therefore the standard material usage per unit of product = 144,000 kilos/18,000 units = 8 kilos per unit.

Direct labour rate variance

	£
32,000 hours of labour did cost	136,000
Direct labour rate variance	8,000(A)
32,000 hours of labour should cost	128,000

Therefore the standard direct labour rate per hour = £128,000/32,000 hours = £4 per hour.

Direct labour efficiency variance

Labour efficiency variance in £ = £16,000 (F)
Standard rate per hour = £4
Labour efficiency variance in hours = 16,000/4 = 4,000 hours (F)

	hours
18,000 units of the product did take	32,000
Labour efficiency variance in hours	4,000(F)
18,000 units of the product should take	36,000

Therefore the standard time per unit of product = 36,000 hours/18,000 units = 2 hours per unit.

This number of hours per unit also applies to variable production overheads.

Variable overhead expenditure variance

	£
32,000 hours did cost	38,000
Variable overhead expenditure variance	6,000(A)
32,000 hours should cost	32,000

Therefore the variable production overhead rate per hour = £32,000/32,000 hours = £1 per hour.

Standard marginal production cost

		£
Direct materials	(8 kilos at £1.50 per kilo)	12.0
Direct labour	(2 hours at £4 per hour)	8.0
Variable production overhead	(2 hours at £1 per hour)	2.0
Standard marginal production cost		22.0

39   Variances

Workings

Sales price variance

	$
5,700 units should sell for (× $50)	285,000
They did sell for	288,300
Sales price variance	3,300(F)

Sales volume variance

	units
Budgeted sales	6,000
Actual sales	5,700
Sales volume variance in units	300(A)

Standard profit per unit ($50 - $32)	$18
Sales volume variance in $	$5,400(A)

	$
Direct materials price variance	
23,200 metres should cost (× $3)	69,600
They did cost	70,500
Direct materials price variance	900(A)

	metres
Direct materials usage variance	
5,700 units should use (× 4 metres)	22,800
They did use	23,200
Materials usage variance in metres	400(A)

Standard cost per metre	$3
Direct materials usage variance in $	$1,200(A)

	$
Direct labour rate variance	
2,740 hours should cost (× $16)	43,840
They did cost	47,900
Direct labour rate variance	4,060(A)

	hours
Direct labour efficiency variance	
5,700 units should take (× 0.5 hours)	2,850
They did take	2,740
Efficiency variance in hours	110(F)

Standard cost per labour hour	$16
Direct labour efficiency variance in $	$1,760(F)

	$
Variable overhead expenditure variance	
2,740 hours should cost (× $4)	10,960
They did cost	10,600
Variable overhead expenditure variance	360(F)

Variable overhead efficiency variance

In hours (see above): 110 hours (F)

In $: (110 hours × $4): $440 (F).

	$
Fixed overhead expenditure variance	
Budgeted fixed overheads (6,000 units × $10)	60,000
Actual fixed overheads	65,000
Fixed overhead expenditure variance	5,000(A)

Fixed overhead efficiency variance

In hours (see above): 110 hours (F)

In $: (110 hours × $20): $2,200 (F).

	hours
Fixed overhead capacity variance	
Budgeted hours of work (6,000 units × 0.5)	3,000
Actual hours of work	2,740
Capacity variance in hours	260(A)

Fixed overhead rate per hour	$20
Fixed overhead capacity variance in $	$5,200(A)

Solution

Operating statement

	$	$
Budgeted profit (6,000 units × $18)		108,000
Sales variances		
Sales price variance	3,300(F)	
Sales volume variance	5,400(A)	
		2,100(A)
Actual sales minus the standard cost of sales		105,900

	$ (F)	$ (A)	
Cost variances			
Direct materials price		900(A)	
Direct materials usage		1,200(A)	
Direct labour rate		4,060(A)	
Direct labour efficiency	1,760(F)		
V'ble overhead expenditure	360(F)		
Variable overhead efficiency	440(F)		
Fixed overhead expenditure		5,000(A)	
Fixed overhead efficiency	2,200(F)		
Fixed overhead capacity		5,200(A)	
	4,760(F)	16,360(A)	
Total cost variances			11,600(A)
Actual profit			94,300

40 Standard costing

(a)

	$	$
Budgeted net profit (10,000 units × $16)		160,000
Sales variances:		
Sales price variance	36,000(F)	
Sales volume variance	16,000(A)	
		20,000(F)
		180,000
Cost variances:		
Materials variances:		
Material A price variance	3,800(A)	
Material B price variance	4,040(F)	
Total material price variance		240(F)
Material A usage variance	2,000(A)	
Material B usage variance	6,600(A)	
Total material usage variance		8,600(A)
Labour variances:		
Rate variance	11,400(A)	
Efficiency variance	9,000(A)	
		20,400(A)
Variable overhead variances:		
Expenditure variance	10,000(F)	
Efficiency variance	6,000(A)	
		4,000(F)
Fixed overhead variances:		
Expenditure variance	8,000(F)	
Efficiency variance	12,000(A)	
Capacity variance	12,000(A)	
		16,000(A)
Actual profit		$139,240

Workings

Sales price variance	$
9,000 units should sell for (× $80)	720,000
They did sell for	756,000
Sales price variance	36,000(F)

Sales volume variance	units
Budgeted sales units	10,000
Actual sales units	9,000
Sales volume variance in units	1,000(A)
Standard profit per unit	$16
Sales volume variance in $	$16,000(A)

Materials price variances	$
19,000 kilos of Material A should cost (× $2)	38,000
They did cost	41,800
Material A price variance	3,800(A)
10,100 kilos of Material B should cost (× $6)	60,600
They did cost	56,560
Material B price variance	4,040(F)

Materials usage variances	Material A	Material B
	kilos	kilos
9,000 units of product should use (× 2 kg/1kg)	18,000	9,000
They did use	19,000	10,100
Material usage variance in kilos	1,000(A)	1,100(A)
Standard cost per kilo	$2	$6
Material usage variance in $	$2,000(A)	$6,600(A)

Labour rate variance	$
28,500 hours of labour should cost (× $6)	171,000
They did cost	182,400
Labour rate variance	11,400(A)

Labour efficiency variances	hours
9,000 units of product should take (× 3 hours)	27,000
They did use	28,500
Efficiency variance in hours	1,500(A)
Standard cost per hour	$6
Labour efficiency variance in $	$9,000(A)

Variable overhead expenditure variance	$
28,500 hours should cost (× $4)	114,000
They did cost	104,000
Labour rate variance	10,000(F)

Variable overhead efficiency variance:

Efficiency variance in hours (see above): 1,500 hours (A)

Efficiency variance = 1,500 hours (A) × $4 per hour = $6,000 (A).

Fixed overhead expenditure variance	$
Budgeted fixed overheads (10,000 units × $24)	240,000
Actual fixed overheads	232,000
Fixed overhead expenditure variance	8,000(F)

Fixed overhead efficiency variance:

Efficiency variance in hours (see above): 1,500 hours (A)

Efficiency variance = 1,500 hours (A) × $8 per hour = $12,000 (A).

Fixed overhead capacity variance	hours
Budgeted hours of work (10,000 units × 3 hours)	30,000
Actual hours of work	28,500
Capacity variance in hours	1,500(A)
Standard fixed overhead cost per hour	$8
Fixed overhead capacity variance in $	$12,000(A)

(b) **Standard marginal costing**

In a standard marginal costing system, the sales volume variance would be evaluated using standard contribution per unit. The sales volume variance would be 1,000 units (A) × standard contribution per unit $40 = $40,000 (A).

This is $24,000 higher than the sales volume variance in an absorption costing system.

There would be no fixed overhead volume variances in marginal costing. There would therefore be no fixed overhead efficiency or capacity variance, totalling $12,000 + $12,000 = $24,000 (A).

Since sales and production volumes are the same, the net profit in marginal costing is the same as the net profit in absorption costing.

41 Sales variances

Sales price variances	$	$
520 units of Q should sell for (× $30)	15,600	
They did sell for	14,560	
Product Q sales price variance		1,040(A)
290 units of R should sell for (× $45)	13,050	
They did sell for	14,210	
Product R sales price variance		1,160(F)
90 units of S should sell for (× $65)	5,850	
They did sell for	5,670	
Product S sales price variance		180(A)
Total sales price variances		60(A)

	Product Q	Product R	Product S	Total
	units	units	units	
Budgeted sales	600	300	100	
Actual sales	520	290	90	
Sales volume variance (units)	80(A)	10(A)	10(A)	
Standard margin per unit	$10	$15	$25	
Sales volume variance ($)	$800(A)	$150(A)	$250(A)	$1,200(A)

The sales volume variance can be analysed between a sales mix and a sales quantity variance:

Mix variance

	Actual mix	Actual total quantity in standard mix	Mix variance	Standard margin per unit	Mix variance
	units	units	units	$	$
Q	520	540	20 (A)	10	200(A)
R	290	270	20 (F)	15	300(F)
S	90	90	-	25	0
	900	900			100(F)

Average standard margin per unit = $(6,000 + 4,500 + 2,500)/1,000 units = $13 per unit

	Total
	units
Budgeted sales	1,000
Actual sales	900
Sales volume variance (units)	100(A)
Average standard margin per unit	$13
Sales volume variance ($)	$1,300(A)

42 Mix and yield variances

	$
5 litres of material P should cost (× $0.70)	3.50
5 litres of material Q should cost (× $0.92)	4.60
10 litres of input material should cost	8.10
= 9 litres of finished product (lubricant)	

Standard material cost per litre of lubricant = $8.10/9 litres = $0.90 per litre.

Standard average cost per litre of input = $8.10/10 litres = $0.81 per litre.

Total material cost variance	$
92,070 litres of lubricant should cost (× $0.90)	82,863
They did cost ($36,000 + $53,350)	89,350
Total material cost variance	6,487(A)

Materials price variances	$	$
45,000 litres of Material P should cost (× $0.70)	31,500	
They did cost	36,000	
Material P price variance		4,500(A)
55,000 litres of Material Q should cost (× $0.92)	50,600	
They did cost	53,350	
Material Q price variance		2,750(A)
Total material price variances		7,250(A)

Materials usage variances	Material P	Material Q
	litres	litres
92,070 litres of lubricant should use (× 10/9 × 50%)	51,150	51,150
They did use	45,000	55,000
Material usage variance in kilos	6,150(F)	3,850(A)
Standard cost per kilo	$0.70	$0.92
Material usage variance in $	$4,305(F)	$3,542(A)
Total material usage variance = $4,305 (F) + $3,542 (A) =		$763(F)

Mix variance

	Actual mix	Actual total quantity in standard mix	Mix variance	Standard cost per litre	Mix variance
	litres	litres	litres	$	$
P	45,000	50,000	5,000(F)	0.70	3,500(F)
Q	55,000	50,000	5,000(A)	0.92	4,600(A)
	100,000	100,000			1,100(A)

Materials yield variance	litres
92,070 litres of lubricant should use (× 10/9)	102,300
They did use (45,000 + 55,000)	100,000
Yield variance in litres	2,300(F)
Standard average cost per litre of input	$0.81
Materials yield variance in $	$1,863(F)

Summary	$	$
Materials price variances		7,250(A)
Materials mix variance	1,100(A)	
Materials yield variance	1,863(F)	
Materials usage variance		763(F)
Total materials cost variance		6,487(A)

43 More mix and yield

(a)

Direct materials price variance	$	$
6,700 kilos of material X should cost (× $8)	53,600	
They did cost	51,400	
Material X price variance		2,200(F)
2,900 kilos of material Y should cost (× $12)	34,800	
They did cost	39,500	
Material Y price variance		4,700(A)
Total direct materials price variance		2,500(A)

Materials mix variance

Material	Actual usage		Actual usage in standard mix	Mix variance	Standard price per kilo	Mix variance
	kilos		kilos	kilos	$	$
X	6,700	(5)	6,000	700(A)	8	5,600(A)
Y	2,900	(3)	3,600	700(F)	12	8,400(F)
	9,600		9,600			2,800(F)

Standard weighted average cost per kilo of materials = $76/8 kilos = $9.50 per kilo.

Direct materials yield variance	kilos
1,250 units should use (× (3 + 5) kilos)	10,000
They did use	9,600
Materials yield variance in kilos	400(F)
Standard weighted average cost per kilo	$9.50
Direct materials yield variance in $	$3,800(F)

(b)

Summary	$
Standard materials cost of 1,250 units (× 76)	95,000
Materials price variance	2,500(A)
Materials mix variance	2,800(F)
Materials yield variance	3,800(F)
Actual materials cost	90,900

44 Planning and operational variances

(a) **Operational variances** (using the retrospective or ex post standard cost).

Direct labour rate variance	$
8,200 hours should cost (× $15)	123,000
They did cost	120,800
Direct labour rate variance	2,200(F)

Direct labour efficiency variance	hours
2,000 units should take (× 4 hours)	8,000
They did take	8,200
Efficiency variance in hours	200(A)
Standard cost per labour hour	$15
Direct labour efficiency variance in $	$3,000(A)

Planning variance	$
Standard cost of 2,000 units:	
Original (ex ante) standard (× 3 hours × $15)	90,000
Revised (ex post) standard (× 4 hours × $15)	120,000
Planning variance	30,000(A)

The planning variance is adverse because the original standard cost was too optimistic.

Summary	$
Original standard cost of 2,000 units	90,000
Planning variance	30,000(A)
Revised standard cost of 2,000 units	120,000
Operational variances	
Direct labour rate	2,200(F)
Direct labour efficiency	3,000(A)
Actual direct labour cost	120,800

(b)

Direct labour rate variance	$
8,200 hours should cost (× $12)	98,400
They did cost	101,600
Direct labour rate variance	3,200(A)

Direct labour efficiency variance	hours
2,000 units should take (× 4 hours)	8,000
They did take	8,200
Efficiency variance in hours	200(A)
Standard cost per labour hour	$12
Direct labour efficiency variance in $	$2,400(A)

Planning variance	$
Standard cost of 2,000 units:	
Original (ex ante) standard (2,000 × 3 hours × $15)	90,000
Revised (ex post) standard (2,000 × 4 hours × $12)	96,000
Total planning variance	6,000(A)

The planning variance can be analysed into:

- a planning variance caused by a change in the time for each unit. This is (4 hours – 3 hours) = 1 hour per unit (A)

- a planning variance caused by a change in the rate per hour. This is ($15 – $12) = $3 per hour (F).

(Note: A planning variance is adverse if the ex ante standard is too optimistic and favourable if it over-estimates costs).

However, there are two ways of analysing the total planning variance:

- Efficiency planning variance = 2,000 units × 1 hour per unit (A) × $15 per hour = $30,000 (A)

- Labour rate planning variance = 2,000 units × 4 hours per unit × $3 per hour (F) = $24,000 (F)

- Alternatively:

- Efficiency planning variance = 2,000 units × 1 hour per unit (A) × $12 per hour = $24,000 (A)

- Labour rate planning variance = 2,000 units × 3 hours per unit × $3 per hour (F) = $18,000(F).

Summary	$
Original standard cost of 2,000 units	90,000
Efficiency planning variance	30,000(A)
Rate per hour planning variance	24,000(F)
Revised standard cost of 2,000 units	96,000
Operational variances	
Direct labour rate	3,200(A)
Direct labour efficiency	2,400(A)
Actual direct labour cost	101,600

45 Sam

Ratios

	Year 7	Year 6
Gross profit % =		
$\dfrac{\text{Gross profit}}{\text{Sales}} \times 100$	$\dfrac{405}{2{,}160} \times 100 = 19\%$	$\dfrac{362}{1{,}806} \times 100 = 20\%$
Net profit % =		
$\dfrac{\text{Net profit}}{\text{Sales}} \times 100$	$\dfrac{9}{2{,}160} \times 100 = 0.4\%$	$\dfrac{53}{1{,}806} \times 100 = 2.9\%$
Return on capital employed =		
$\dfrac{\text{Profit before interest and tax}}{\text{Share capital and reserves} + \text{Long-term debt capital}}$	$\dfrac{15}{246} \times 100 = 6\%$	$\dfrac{56}{190} \times 100 = 29\%$
Asset turnover =		
$\dfrac{\text{Sales}}{\text{Share capital and reserves} + \text{Long-term debt capital}} \times 100$	$\dfrac{2{,}160}{246} = 8.8 \text{ times}$	$\dfrac{1{,}806}{190} = 9.5 \text{ times}$
Current ratio =		
$\dfrac{\text{Current assets}}{\text{Current liabilities}}$	$\dfrac{422}{254} = 1.7 \text{ times}$	$\dfrac{265}{147} = 1.8 \text{ times}$
Quick ratio =		
$\dfrac{\text{Current assets excluding inventory}}{\text{Current liabilities}}$	$\dfrac{422 - 106}{254} = 1.2 \text{ times}$	$\dfrac{265 - 61}{147} = 1.4 \text{ times}$
Average time to collect =		
$\dfrac{\text{Trade receivables}}{\text{Sales}} \times 365$	$\dfrac{316 \times 365}{2{,}160} = 53 \text{ days}$	$\dfrac{198 \times 365}{1{,}806} = 40 \text{ days}$

Average time to pay =

$$\frac{\text{Trade payables}}{\text{Cost of purchases}} \times 365 \qquad \frac{198 \times 365}{1{,}755} = 41\,\text{days} \qquad \frac{142 \times 365}{1{,}444} = 36\,\text{days}$$

Inventory turnover =

$$\frac{\text{Inventory}}{\text{Cost of sales}} \times 365 \qquad \frac{106 \times 365}{1{,}755} = 22\,\text{days} \qquad \frac{61 \times 365}{1{,}444} = 15\,\text{days}$$

Commentary

Profitability

Although revenue has increased by 20% this has not led to increased profitability, as shown by the gross profit and net profit percentages.

The gross profit percentage is largely unchanged suggesting that Sam has maintained its profit margins.

However, the net profit percentage has fallen significantly (from 2.9% to 0.4%). There may be increased costs because of the increased level of business (e.g. recruitment of new employees) but it may also mean that overheads are getting out of control.

Return on capital employed has fallen even more significantly (from 29% to 6%). The asset base has increased over the last year and revenue has increased accordingly, but the company has not been able to maintain its profitability.

Efficiency/liquidity

Inventory turnover has also fallen (from 15 days to 22 days) showing that, whilst there has been an increased volume of business, Sam is exercising less control over working capital as the amount tied up in inventory has increased.

However, the main indicators of liquidity, the current and quick ratios, show that there has been little change in the last year, suggesting that Sam is not having problems meeting its debts as they fall due.

The average time to collect debts has worsened from 40 days to 53 days. This may indicate a loss of credit control or that more favourable terms have been given to customers in order to gain sales. In either case, it indicates an increased bad debt risk, although, to some extent, it is mitigated by the small increase in average time to pay from 36 to 41 days.

46 | **Chris and Caroline**

Ratios

	Chris	Caroline
Gross profit % = $\dfrac{\text{Gross profit}}{\text{Sales}} \times 100$	$\dfrac{90,000}{150,000} \times 100 = 60\%$	$\dfrac{490,000}{700,000} \times 100 = 70\%$
Net profit % = $\dfrac{\text{Net profit}}{\text{Sales}} \times 100$	$\dfrac{44,895}{150,000} \times 100 = 30\%$	$\dfrac{270,830}{700,000} \times 100 = 39\%$
Return on capital employed = $\dfrac{\text{Profit before interest and tax}}{\text{Share capital and reserves} + \text{Long - term debt capital}} \times 100$	$\dfrac{61,500 + 500}{207,395 + 10,000} \times 100 = 28.5\%$	$\dfrac{371,000 + 12,000}{565,580 + 250,000} \times 100 = 47\%$
Asset turnover = $\dfrac{\text{Sales}}{\text{Share capital and reserves} + \text{Long - term debt capital}} \times 100$	$\dfrac{150,000}{207,395 + 10,000} = 0.7 \text{ times}$	$\dfrac{700,000}{565,580 + 250,000} = 0.85 \text{ times}$
Current ratio = $\dfrac{\text{Current assets}}{\text{Current liabilities}}$	$\dfrac{50,000}{22,605} = 2.2 \text{ times}$	$\dfrac{153,250}{117,670} = 1.3 \text{ times}$
Quick ratio = $\dfrac{\text{Current assets excluding inventory}}{\text{Current liabilities}}$	$\dfrac{50,000 - 12,000}{22,605} = 1.7 \text{ times}$	$\dfrac{153,250 - 26,250}{117,670} = 1.1 \text{ times}$

Table continues

	Chris	Caroline
Average time to collect = $\dfrac{\text{Trade receivables}}{\text{Sales}} \times 365$	$\dfrac{37{,}500}{150{,}000} \times 365 = 91\text{ days}$	$\dfrac{105{,}000}{700{,}000} \times 365 = 55\text{ days}$
Average time to pay = $\dfrac{\text{Trade payables}}{\text{Cost of purchases}} \times 365$	$\dfrac{22{,}605}{60{,}000} \times 365 = 137\text{ days}$	$\dfrac{117{,}670}{210{,}000} \times 365 = 204\text{ days}$
Inventory turnover = $\dfrac{\text{Inventory}}{\text{Cost of sales}} \times 365$	$\dfrac{12{,}000}{60{,}000} \times 365 = 73\text{ days}$	$\dfrac{26{,}250}{210{,}000} \times 365 = 46\text{ days}$
Gearing ratio = $\dfrac{\text{Long - term debt}}{\text{Share capital and reserves}} \times 100$	$\dfrac{10{,}000}{207{,}395} \times 100 = 4.8\%$	$\dfrac{250{,}000}{565{,}580} \times 100 = 44\%$
Interest cover = $\dfrac{\text{Profit before interest and tax}}{\text{Interest charges in the year}}$	$\dfrac{61{,}500 + 500}{500} = 124\text{ times}$	$\dfrac{371{,}000 + 12{,}000}{12{,}000} = 32\text{ times}$

Commentary

Profitability

The return on capital employed achieved by Chris (28.5%) is substantially lower than that achieved by Caroline (47%). This variation in performance is also seen at the gross profit (60% compared to 70%) and net profit levels (30% compared to 39%).

The variation in gross profit percentage could be caused by differences in sales mix, inventory valuation methods or mark-up.

Since these entities operate in the same sector it is unlikely that their selling prices differ significantly. However, Caroline, as a much larger entity, may be able to negotiate better prices from its suppliers.

Caroline is also more efficient at using its assets. It is generating 85c per $1 of assets whereby Chris is only generating 70c per $1.

Efficiency/liquidity

The liquidity of both entities appears satisfactory, although Caroline has less funds tied up in its current assets. Caroline is also more efficient at collecting its debts (55 days compared to Chris's 91 days), and takes a longer credit period from its suppliers.

Solvency

Caroline is much more highly geared than Chris (44% compared to 4.8%). Caroline has the ability to raise debt more easily because of its greater profitability and its property, on which debt can be secured. Both companies can easily cover their interest payments suggesting that neither entity's debt is at risk.

Conclusion

Caroline is the stronger entity.

47 Balanced

(a) The four perspectives for performance targets and measuring performance in a balanced scorecard approach are:

(1) a customer perspective: identifying what customers value most

(2) an internal systems perspective: identifying the processes that must be performed with excellence to satisfy customers

(3) an innovation and learning perspective: what must the organisation do to innovate or add to its knowledge and experience

(4) a financial perspective.

(b) **A professional football club**

Here are some suggestions

Customer perspective

Customers value:

- results, winning

- an enjoyable time at football matches: being entertained (for example, with food and drink).

Targets for performance might be:

- the size of attendances at matches

- results (points, position in the league table, promotion)

- revenue from catering: number of meals sold before matches.

Internal processes perspective

Processes that must be excellent to support customer expectations might include ticket selling, getting customers into the ground quickly on match days, catering efficiency, effective security and policing, and so on.

Targets for performance might be:

- number of season ticket sales

- targets for number of spectators per minute going through each turnstile

- speed of producing meals in the catering area

- number of incidents and police arrests on match days.

Innovation and learning perspective

Value can be created by developing well-trained footballers through coaching and training, and possibly selling them in the transfer market to make profits.

Targets for performance might be:

- average fitness levels for players

- average number of hours of training each week per player

- revenue from transfers

Financial perspective

Presumably, the football club will be expected to make profits for its owners. Targets for performance might be profits each year, and return on investment.

Subsidiary financial targets might be average wages per player, and revenue from sponsorship deals.

48   Pyramid

(a)   The performance pyramid describes a view that all measures of performance for an organisation should be linked and consistent with each other. There is a hierarchy of suitable measures of performance, with performance measures at lower levels in the hierarchy (or pyramid) supporting performance measures at a higher level.

(1) At the bottom of the pyramid, there are operational performance measures, relating to external effectiveness and internal efficiency.

(2) Operational performance measures support higher-level measures that should relate to quality, delivery, production or service cycle time and waste.

(3) These measures of performance support measures of performance at an even higher level in the pyramid, relating to customer satisfaction, flexibility and productivity.

(4) These measures of performance support measures relating to market satisfaction and financial performance.

(5) Together, measures of market satisfaction and financial performance support the achievement of the organisation's objectives.

The performance pyramid recognises that external and market measures of performance are as important as financial performance and internal efficiency in achieving the long-term objectives of the organisation.

(b) Dimensions of performance in service industries may be measured primarily by:

(1) financial performance and

(2) competitiveness.

These should be supported by performance in four other dimensions:

(1) service quality

(2) flexibility

(3) resource utilisation and

(4) innovation.

49 Three services

(a) Workings

Revenue:

Service A: contract customers – 350,000 × 60% × \$9 × 1.03 = \$1,946,700

Service A: non-contract customers – 350,000 × 40% × \$9 × 1.30 × 1.03 = \$1,687,140

Service B: contract customers – 250,000 × 60% × \$15 × 1.03 = \$2,317,500

Service B: non-contract customers – 250,000 × 40% × \$15 × 1.50 × 1.03 = \$2,317,500

Service C: contract customers – 20,000 × 80% × \$300 × 1.03 = \$4,944,000

Service C: non-contract customers 20,000 × 20% × \$300 × 1.20 × 1.03 = \$1,483,200

Salaries: $45,000 × 85 employees × 1.05 = $4,016,250

Sundry operational costs: $4,000,000 ×1.05 = $4,200,000

Fuel

Services A and B – 400 km × 50 vehicles × 300 days × $0.40 = $2,400,000

Service C – 600 km × 18 vehicles × 300 days × $0.80 = $2,592,000

Budgeted income statement for the year to 31st December Year 2

	Service A	Service B	Service C	Total
Revenue:	$	$	$	$
Contract customers	1,946,700	2,317,500	4,944,000	9,208,200
Non-contract customers	1,687,140	2,317,500	1,483,200	5,487,840
Total revenue	3,633,840	4,635,000	6,427,200	14,696,040
Costs:				
Salaries			4,016,250	
Fuel:				
Services A and B		2,400,000		
Service C		2,592,000		
			4,992,000	
Sundry operational costs			4,200,000	
Total costs				13,208,250
Net profit				1,487,790

(b) **Vehicle utilisation**

There is no information about weight carried, only about distance travelled.

All vehicles were used for 300 days in the year. Presumably, vehicles might be used for 365 days per year, indicating an overall utilisation ratio for all vehicles of 82.2%.

Other utilisation measure: a revenue measure might be used as an indication of the utilisation of vehicles.

	Services A and B	Service C
Revenue per vehicle	($8,268,840/50)	($6,427,200/18)
	$165,377	$357,067

Kilometres travelled each year might also be a measure of utilisation:

■ Service A and B vehicles travel on average (400 × 300) = 120,000 kilometres each year.

■ Service C vehicles travel on average (600 × 300) = 180,000 kilometres each year.

50 Private medical practice

Workings

Total number of patients per year = 5 doctors × 18 patients per day × 5 days per week × 46 weeks per year = 20,700.

| | Total | Patients | | |
		Adults	Children	65 years and over
	20,700	(45%) = 9,315	(25%) = 5,175	(30%) = 6,210
Treatment				
None: 20%		1,863.0	1,035.0	1,242
Minor: 70%		6,520.5	3,622.5	4,347
Major: 10%		931.5	517.5	621

Revenue:

Adults, no treatment: 1,863 × $50 = $93,150
Adults, minor treatment: 6,520.5 × $200 = $1,304,100
Adults, major treatment: 931.5 × $600 = $558,900
Children, no treatment: 1,035 × $30 = $31,050
Children, minor treatment: 3,622.5 × $120 = $434,700
Children, major treatment: 517.5 × $280 = $144,900
65 years and over, no treatment: 1,242 × $30 = $37,260
65 years and over, minor treatment: 4,347 × $120 = $521,640
65 years and over, major treatment: 621 × $280 = $173,880.

Budgeted income statement for the year to [...]

	Adults	Children	Aged 65 years and over	Total
Revenue:	$	$	$	$
No treatment	93,150	31,050	37,260	161,460
Minor treatment	1,304,100	434,700	521,640	2,260,440
Major treatment	558,900	144,900	173,880	877,680
Total revenue	1,956,150	610,650	732,780	3,299,580
Costs:				
Salaries				
Doctors (5 × $240,000)		1,200,000		
Assistants (5 × $100,000)		500,000		
Administrators (2 × $80,000)		160,000		
		1,860,000		
Bonus		93,000		
			1,953,000	
Materials costs			414,300	
Other costs			733,600	
Total costs				3,100,900
Net profit				198,680

51 Train times

| | Northern Region | | Southern Region | |
	Inter-city services	Suburban services	Inter-city services	Suburban services
Target for completion on time	90%	95%	90%	95%
Actual % on time	82.7%	73.8%	88.3%	91.9%
% not on time, but less than 5 minutes late	7.3%	12.9%	5.6%	4.0%
% between 5 and 10 minutes late	6.0%	10.6%	2.2%	2.9%
% cancelled	3.2%	1.2%	0.1%	0.5%
	99.2%	98.5%	96.2%	99.3%
Over 10 minutes late (balance)	0.8%	1.5%	3.8%	0.7%
	100.0%	100.0%	100.0%	100.0%

Assessment of performance

Neither region has achieved its target for journeys completed on time, although Southern Region appears to be closer to achieving its targets.

Most of the late-completed journeys were completed within ten minutes of the scheduled time.

Northern Region has a fairly large proportion of cancelled trains – certainly much higher than Southern Region. However, Southern Region has a comparatively high proportion of inter-city journeys finishing over ten minutes late.

The managers of the two regions should be asked to provide a report on these aspects of performance.

52   Growth objective

Sales

Sales growth: Year 2 compared with Year 1	20.0%
Sales growth: 1- six months of Year 2 compared with 1- six months of Year 1	28.1%
Sales growth: 2- six months of Year 2 compared with 2- six months of Year 1	5.0%

Sales increased by 20% in Year 2 compared with Year 1. However, the strong growth in sales occurred in the first six months of the year (28% compared with the same period in Year 1). In the second half of the year, sales growth compared with the same period in Year 1 was down to 5%. There is insufficient information to judge whether the growth in sales revenue is slowing down or coming to an end.

Net profit

There was no increase in net profit between Year 1 and Year 2. The increase in sales (20%) is offset by an increase of 30.4% in operating costs and some interest charges. In terms of annual net profit, the business is therefore not growing.

If a part-time employee is the equivalent of 50% of a full-time employee, there were 415 equivalent full time employees in Year 1 (260 + 50% × 310). There were 565 equivalent full time employees in Year 2 (318 + 50% × 494). Sales revenue per equivalent full-time employee was therefore $62,651 in Year 1 and $55,221 in Year 2. This fall in employee productivity is one reason for the failure to achieve growth in the annual net profit.

Investment

The investment in non-current assets has risen by just 5%, but the investment in working capital has doubled. The increase in net assets has been almost entirely financed by borrowing. (Presumably, this means that most of the profits earned in Year 1 have been paid in taxation or distributed as dividends to shareholders.)

It is difficult to draw definite conclusions from the limited amount of data, but management should be concerned about a 100% increase in working capital, when the increase in annual sales is only 20%. Could there be large quantities of unsold inventory as a result of the decline in sales growth in the second half of the year?

It is not clear why it was considered necessary to borrow $9,000,000 when increases in non-current assets have been only $1,300,000. It would appear that the new borrowing might be financing unnecessary working capital investment, and not investment in non-current assets for longer-term development.

On the other hand, investment in non-current assets will probably need to exceed 5% per year (by a large amount) if the company is to achieve significant long-term growth in its business.

Product range/new product sales

The data about new products is difficult to interpret, because there is no information about the total size of the product portfolio and no information about whether the new products sold well or badly.

53   Responsibility

(a)   We are told that decisions about capital investment and borrowing are taken at head office. It would therefore be appropriate to look at the performance of the division over which the managing director has control – sales revenue and operating costs, but not depreciation or interest.

Sales revenue minus operating costs provides a measure of **profit or earnings before interest, depreciation and amortisation (EBITDA).**

	Year 1	Year 2	Year 3	Year 4
	$000	$000	$000	$000
Sales revenue	172	646	810	1,792
Operating costs	167	620	718	1,490
EBITDA	5	26	92	302

This indicates improving performance over each year of the four-year period.

(b)   Controllable performance has been improving each year. There has also been a continuing improvement in the ratio of EBITDA to sales revenue.

On the basis of the information available, the managing director's view is justified.

However, senior management should assess the return that the company is obtaining on its investment in the Fenland Division. Presumably, there was an investment plan for the project, containing an estimate of the profits that the division should be expected to make.

■ If sales are lower than expected, or if costs are higher than expected, the managing director of the division might be asked to give reasons why performance has not been better.

■ If the size of the investment or the cost of borrowing has been more than expected, the poor performance should be attributed to the managers responsible for the investment and borrowing decisions.

54   Cross Streets Hotel

A well-designed management information system should provide relevant, accurate and timely information to all levels of management. Hence the introduction of a new system should not only allow the directors to monitor performance, but may actively help to address the issue of declining profits by providing greater feedback to tactical and operational managers.

(a)   Periodic reports

The computerisation of hotel records and the online link to head office allow the latter to acquire and assimilate large volumes of data rapidly. This would permit monthly financial statements to be produced for each hotel in time for directors to review them and action their findings whilst the implications are still relevant.

The statements should comprise balance sheet, cash flow and income statement, and would enable directors to gain an overview of the effects of local management decisions and the effectiveness of corporate policy on a regional basis.

These periodic reports should include comparative data in addition to actual data. Figures could be included for budget/previous periods/industry data. Variances could be reported.

(b)   Demand reports

The new system should also be capable of producing a range of reports on demand, so that senior management can assess high-risk aspects of the business by obtaining information whenever they need it.

(i)   Room occupancy report

This report gives details of the proportion or percentage of a hotel's available rooms that were occupied. By using information from registration cards, it should be possible to split this figure between business and non-business users.

The incorporation of room charge-out rates into the same report would enable management to:

■ assess the accuracy of revenues from room-letting

■ identify if variations in regional rates have a significant impact on occupancy rates and overall profitability

■ identify any trends in business/non business usage and the opportunity for differential pricing and attracting more guests.

Room rates should also be compared to a centralised master file of approved rates and discounts to ensure hotel managers are not offering rooms at below cost in an attempt to attract business.

To ensure all income from rooms let is recorded, the room occupancy report should compare rooms for which income has been recorded to a housekeeper's report giving details of the rooms cleaned.

(ii) **Bad debts report**

This report should highlight all debts more than (say) 60 days overdue.

Bad debts could be a major contributor to declining profits, particularly if the hotels catering for business travellers are taking block corporate bookings.

As an additional control to ensure that all reported bookings are genuine, this report should also include a comparison of revenues with a direct room cost such as laundry bills.

(iii) **Restaurant sales report**

This should compare total revenues from the restaurant to the number of bills raised and occupancy rate, thereby allowing the directors to ascertain if unduly preferential arrangements are being allowed by some of their hotels.

Differentiation should also be made between billings to non-residents, as this will enable attention to be focused on this separate revenue source. This is important if the restaurant is not being operated at capacity such that non-residents could be a useful source of income.

(iv) **Bar sales report**

Total billing should be compared as for restaurant sales, but without the division between residents and non-residents, as the latter would be difficult to obtain in view of the large number of cash transactions.

(v) **Restaurant and bar inventories report**

Physical control over bar and restaurant inventories is difficult to maintain and yet losses represent a potentially significant restriction on profits.

An official from head office should attend a physical count at each hotel, and this figure should then act as the benchmark for subsequent movements and be "enforced" by random spot checks.

The inventories report should compare the verified figure as adjusted for subsequent purchases and sales to occupancy rate and highlight any significant percentage variation from preceding months (indicating pilferage and misappropriation). The overall holding of inventory in each hotel should be compared to inventory turnover to ensure the former does not represent an excessive usage of working capital.

(vi) **Cash availability report**

Many of the bar and restaurant takings of each hotel will be in cash; as with inventories, cash is easily susceptible to misappropriation.

The head office directors will require a report that summarises the cash takings and receipts, and makes a comparison between hotels making allowances for differences in the number and type of resident (for example, business users may utilise corporate client cards rather than their own cash).

(vii) **Wages report**

Given that wages, often casual wages, represent a significant item of cash expenditure for hotels and one which can be directly related to revenue, a report should be produced detailing the number of waged staff per week and their wages.

This could then be compared to revenue reports to identify any significant departures from the expected relationship. This may indicate general inefficiency capable of improvement or fraud.

(c)   Error/exception reports

A unique feature of computerised systems is their ability to search through large volumes of data and extract only those figures of significance to users.

These exception reports should be produced automatically to highlight matters such as:

- hotel revenue falling below budget (for example, by more than 10%)
- group cash reserves/funding requirements exceeding available limits
- hotels selling room accommodation below the approved room rate.

55   Non-financial performance measurements

Service quality

(1)   The percentage of customers who take their account away in a period (the rate of 'churn')

(2)   The number of complaints in a period

(3)   A measure of 'satisfaction' from responses by customers to a questionnaire about the bank's services

(4)   In some aspects of service, speed of response (for example, the average time to answer telephone calls from customers: these time measures can be obtained from the bank's telephone systems).

Marketing effectiveness

(1)   The number of new accounts or growth rate in new accounts in the period

(2)   The growth in major business activities in the period (lending, foreign exchange dealing, and so on)

(3)   Market share

Personnel

(1)   The rate of absenteeism in the period

(2)   The amount of staff training in the period (total training days, for example)

(3)   The rate of staff turnover

(4)   It might be possible to identify ways of measuring staff efficiency, but this can be difficult when much of the work is non-standard or non-routine.

56   Decentralisation

(a)   (i)   **Responsibility accounting** is the structuring of performance reports for individual managers in a way that identifies the factors that are controllable by them and for which they are responsible. Depending on the factors under the control of the manager, responsibility accounting reports may be prepared for cost centres, revenue centres, profit centres or investment centres.

(ii)   An **investment centre** is an operating division within an organisation whose manager has responsibility for both the profits of the division and the investments that it makes.

(iii)   **Return on investment (ROI)** The divisional profit divided by the capital employed within that division.

(iv)   **Residual income** = Divisional income – a notional interest charge for the investment in capital investment in the division

Residual income = Divisional income – Divisional investment × cost of capital

Note: Both ROI and residual income can be used as:

- ex ante targets (planning targets) – in order to motivate divisional managers and to guide their decision-making

- ex post appraisal measures (actual performance measures) – to evaluate the divisional manager's performance.

(b)   **Divisions M and W**

The performance of the two divisions will be evaluated using both ROI and residual income. There is no specific performance target for either division. To compare divisional performance, it is assumed that the division with the higher ROI or residual income has performed 'better'.

	Division M	Division W
ROI	20/200	410/5,000
	10%	8.2%
	$000	$000
Profit	20	410
Less: Interest on investment at 8%	(16)	(400)
Residual income	4	10

Division M has a higher ROI than Division W. However, the reason for this difference in performance may be that Division M has older non-current assets, and is reluctant to invest in new capital equipment. New investments would increase the division's profit but reduce its ROI in the short-term (because capital investment will also be higher).

Division M has a higher residual income than Division W. Therefore, in a situation where both divisional managers are motivated to accept projects that meet the firm's investment criteria (i.e. cost of capital): Division W may have been more successful in finding investments that earn a return above the cost of capital. However, the difference in residual income is only $6,000, but Division W has invested $4.8 more than Division M.

Both divisions have a positive residual income, which means that they have succeeded in investing in projects with accounting returns higher than the company's cost of capital.

A change in the company's cost of capital will only affect the residual income figure; it has no effect on the ROI. The revised residual income figures for cost of capital at 6% and 10% respectively are as follows:

	Division M	Division W
	$000	$000
Cost of capital 6%		
Profit	20	410
Less Interest on investment at 6%	(12)	(300)
Residual income	8	110
Cost of capital 10%		
Profit	20	410
Less Interest on investment at 10%	(20)	(500)
Residual income	0	(90)

If the cost of capital for the company is only 6%, the residual income of both Division M and Division W is higher. The larger size of the investment in Division W results in a proportionally higher RI figure.

On the other hand, if the cost of capital is raised to 10%, Division M is the better performer with a residual income of 0 compared with a negative residual income (a residual loss) of $90,000 for Division W.

57   West Division

	Sales price	Variable cost	Contribution per unit	Sales	Total contribution
	$ per unit	$ per unit	$ per unit	units	$
Product A:					
Titan brand	2.50	1.50	1.00	160,000	160,000
Unbranded	1.50	1.30	0.20	450,000	90,000
Product B:					
Titan brand	3.20	2.00	1.20	120,000	144,000
Unbranded	2.00	1.80	0.20	600,000	120,000
Product C:					
Titan brand	5.00	3.00	2.00	50,000	100,000
					614,000
				$	
Marketing costs				180,000	
Other fixed costs				375,000	
					555,000
					59,000
Notional interest: 10% × $400,000					(40,000)
Residual income					19,000

(a)   ROI = 59,000/400,000 = 14.75%.

(b)   Residual income (see above) = $19,000.

58   Residual

(a) **ROI**

Annual depreciation (straight-line) = $42,000/3 = $14,000.

Annual accounting profit = $5,000

Year	Profit	Average investment	ROI
	$	$	
1	5,000	35,000	14.3%
2	5,000	21,000	23.8%
3	5,000	7,000	71.4%
Average	5,000	21,000	23.8%

Note: Average investment, measured as the net book value of the asset, is the mid-point between $42,000 and $28,000 in Year 1, the mid-point between $28,000 and $14,000 in Year 2, and the mid-point between $14,000 and $0 in Year 3.

(b) The investment centre has been achieving a ROI in excess of 35% each year for several years. Investing in this project will therefore have the effect of bringing ROI down, although the investment is probably quite small in relation to the total size of the investment centre and its assets. The managers of the investment centre would therefore have no particular reason to undertake the investment, even though it has a positive NPV when the cash flows are discounted at 12%.

(c) **Residual income**

For each year, Years 1 – 3, the residual income would be as follows:

	Year 1	Year 2	Year 3
Average investment	$35,000	$21,000	$7,000
	$	$	$
Profit after depreciation	5,000	5,000	5,000
Notional interest (12% of investment)	4,200	2,520	840
Residual income	800	2,480	4,160

The residual income is positive in each of the three years, although it increases each year as the value of the investment declines.

If the performance of the investment centre is measured by residual income, its managers would be willing to undertake the investment because it will improve the divisional performance by increasing the residual income.

59   Two divisions

(a) An optimal transfer price (or range of transfer prices) is a price for an internally-transferred item at which:

- the selling division will want to sell units to the other profit centre, because this will add to its divisional profit

- the buying division will want to buy units from the other profit centre, because this will add to its divisional profit

- the internal transfer will be in the best interests of the entity as a whole, because it will help to maximise its total profit.

(b)   When Division X has spare capacity, its only cost in making an selling extra units of Product B is the variable cost per unit of production, $48. Division Y can buy the product from an external supplier for $55.

It follows that a transfer that is higher than $48 but lower than $55, for additional units of production, will benefit both profit centres as well as the company as a whole. (It is in the best interests of the company to make the units in Division X at a cost of $48 than to buy them externally for $55.)

(c)   When Division X is operating at full capacity and has unsatisfied external demand for Product A, it has an opportunity cost if it makes Product B for transfer to Division Y. Product A earns a contribution of $16 per unit ($62 – $46). The minimum transfer price that it would require for Product B is:

	$
Variable cost of production of Product B	48
Opportunity cost: lost contribution from sale of Product A	16
Minimum transfer price to satisfy Division X management	64

Division Y can buy the product from an external supplier for $55, and will not want to buy from Division X at a price of $64. The maximum price it will want to pay is $55.

The company as a whole will benefit if Division X makes and sells Product A.

■ It makes a contribution of $16 from each unit of Product A.

■ If Division X were to make and sell Product B, the company would benefit by only $7. This is the difference in the cost of making the product in Division X ($48) and the cost of buying it externally ($55).

The same quantity of limited resources (direct labour in Division X) is needed for each product, therefore the company benefits by $9 ($16 – $7) from making units of Product A instead of units of Product B.

On the basis of this information, the transfer price for Product X should be $64 as long as there is unsatisfied demand for Product A. At this price, there will be no transfers of Product B.

60   Training company

(a)   If the Liverpool centre has spare capacity, it will be in the best interest of the company for the London centre to use Liverpool trainers, at a variable cost of £450 per day including travel and accommodation, instead of hiring external trainers at a cost of £1,200.

Since the Liverpool centre will have to pay £450 per trainer day, any transfer price per day/daily fee in excess of £450 would add to its profit.

Since the London centre can obtain external trainers for £1,200 per day, any transfer price below this amount would add to its profit.

An appropriate transfer price would therefore be a price anywhere above £450 per day and below £1,200 per day.

(b)   If the Liverpool centre is operating at full capacity and is charging clients £750 per trainer day, there will be an opportunity cost of sending its trainers to work for the London centre. The opportunity cost is the contribution forgone by not using the trainers locally in Liverpool. Assuming that the variable cost of using trainers in Liverpool would be £200 per day, the opportunity cost is £550 (£750 – £200).

The minimum transfer price that the manager of the Liverpool centre would want is:

	£
Variable cost of trainer day	200
Travel and accommodation	250
Opportunity cost: lost contribution	550
Minimum transfer price	1,000

The maximum price that the London centre would be willing to pay is £1,200, which is the cost of using an external trainer.

The company should encourage the use of Liverpool trainers by the London centre, because this will add to the total company profit.

The optimal transfer price is above £1,000 per day, so that the Liverpool centre will benefit from sending trainers to London, but below £1,200 so that the London centre will also benefit.

A transfer price of £1,000 per day might be agreed.

(c)   If the Liverpool centre is operating at full capacity and is charging clients £1,100 per trainer day, the opportunity cost of sending its trainers to work for the London centre is £900 (£1,100 – £200).

The minimum transfer price that the manager of the Liverpool centre would want is:

	£
Variable cost of trainer day	200
Travel and accommodation	250
Opportunity cost: lost contribution	900
Minimum transfer price	1,350

The maximum price that the London centre would be willing to pay is £1,200, which is the cost of using an external trainer.

It would be in the best interests of the company as a whole to use the Liverpool trainers to work for Liverpool clients, earning a contribution of £900 per day, rather than use them in London to save net costs of £750 per day (£1,200 – £200 – £250).

The transfer price should be set at £1,350 per trainer day. At this rate, the London centre will use external trainers, and all the Liverpool trainers will be used in Liverpool.

61 Shadow price

(a) The shadow price of the special chemical is the amount by which total contribution would be reduced (or increased) if one unit less (or more) of the chemical were available.

1 kilogram = 1,000 grams; therefore one kilogram of special chemical will produce 100 tablets (1,000/10 grams per tablet).

Shadow price of the chemical	$
Sales value of 100 tablets (× $10)	1,000
Further processing costs in B (× $2)	200
	800
Variable cost of making the chemical in A	500
Shadow price per kilogram of chemical	300

(b) The special chemical does not have an intermediate market.

■ The ideal transfer price for A is therefore any price above the variable cost of making the chemical, which is $500 per kilogram.

■ The ideal transfer price for B is anything below the net increase in contribution from processing a kilogram of the chemical. This is $1,000 – $200 = $800 per kilogram.

■ There is no single ideal price. Any price in the range above $500 and below $800 should make the managers of both profit centres want to produce up to the capacity in division A.

■ A transfer price in the middle of the range, say $650, might be agreed.

(c) The transfer price is needed to share the profit from selling the tablets between divisions A and B. It is an internally negotiated price. Changing the price will not affect the total profit for the company as a whole, provided that division A produces the chemical up to its production capacity.

The transfer price itself should not be used as a basis for judging performance. Having agreed a transfer price, key financial measures of performance will be control over costs for division A and control over costs and the selling price for tablets for division B.

(The divisions are profit centres, and so the performance of the divisional managers should not be assessed on the basis of ROI or residual income.)

62 Bricks

(a) **Profit statements**

(i) *Operating at 80% capacity*

	Transfer price $200			Transfer price $180		
	Group X	Group Y	Total	Group X	Group Y	Total
Sales:						
External	180	240	420	180	240	420
Transfers	120	-	0	108	-	0
Total	300	240	420	288	240	420
Costs						
Transfers	-	(120)	0	-	(108)	0

	Variable	(112)	(36)	(148)	(112)	(36)	(148)
	Fixed	(100)	(40)	(140)	(100)	(40)	(140)
	Total	(212)	(196)	(288)	(212)	(184)	(288)
	Profit	88	44	132	76	56	132

(ii)   *Operating at 100% capacity*

	Transfer price $200			Transfer price $180		
	Group X	**Group Y**	**Total**	**Group X**	**Group Y**	**Total**
Sales:						
External	180	320	500	180	320	500
Transfers	200	-	0	180	-	0
Total	380	320	500	360	320	500
Costs						
Transfers	-	(200)	0	-	(180)	0
Variable	(140)	(60)	(200)	(140)	(60)	(200)
Fixed	(100)	(40)	(140)	(100)	(40)	(140)
Total	(240)	(300)	(340)	(240)	(280)	(340)
Profit	140	20	160	120	40	160

(b)   The effect of a change in the transfer price from $200 to $180 will result in lower profit for Group X and higher profit for Group Y, but the total profit for the company as a whole will be unaffected.

A reduction in the transfer price to $180 (or possibly lower) is recommended, because this is the price at which Group Y can buy the materials externally. At any price above $180, Group Y will want to buy externally, and this would not be in the interests of the company as a whole.

Significantly, at a transfer price of both $200 and $180, Division Y would suffer a fall in its divisional profit if it reduced the selling price of bricks to $0.32 and increased capacity by 400,000 bricks each month. A reduction in price would be in the best interests of the company as a whole, because total profit would rise from $132,000 per month to $160,000.

(c)   Ignoring the transfer price, the effect on Division Y of reducing the sale price of bricks to $0.32 would be to increase external sales by $80,000 and variable costs in Division Y by $24,000 (400 tonnes × $60). Cash flows would therefore improve by $56,000 per month. To persuade Division Y to take the extra 400 tonnes, the transfer price should not exceed $140 ($56,000/400). This is below the current external market price, although there is strong price competition in the market.

The transfer price for Division X should not be less than the variable cost of production in Division X, which is $70 per tonne.

However, if the transfer price is reduced to $140 per tonne or less, Division X might try to sell more materials in the external market, by reducing the selling price.

It would appear that although the ideal transfer price might be $140 or below, this will not be easily negotiated between the group managers. An imposed settlement may be necessary. Intervention by head office might be needed to impose a transfer price, and require Division Y to reduce its sales price to $0.32.

63   International transfers

(a)   The transfer price for Product P would be $9 less 40% = $5.40.

Division Y could buy from an external supplier at $5 per unit.

The manager of Division Y will want to maximise the profits of the division. The decision will therefore be to purchase Product P from the external supplier. This will be $0.40 per unit cheaper than buying from Division X.

This decision will be made regardless of the annual purchase quantity.

(b)   The annual profit of the company as a whole will be maximised if the marginal revenue for the company from making the transfers exceeds the opportunity cost.

(i)   **Annual purchases: 50,000 units of Product P**

Division X has spare production capacity for 50,000 units of Product P.

The marginal cost to Division X and to the company as a whole from making and transferring 50,000 units of Product P is therefore the marginal cost of producing them, $3.40 per unit.

A transfer price anywhere above $3.40 and below $5 would increase the annual profit of Division X and would make Division Y want to buy the units from Division X and not externally at $5.

(ii)   **Annual purchases: 120,000 units of Product P**

Division X has spare production capacity for 50,000 units of Product P, but producing the additional 70,000 units means that production and sales of Product Q would have to be reduced by 70,000 units.

The opportunity cost for Division X and for the company as a whole of transferring 120,000 units to Division Y is therefore:

		$
Variable cost of making 120,000 units	× $3.40	408,000
Contribution lost: 70,000 units of Product Q	× $0.50	35,000
		443,000

The minimum transfer price should be excess of $443,000/120,000 units = $3.692 per unit.

The transfer price should therefore be negotiated in the range $3.70 to $5. Any transfer price between these two amounts would result in higher profits for the company, Division X and Division Y (on the reasonable assumption that Division Y will sell Product P at a price higher than the transfer price.)

(c)   If Division Y buys 120,000 units of Product P externally at $5 per unit, the after-tax position of the company as a whole would be as follows:

	$	$
Division X		
Contribution from selling 70,000 units of Product Q		35,000
Less tax at 50%		(17,500)
After-tax contribution, Division X		17,500

Division Y

Cost of buying 120,000 units of P externally (at $5)	(600,000)	
Less tax at 30%	180,000	
Cost net of tax, Division Y		(420,000)
Cost to the company		(402,500)

(**Tutorial note:** Revenue from selling the units of Product P in Country Y can be ignored because this is the same regardless of whether the units are transferred from Country X or bought externally.)

If Division Y buys 120,000 units of Product P from Division X at $5.40 per unit, the after-tax position of the company as a whole would be as follows:

	$	$
Division X		
Transfer of 120,000 units of P at $5.40		648,000
Variable cost of 120,000 units of P at $3.40		408,000
Contribution from 120,000 units of Product P		240,000
Less tax at 50%		(120,000)
After-tax contribution, Division X		120,000
Division Y		
Cost of buying 120,000 units of P (at $5.40)	(648,000)	
Less tax at 30%	194,400	
Cost net of tax		(453,600)
Total cost to the company		(333,600)

Conclusion

It is in the best interests of the company as a whole for Division Y to purchase the units of Product P from Division X. This will result in an annual profit after tax that is higher by $68,900 ($402,500 – $333,600).

64 Long and Short

(a) **Group contribution (per unit and in total)**

	RDZ		BL	
	$	$	$	$
Selling price		45		54
Components used				
S (3 : 2)	18		12	
M (2 : 4)	8		16	
Processing costs	12		14	
Cost		38		42
		7		12
		(× 200)		(× 300)
Group contribution		1,400		3,600

Total contribution = $1,400 + $3,600 = $5,000

(b) Divisional contribution

(i) *Transfer price (variable cost + shadow price): supplying divisions*

	A	B
	$	$
S: (6 + 0.5)	6.50	
M: (4 + 2.75)		6.75
Less variable cost	6.00	4.00
Contribution per unit	0.50	2.75

(ii) *Buying divisions*

	RDZ		BL	
	$	$	$	$
Selling price		45.0		54.0
Less				
Transfer price				
S: (3:2)	19.5		13.0	
M: (2:4)	13.5		27.0	
Processing cost	12.0		14.0	
		45.0		54.0
Contribution per unit		0.0		0.0

(c)

All contribution arises in the supplying divisions. This will be unacceptable to the buying divisions, and so will have an adverse affect on the promotion of these two products.

(d) Transfer price

$$\text{Transfer price} = \frac{\text{Variable cost} + \text{Opportunity cost}}{(\text{or} = \text{Market clearing price})}$$

S   = \$6.00 + (5% × \$6.00) = \$6.30

M   = \$7.50 – \$0.50   = \$7.00

Contribution of end-products in buying divisions

	RDZ		BL	
	$	$	$	$
Selling price		45.0		54.0
Less				
Transfer price				
S: (3:2)	18.9		12.6	
M: (2:4)	14.0		28.0	
Processing cost	12.0		14.0	
		44.9		54.6
Contribution per unit		0.1		(0.6)

Therefore do not produce BL.

Strategy

Produce RDZ: Maximum possible.

Constraint?

S   2,400 units/3 units of S per unit of RDZ =   800 units

M   3,200 units/2 units of M per unit of RDZ =   1,600 units

Therefore produce 800 units of RDZ and sell the remaining 1,600 units of M externally.

Total contribution for group

	$
800 units of RDZ × $7/unit (see part (a))	5,600
1,600 units of M × $3/unit ($7 − $4)	4,800
Total group contribution	10,400

Index